THE COMPLETE
IDIOT'S
GUIDE® TO

Easy Freezer Meals

by Cheri Sicard

ALPHA

A member of Penguin Group (USA) Inc.

For Mitch Mandell, my best friend, partner in crime, chief recipe taster, and fellow collector of points in the game of life.

ALPHA BOOKS

Published by the Penguin Group

Penguin Group (USA) Inc., 375 Hudson Street, New York, New York 10014, USA

Penguin Group (Canada), 90 Eglinton Avenue East, Suite 700, Toronto, Ontario M4P 2Y3, Canada (a division of Pearson Penguin Canada Inc.)

Penguin Books Ltd., 80 Strand, London WC2R 0RL, England

Penguin Ireland, 25 St. Stephen's Green, Dublin 2, Ireland (a division of Penguin Books Ltd.)

Penguin Group (Australia), 250 Camberwell Road, Camberwell, Victoria 3124, Australia (a division of Pearson Australia Group Pty. Ltd.)

Penguin Books India Pvt. Ltd., 11 Community Centre, Panchsheel Park, New Delhi—110 017, India

Penguin Group (NZ), 67 Apollo Drive, Rosedale, North Shore, Auckland 1311, New Zealand (a division of Pearson New Zealand Ltd.)

Penguin Books (South Africa) (Pty.) Ltd., 24 Sturdee Avenue, Rosebank, Johannesburg 2196, South Africa

Penguin Books Ltd., Registered Offices: 80 Strand, London WC2R 0RL, England

Copyright © 2011 by Cheri Sicard

THE COMPLETE IDIOT'S GUIDE TO and Design are registered trademarks of Penguin Group (USA) Inc.

International Standard Book Number: 978-1-61564-064-5
Library of Congress Catalog Card Number: 2010913758

13   8 7 6 5 4 3 2

Interpretation of the printing code: The rightmost number of the first series of numbers is the year of the book's printing; the rightmost number of the second series of numbers is the number of the book's printing. For example, a printing code of 11-1 shows that the first printing occurred in 2011.

Printed in the United States of America

Note: This publication contains the opinions and ideas of its author. It is intended to provide helpful and informative material on the subject matter covered. It is sold with the understanding that the author and publisher are not engaged in rendering professional services in the book. If the reader requires personal assistance or advice, a competent professional should be consulted.

The author and publisher specifically disclaim any responsibility for any liability, loss, or risk, personal or otherwise, which is incurred as a consequence, directly or indirectly, of the use and application of any of the contents of this book.

Most Alpha books are available at special quantity discounts for bulk purchases for sales promotions, premiums, fund-raising, or educational use. Special books, or book excerpts, can also be created to fit specific needs.

For details, write: Special Markets, Alpha Books, 375 Hudson Street, New York, NY 10014.

Publisher: *Marie Butler-Knight*

Associate Publisher: *Mike Sanders*

Senior Managing Editor: *Billy Fields*

Senior Acquisitions Editor: *Paul Dinas*

Senior Development Editor: *Christy Wagner*

Production Editor: *Kayla Dugger*

Copy Editor: *Monica Stone*

Cover Designer: *Kurt Owens*

Book Designers: *William Thomas, Rebecca Batchelor*

Indexer: *Heather McNeill*

Layout: *Ayanna Lacey*

Proofreader: *Laura Caddell*

Contents

Introduction

When you think of "easy freezer meals," you might think, *Why cook for the freezer?* The better question might be, why *wouldn't* you cook for the freezer? The benefits of cooking and then freezing the dishes for later are many, and I can't wait to share them all with you in the following chapters. But if I had to boil freezer cooking down to a single word, it's this: *freedom*.

By using the easy recipes and meal plans in this book, you can actually gain more free time in your life, every day. This isn't a vague concept or an empty promise. Once you get rolling with freezer meals, you can take nights off from kitchen chores anytime you choose. By allowing your freezer to act as your personal home chef, it's easy to shave an hour or more off your daily chores. What will you do with that extra free time?

While you save time, you're also building your personal food bank. Anytime you cook food for the freezer, you'll be making more than your family can consume in a single serving. That means you cook once, but your family eats two, three, four, or more times as a result of that single effort. Not only will you save time by cooking several meals at once, you'll also only have to clean the kitchen, stove, appliances, and utensils once. The rest is a matter of heating and eating.

Another benefit of freezer meals is that you know the food you're feeding your family is delicious as well as nutritious. Too often, busy people resort to fast food or processed convenience foods and sacrifice good nutrition in the process. I'm not claiming all the recipes in this book constitute "health food," but they *are* all made with real, wholesome ingredients. No chemicals, preservatives, or high-fructose corn syrup here.

With freezer cooking you are also in control of how much salt, sugar, or excess fat goes into the food. You can have the freedom to enjoy convenient foods from your freezer made with locally grown or organic ingredients instead of those trucked in from far away. If you have a garden, you'll easily be able to extend its usefulness and preserve its bounty for delicious use all year long. Furthermore, by packaging your freezer meals in appropriate portions for your family's needs, you'll find it easy to control portions—one of the biggest challenges facing anyone trying to lose pounds or maintain a healthy weight.

Cooking for the freezer saves you money. Anytime you find grocery bargains, you'll now have a plan of how to use them, not only for now, but for delicious and economical meals down the road. Shop wisely and deposit extra meals in your freezer food bank, and you'll also be keeping more money in your actual bank account. With just a little planning to take advantage of supermarket sales, it's easy to knock 10 to 20 percent or more off your grocery bill!

You can also save by shopping at warehouse stores. Buying in bulk used to only be practical for large families. By planning how to use ingredients in advance and filling the freezer, even people living alone can take advantage of the lower prices offered at warehouse stores, without any fear of wasting food.

Freezer cooking isn't difficult. For the most part, if you know how to cook, you know how to cook for the freezer.

If you just can't wait to get started, pick a recipe and jump right in. Before you actually send your recipe creation to the freezer, however, you might want to take a few minutes to learn some important basics—easy techniques that can make the difference between a delicious dish that's heated after freezing and comes out with a freshly made taste and texture, or a recipe that comes out watery, mushy, or dry. (That's where the chapters in Part 1 come into play.)

As you flip through the recipe chapters in Parts 2 through 5, which contain over 100 recipes that have been specifically tested for going through the freezing process and coming out delicious on the other side, you'll notice that some meals are cooked before freezing, while other times the first heat a dish feels is after it's gone through a stint in the freezer. And some recipes need nothing more than thawing before they can be enjoyed. In all cases, the lion's share of the work is done far in advance of when you'll be enjoying the food. That leaves you, the cook, with plenty of time to relax and enjoy the meal like everyone else at the table.

How to Use This Book

I've divided the book into five parts to help you find what you're looking for quickly and easily:

The chapters in **Part 1, Freezer Cooking Essentials,** give you the lowdown on freezer food basics, including what does and does not freeze well, as well as steps you can take to ensure your freezer food comes out tasting like it was made fresh on the spot. You'll also discover tips for getting the most mileage possible from your freezer. And while you don't need any fancy equipment for freezer cooking, I show you some items you'll find handy as well as information on packaging foods for the freezer.

Part 2, From-the-Freezer Morning Meals, gives you a great place to start practicing freezer cooking skills, starting with breakfast, the most important meal of the day—and also often the most rushed and, therefore, most skipped meal.

Part 3, Lunches, Appetizers, and Snacks, gives you dozens of recipes for knock-out light meals and starters. Don't want to eat from the office vending machine? Need to pull together some quick party food when unexpected guests drop by? The chapters in this part have you covered.

Part 4, What's for Dinner?, answers that age-old question simply and deliciously. The recipes in these chapters enable you to cook once, freeze, and then have your pick of delicious, good-for-you entrées to feed your family come dinnertime.

Finally, **Part 5, Sweet Endings,** gives you recipes for the finishing touches, whether you want a sweet treat, or need a fantastic sauce.

At the end of the book, I've provided several appendixes, including a glossary of terms and a list of further resources you might want to check out. I've also included a checklist to help you stock your pantry with everything you need to cook for the freezer, and a worksheet for planning out your menus. Last but not least is a freezing timetable to give you at-a-glance information on recommended freezer storage times for different foods.

Extras

Throughout the book, I've included informative sidebars that give extra insight:

COLD FACT

Check these sidebars for informative fun facts about ingredients and cooking techniques that add to your arsenal of culinary and nutritional knowledge.

COOL TIP

These sidebars offer handy time-saving, money-saving, or kitchen-efficiency suggestions.

FREEZER BURN

Heed the important information concerning food safety or recipe troubleshooting in these sidebars.

TABLE TALK

These sidebars contain explanations of important terms and techniques needed to accomplish the recipes.

Acknowledgments

I would like to thank the following people who helped in the production of this book and/or who support me and make my life a better place every day, including but not limited to: Janet Rosen, Paul Dinas, Christy Wagner, Sheree Bykofsky, Richard Burnes, Tracy Burnes, Madison Burnes, Bambi Burnes, Chuck Burnes, Ethan Burnes, Lisa Casullo Burnes, Chipper Lowell, Rick Duffy, Wini McKay, Chester Cable, Kiyomi Hara, Lee Maloney, Tom Conley, Susan Conley, Sarah Conley, Nick Conley, Oliver de la Torre, and Steve Conti.

Special Thanks to the Technical Reviewer

The Complete Idiot's Guide to Easy Freezer Meals was reviewed by an expert who double-checked the accuracy of what you'll learn here, to help us ensure that this book gives you everything you need to know about preparing delicious dishes you can pull from the freezer, heat, and eat. Special thanks are extended to Leslie Bilderback.

A Certified Master Baker and culinary instructor, Chef Bilderback has written six *Complete Idiot's Guides* on cooking, as well as a monthly column in a local Los Angeles magazine, *The Arroyo*. She teaches baking and pastry at Ecole de Cuisine in Pasadena, travels through the LA Unified School District teaching nutrition to kids, and trains chefs for the U.S. Navy.

Trademarks

All terms mentioned in this book that are known to be or are suspected of being trademarks or service marks have been appropriately capitalized. Alpha Books and Penguin Group (USA) Inc. cannot attest to the accuracy of this information. Use of a term in this book should not be regarded as affecting the validity of any trademark or service mark.

Freezer Cooking Essentials

Wait! Before you start stocking your freezer with delicious dishes to freeze and eat later, take some time to look over the tips and techniques in Part 1. They're not difficult to implement, and they'll make a major difference in the final quality of your from-the-freezer food.

The chapters in this first part cover the science of freezing. You'll understand what actually happens to food as the temperature drops in order to make sense of how a few extra steps when preparing and packing foods can have a huge impact on the quality of a finished dish. You'll know what can go wrong when freezing foods while being armed with the necessary knowledge to avoid any possible pitfalls.

Familiarize yourself with the simple principles in these chapters and you'll also have the knowledge you need to start adapting favorite family recipes for freezer storage. You'll know which foods do and do not freeze well, how to prepare foods for the freezer, how long foods keep, and even what to do if the power goes out on your freezer full of food.

Freezing 101

In This Chapter

- How freezing works
- What to freeze
- What not to freeze
- Preparing foods for freezing
- How long to freeze foods

What actually happens to food as temperatures drop, and how do these changes affect the quality of frozen foods? These and other important questions and answers are covered in this chapter. You'll learn the hows and whys and ins and outs of preparing foods for freezing, so you'll always achieve great results after reheating your freezer meal creations. Armed with this important knowledge, you'll also be ready to start adapting your own favorite recipes for the freezer.

The Science of Freezing Foods

Freezing occurs when water—in this case, the water within a food—reaches a temperature below 32°F (0°C) and becomes ice. Freezing is a convenient way to keep food because, in a frozen state, bacterial spoilage stops. Enzyme reactions also slow, so by doing a little prefreezer prep, you can preserve foods like fruit and vegetables that typically fall prey to enzymatic spoilage.

As water cools, its molecules start moving more slowly. Eventually, the movement becomes so slow the molecules begin to gather in loose clusters. As the temperature continues to drop, more water molecules join in the clusters, and together they all form rigid ice crystals. How large or small those crystals become depends on how long it took for the water to transform into the frozen state. The longer it takes for an ice crystal to form, the larger that crystal will be.

Large crystals may be a good thing when it comes to rock hunting, but they're not when it comes to freezing foods. In fact, freezer cooks should look at large ice crystals as their nemesis. Nothing will ruin the texture of a frozen food quicker.

Ice takes up more space than water. For example, water frozen at sea level takes up about 8 percent more space in its frozen state than it does as a liquid. When food is frozen, the expanding ice crystals put pressure on the food's cell walls. As long as the cell walls are flexible enough, they stretch and contract with the ice. But if they lack flexibility, the ice crystals break the cell walls and water leaks out. This devastation and destruction taking place at the molecular level is what causes some foods to emerge from the freezer in a less-than-appetizing state.

Many foods can go directly into the freezer and come out as fresh and delicious as if they'd never been frozen. Some need just a little extra prep before going into a deep freeze in order to successfully survive the ordeal. Others just don't work well, no matter what you do. Learn these simple freezer facts, and you'll always know what to expect when attempting to freeze your own recipes.

Foods That Freeze Well

Some foods can go directly into the freezer with no special preparation other than wrapping and come out as good as new. How many of these foods are already in your freezer?

Most baked goods freeze well. Generally speaking, the lower the moisture content in the baked good, the longer it keeps. Freeze baked breads, muffins, cookies, cakes, and cheesecakes. Avoid pastries with a custard or jelly filling because these turn into a watery mush after freezing and thawing. Freeze cakes plain or frosted with a butter cream icing. (Other types of icings may or may not successfully survive the ordeal, so experiment with your favorites.) Many unbaked baked goods also do well in the freezer. Freeze yeast doughs for breads, pizzas, or pastries. Thaw in the refrigerator, and bring to room temperature before continuing with the recipe. Freeze unbaked logs of cookie dough and then slice off the portions you need and bake.

Unbaked pie shells also freeze well, and pies that require a prebaked crust before filling should go directly from the freezer to the oven without thawing in between.

Some people like to freeze whole unbaked fruit pies, but I find the crust becomes too soggy after baking. Better to freeze the crust and filling separately, remove the filling from the freezer, thaw, fill the frozen unbaked pie shell, and bake. It takes only a little more time, and the results are far superior.

Some nuts work well frozen. For example, buy pecans and walnuts at harvest time, and keep them fresh all year long by storing them in the freezer.

Baker's yeast stays fresh and potent for years when frozen.

Cooked eggs or uncooked scrambled eggs freeze well. So do egg whites, a handy thing to keep in mind when making recipes that call for only yolks.

COOL TIP

Freeze extra egg whites in ice cube trays, one per cup. When frozen, pop out of the tray and store in a zipper-lock plastic freezer bag. Thaw in the refrigerator before using.

Most soups and stews freeze exceptionally well. Those with a heavy dairy or cheese content may separate, but you can usually fix this with a whirl in a blender or food processor after heating.

The higher the fat content in dairy products, the better they freeze. Milk products under 40 percent separate (although you can mix to restore smoothness), but heavy cream freezes well (although its volume upon whipping will be less than nonfrozen cream). The same goes for well-wrapped butter, flavored or compound butter, and cream cheese.

Most mayonnaise-based sauces and the prepared foods and casseroles that use them generally freeze well.

Firmer cheeses freeze well, but their texture changes upon thawing. This presents no problem for cheese destined for cooked recipes or melting. Cheese intended for snacking out of hand, however, should not be frozen. Its grainy, crumbly texture would make it unappetizing.

Freezing also creates a texture change in tofu, making it chewier and more absorbent—qualities that can be helpful in many vegetarian recipes. Freeze tofu in its water and package, and thaw in the refrigerator. Squeeze out all the water, like a sponge, before using in recipes. When frozen, thawed, and then cooked, firm grated tofu takes on the texture of shredded meat.

Wrap uncooked meats well in foil or heavy freezer paper before freezing to prevent *freezer burn*. Freeze well-wrapped uncooked poultry whole or in pieces. If whole, it's best to remove giblets before freezing. Scale and clean fresh uncooked fish before double wrapping in foil and then either paper or plastic and freezing.

Preserve the flavor of fruits and vegetables at the peak of harvest by freezing them when they're at their best. Be sure to blanch produce first (more on blanching coming up).

TABLE TALK

Freezer burn is caused by huge ice crystals permeating the food's cell tissues, which causes water to rise to the surface and freeze outside the food. You can identify freezer-burned food by the dry, discolored spots that form on a food's surface, or a dry surface covered in large ice crystals.

Foods That Don't Freeze Well

Technically, you can safely freeze most any food, with the exception of food in cans and eggs still in their shells. But just because you can doesn't mean you *should*. Some foods—thankfully not many—simply do not emerge unscathed from a stint in the freezer. Their ingredients may separate or turn watery, or they may come out so soggy and lacking texture they're no longer appetizing.

Avoid putting these in the freezer:

- Mayonnaise on its own (mixed in sauces is okay)
- Egg yolks
- Gelatin-based dishes

- Delicate, high-moisture-content vegetables like lettuce and cucumbers
- Cooked meats, unless covered and protected with a sauce or gravy (Freezing tends to dry and toughen cooked meats.)

FREEZER BURN

While trichinae and other parasites can be destroyed by subzero freezing, home freezers cannot be relied upon to safely eliminate all parasites because of their fluctuating temperatures. To be sure, cook meats, even those that have been frozen, and especially pork, thoroughly.

The Importance of Blanching

The condition of fruits and vegetables when they go into the freezer has an enormous impact on the level of quality they have when they come out and thaw. Produce frozen at the peak of freshness and ripeness retains its fabulous flavor, but if you freeze under- or overripe produce, it won't taste any better upon thawing than it did when it went into the freezer.

It's easy to preserve the flavors of fresh fruits and vegetables, but preserving texture is another matter. Nothing presents more of a challenge to freezer cooks.

It's important to realize that no produce emerges from the freezer with the exact same texture it had when fresh. That's just not possible. If you've ever attempted to freeze raw produce, you know what I mean and have witnessed the disappointingly mushy results. You can alleviate this problem by *blanching* fresh fruits and vegetables before they go to the freezer. This extra step slows the enzymatic activity that breaks down fruits and veggies and helps them retain their vibrant color and valuable nutrients.

TABLE TALK

Blanching involves partially cooking the exterior of a food by submerging it in boiling water for a short period and then immediately rinsing it in ice water to halt the cooking process. After the produce has completely cooled, you can package and freeze it. Blanching comes from the French word *blanche,* meaning "white." Its culinary use stems from the technique of boiling almonds until their skins fall off, transforming the nut from brown to white.

Blanch produce between 1 and 5 minutes, depending on how hardy it is or how large the pieces are you're blanching. Delicate veggies like tomato slices or asparagus only need 1 or 2 minutes; give carrots and cauliflower up to 5 minutes.

The hardier the produce, the better results you can expect after freezing. Vegetables like carrots or broccoli stay far more intact than delicate fruits like raspberries or strawberries, even with a dip in the blanching pot.

Pre- and Postfreezer Prep

Before you stick the pan of food you just made in the freezer, wait! Besides properly packaging and labeling (more on this in Chapter 2), there are a few more considerations to keep in mind before filling the freezer with your homemade culinary masterpieces.

Cool First

It's essential to always completely cool foods before placing them in the freezer. If necessary, you can wrap and package room-temperature foods, but better still, chill them in the refrigerator before freezing. This extra step helps keep freezer temperatures stable and helps the food freeze faster.

Both factors contribute to better-quality food when thawed and reheated, plus a decreased chance of freezer burn occurring both in the new dish and those already in the freezer.

Avoiding Freezer Burn

What's all this about freezer burn, and what causes it? Let's take a closer look at this freezer cook's foe.

Anytime a freezer's temperature fluctuates, any new food placed within freezes more slowly. Even worse, the food that's already inside can partially thaw. Both of these make your food prime candidates for the dreaded freezer burn.

COLD FACT

You'll have less trouble with freezer burn in a manual defrost freezer than in a "frost-free" model with an automatic thaw cycle.

Freezer-burned food is technically safe to eat, but it probably won't taste all that great. Better to avoid freezer burn in the first place by following these tips:

- Wrap foods, like meats, tightly. Air contains moisture, and the less air surrounding a food, the less chance of freezer burn. When storing food in plastic freezer bags, be sure to remove all the air before sealing.

- When buying frozen foods at the store, be sure they're frozen solid and hard.

- Paper wrappers can help absorb excess moisture, so especially when dealing with expensive foods like fine cuts of meat, wrap in freezer paper and then aluminum foil or plastic.

- Keep your freezer's temperature below 0°F, and keep it stable (see Chapter 2).

To Thaw or Not to Thaw?

Most dishes can be cooked directly from the freezer without thawing first, but unless you're using a microwave oven, it takes substantially longer. A good rule of thumb is to allow about 1½ times longer to cook frozen food than its thawed counterpart.

Some foods, such as meats destined for the grill, require thawing before cooking. Others, like most fried foods or just about anything in a batter, breading, wrap, or coating, turn out far better when cooked from the frozen state.

Aside from that, it's a judgment call whether or not you want to thaw foods before cooking or reheating.

If you do decide upon thawing first, keep in mind that there are only three safe ways to defrost foods:

- In the refrigerator

- In cold water

- In the microwave

If it's not on this list, don't do it! In the refrigerator takes longer, but the food always remains within a safe temperature zone. Small items may defrost overnight, and larger items take a day or two. For really big foods such as whole turkeys or roasts, allow 1 day of thawing time for every 5 pounds of weight.

Hasten thawing raw meats, poultry, and fish by placing the food in a large, leak-proof bag and immersing it in cold water. Change the water every 30 minutes to ensure it stays cold, and be sure to cook the food immediately upon thawing.

> **FREEZER BURN**
>
> When thawing food in cold water, be sure the food is completely sealed and the bag has absolutely no leaks. Thawing foods can absorb extra water like a sponge, making for a water-logged finished dish. And bacteria and microorganisms can be introduced via the air or surrounding environment.

Food defrosted in the microwave should be cooked immediately upon thawing because, even on the defrost cycle, parts of the food will become warmer than others and begin to cook.

How Long Will Frozen Foods Keep?

Contrary to what you might have been told in the past, foods kept at 0°F are safe indefinitely. That's not to say the quality won't degrade with time, especially if there's any freezer burn going on.

In Appendix E, I give you a list of how long foods can keep in the freezer. That list is for quality purposes only, not food safety. If your food is a little over the recommended time, give it a try. If the freezer's temperature has remained consistent, the food should still taste fine.

The major factor affecting properly frozen foods is fat content because fat can still turn rancid even when frozen. According to the experts at the U.S. Department of Agriculture, this won't make you sick and the food is still "safe" to eat, but it's certainly not appetizing or good for you.

If any meats you take out of the freezer have an "off" smell, toss them out.

Cured meats especially have a shorter shelf life because the curing salt hastens the development of rancidity, both in and out of the freezer. To be safe, use cured meats like bacon, sausage, and cold cuts within 1 month of freezing, and all other raw meats within 3 months.

Dealing with Power Outages

Nothing strikes fear in the heart of a cook with a freezer full of prepared meals like a power outage. Even if you avoid a national disaster like a hurricane, earthquake, or tornado, you could still experience an extended outage due to high winds, snow, or ice. Power outages are the one instance when you need to be concerned about the safety of your frozen food.

The most important thing to remember during a power outage is to keep freezer and refrigerator doors closed. If the power remains out for only a few hours, there won't be a problem. An unopened refrigerator keeps foods safely cold for about 4 hours. A full freezer holds its temperature for about 48 hours. If the freezer in question is only half full, cut the time in half, too—24 hours.

Should the power outage continue, you can extend the life of your food if you can get your hands on some blocks of ice or, even better, *dry ice*. Fifty pounds of dry ice holds a full 18-cubic-foot freezer for 2 days.

TABLE TALK

Dry ice is solidified carbon dioxide. When it melts, it turns into colorless, odorless carbon dioxide gas. You can buy dry ice from producers of regular ice.

Exercise caution when using dry ice:

- Dry ice is significantly colder than regular ice, so never touch it with your bare skin or you can get a burn similar to frostbite. Wear insulated gloves when handling.

- Wear safety goggles or a face shield when chopping or chipping dry ice.

- Always keep dry ice away from children.

- Always store dry ice in a container that allows for some ventilation and leakage. If unvented, carbon dioxide gas can build up in a closed jar or container.

- Never eat or swallow dry ice.

- When transporting dry ice, transport within the vehicle (not the trunk), and keep your vehicle windows open for ventilation.

FREEZER BURN

The quantity of dry ice used to keep a home deep freezer cold during a power outage is not sufficient to produce health problems. However, you should never use dry ice in a walk-in freezer, closed car trunk or truck bed, or other small space with poor ventilation. Large amounts of dry ice can produce a great deal of carbon dioxide, which can be fatal to someone entering that space. Symptoms of overexposure to carbon dioxide include headache and difficulty breathing and, with greater exposure, nausea and vomiting.

Of course, access to ice—dry, block, or cubes—is impossible during many emergency situations. If items in your freezer are beginning to thaw, it may be time to cut your losses, pull out the grill, make the best of a bad situation, and have a party.

The Least You Need to Know

- The faster a food freezes, the better quality it will have upon thawing and reheating.
- Always blanch raw fruits and vegetables before freezing.
- Most foods can be cooked directly from freezer to oven without thawing first.
- There are only three safe ways to thaw food: in the refrigerator, sealed in plastic and submerged in cold water, or in the microwave.
- Foods kept at or below 0°F are safe to eat indefinitely.
- Keep refrigerator and freezer doors closed during a power outage to preserve cold temperatures.

Tools of the Trade

In This Chapter

- Refrigerator/freezer care
- Handy kitchen tools
- Proper food packaging
- Efficient freezer packing

In this chapter, we take a look at the necessary hardware for successful freezer cooking. You learn how to choose the best refrigerator or freezer when buying a new one, and how to optimize your current appliances' performance. We also go over food packaging options and kitchen tools and gadgets you may find useful.

Getting the Most Out of Your Refrigerator and Freezer

Ideally, you want your freezer to stay at 0°F or below at all times. Temperature fluctuations can cause freezer burn, which in turn negatively affects the thawed food's texture and taste (see Chapter 1). To avoid freezer temperature fluctuations in both the freezer and refrigerator, it's important to keep the doors closed as much as possible because every time the door opens, cold air escapes. Decide what you need before opening the door and then go in, get it, and get out. The refrigerator and freezer are no place for browsing. (Be sure to tell your kids this, too!)

Refrigerator TLC

Think of how much your family relies on the refrigerator/freezer combo standing in your kitchen. A little TLC can make this workhorse run more efficiently and have a longer productive life.

Clean the exposed coils on the bottom and back of the refrigerator/freezer regularly. As dust builds up, the condenser needs to kick on more often, and the appliance uses more energy. The extra work also causes the condenser to wear out prematurely. Help your refrigerator/freezer help you by cleaning the coils every 3 months. Pull out the refrigerator/freezer from the wall, and dust the coils behind and underneath. A vacuum cleaner with a crevice attachment works if you use a gentle touch.

It also helps to simply move the fridge away from the wall a bit. Even an inch or two (more is better) allows air to flow, reduces the amount of work the motor has to do, and cuts down on energy consumption.

COLD FACT

Top-mount refrigerator/freezers use 10 to 25 percent less energy than bottom-mount or side-by-side models. Automatic ice makers and through-the-door dispensers not only increase purchase price, but use 14 to 20 percent more energy than those without.

Check the seals on your refrigerator and freezer doors by inserting a piece of paper in the door frame and closing the door. If you can easily pull out the paper, the seals have become damaged or weak and it's time to think about replacing them. Repeat the test in several spots to accurately gauge the quality of your appliance's seals.

If the freezer isn't full of food, fill it with water. Less nonfrozen food space, the harder the freezer has to work to chill that space. Empty space probably won't be an issue once you start using this book, but should you ever find your freezer partially empty, help it maintain a steady low temperature by filling empty milk jugs ¾ full with water and freezing.

Freezer Care and Maintenance

If you have a deep freezer, you have one of the handiest appliances around when it comes to easy freezer meals. Imagine—a whole freezer dedicated to your future meals! Take some care in placing and maintaining your deep freezer, and you'll be rewarded with many years of use.

Place the freezer in a cool, dry, well-ventilated place away from stoves, water heaters, direct sunlight, or other sources of heat. For best performance, be sure the freezer sits level. Allow a minimum of 2 inches between the freezer and the wall if your freezer has exposed coils in the back. Dust the coils every 3 months.

Clean frost-free freezers once a year by unplugging them from the wall, emptying the freezer, and wiping the interior surfaces with a mild baking soda solution (2 tablespoons per quart of water). Rewipe the surface with another towel moistened with clean water. Towel dry, replace the food, and plug in. You're good to go until next year. (More on defrosting your freezer coming up in the following section.)

Defrost manual freezers when the ice buildup is more than ¼ inch thick. Don't procrastinate on this! The thicker the layer of ice, the less efficiently the freezer runs.

COLD FACT

A certain amount of moisture is always present within a freezer. Over time, this moisture freezes and forms a layer of ice on the freezer's interior surface. Frost-free freezers come programmed with a defrost cycle that quickly melts any accumulated ice (which then drains outside the freezer and evaporates). After the defrost cycle, the freezer returns to its regular cooling cycle. The process automatically repeats every 6 to 8 hours, stopping any significant ice buildup before it happens.

Freezer Defrosting

Try to schedule defrosting when the freezer's inventory is low because the job can take about 2 hours to complete. Store any perishable foods in a cooler chest with ice during the process.

Unplug the freezer from the power source, and follow the manufacturer's instructions for defrosting your type of freezer. Place towels in the bottom to catch water and frost, and use a plastic scraper tool to pry loose any frost from the sides of the freezer.

When all frost is removed, wipe down the freezer with a mild baking soda solution and dry with absorbent towels. Plug in the freezer, close the door, and allow the freezer to chill for 15 minutes before refilling with food.

When returning previously frozen food to a freezer after defrosting, take care to scrape as much frost and moisture off the packages as possible. Earmark these packages for first use.

COOL TIP

Is a separate deep freeze appliance really worth it? Maybe and maybe not. It depends on how, and how much, you use it. If you enjoy cooking large, shopping for sales, shop infrequently, have a vegetable garden or fruit trees, or have a large family, one of today's new energy-efficient freezers is probably a good investment. If you can't manage to keep it filled though, you'll probably waste more money than you save. Buy an appropriate-size freezer for your family's needs, and don't buy any at all if your refrigerator's freezer compartment suffices.

Thinking of Buying a New Freezer?

If you're considering buying a new deep freezer, here's some good news: you'll have much less to consider with this purchase than with many other major appliances.

For the most part, a deep freezer is nothing more than a plastic-lined box that has freezing capabilities. It may open from the top like a chest or have a door like a refrigerator. It may have adjustable shelves or removable storage baskets. But other than that, there just aren't a lot of gizmos, gadgets, or special features to sort out. More often than not, the freezer will remain hidden in a basement or garage, so aesthetics don't even come into play.

As simple as freezers are, it still pays to take your time, comparison shop, and do a little research before you buy so you get the best freezer for your needs. For example, check the yellow Energy Guide label and compare the model you're interested in against similar models. The more energy-efficient an appliance, the less it costs to operate.

COLD FACT

Appliances bearing a yellow ENERGY STAR label have met strict guidelines set by the U.S. Environmental Protection Agency and the Department of Energy that ensure the product saves the consumer money over a lower-priced but less-efficient model.

Upright freezers generally cost more and use more energy than chest-type freezers. On the plus side, the latter make it easier to locate and retrieve what's inside.

Buy the size freezer that meets your storage needs. As mentioned earlier, too much empty space in a refrigerator or freezer makes the motor work harder and wastes energy.

Frost-free and automatic-defrost models cost more to buy and consume more energy than their manual-defrost counterparts. However, if you know you don't have the time or discipline to regularly defrost the freezer, it may be worth it. A freezer in need of defrosting uses more energy than a frost-free one.

More Useful Tools for Freezer Cooks

If you cook regularly, you probably already have everything you need to prepare a variety of freezer-friendly meals. Other than packaging materials, no special tools or equipment are required.

That said, some items make kitchen chores infinitely easier and more time-efficient. If you don't already have the following items in your kitchen arsenal, I highly recommend picking them up when you can.

Food Processor

If I had to pick only one kitchen gadget to help me in food preparation, it would be a food processor. Tedious tasks like chopping vegetables take seconds in it. It blends. It purées. It chops, minces, grates, and shreds. You can even knead bread dough in it!

Buy the most powerful and largest model you can afford because you'll put this appliance through a workout, and you don't want to burn up a motor before its time.

A mini food processor can also be handy for chopping herbs and garlic and mixing salad dressing, but isn't essential.

Toaster and Convection Ovens

I assume your kitchen already contains an oven, so I won't go into those here. I will share some options—big and small—you might want to consider.

Convection ovens use a fan to circulate the hot air within the oven. With hot air constantly dancing around it, food cooks at a 20 percent lower temperature and about 20 percent faster in a convection oven than in a conventional oven. Many new ovens these days come with a convection oven option, so if you're buying new appliances or remodeling the kitchen anyway, it's a good choice.

You can also find portable, countertop convection ovens that work well, but they do take up a lot of counter real estate. Unless you need extra oven space, or your regular oven is on the blink and you can't afford to replace it yet, this is an optional purchase.

If you often cook for just one or two people, a toaster oven makes a great investment because it saves the time and energy that goes into heating a large oven to cook a small amount of food. It also makes toast, so you can save some counter space and ditch your regular toaster. Some toaster ovens even offer a convection feature for faster, more-efficient cooking.

Microwave Ovens

If you cook a lot of freezer foods, a microwave is almost essential. I rarely do actual cooking in the microwave, but I find it invaluable for reheating.

Foods reheat quickly of course, but for some dishes, the microwave provides the best method of reheating from a quality perspective.

Buy the most powerful model you can afford. A defrost option is nice if you regularly like to use the microwave for this function.

FREEZER BURN

Microwave oven cooking times vary greatly from oven to oven. Always take the microwave cooking times given with a recipe as a rough guideline. A better method is to become familiar with how your oven cooks and judge cooking times accordingly. Always err on the side of undercooking because you can add more time if needed, but too much time in the microwave renders many dishes rubbery and unappetizing.

Slow Cookers and Pressure Cookers

Slow cookers and pressure cookers are capable of turning out similar dishes, but they take different routes to get there. The slow cooker works by cooking foods for long periods of 3 to 8 hours at low temperatures. After you set up everything in the slow cooker, you can more or less forget it until it's time to eat. The pressure cooker reduces cooking times over conventional methods by cooking foods under pressure at high temperatures.

If you're a fan of either appliance, know that most of the foods cooked via these methods freeze beautifully. So load up your freezer cooking repertoire with slow cooker and pressure cooker recipes. *The Complete Idiot's Guide to Slow Cooker Cooking, Second Edition,* and *The Complete Idiot's Guide to Pressure Cooking* are packed full with delicious recipes for each appliance.

Anyone planning to cook several dishes at once in order to get ahead on kitchen chores (see Chapters 3 and 4) will especially benefit from owning a large slow cooker. One dish can be merrily cooking away while you go about accomplishing the rest of your chores.

COLD FACT

An inexpensive probe-style kitchen thermometer is especially helpful for freezer cooks, not only for checking if meats are cooked to proper tempera-tures, but also for determining if that previously frozen but now perfectly browned casserole is actually heated all the way through.

Packing It Up

Foods inside your freezer live in a cold, dry climate. In order to survive and come out appetizing, they need protection while they're in deep freeze. The proper packaging helps preserve moisture content, color, texture, and nutritional value.

Supermarket shelves are filled with packaging options in virtually every size and shape. The types you use depend upon your family's needs, but generally speaking, good freezer packaging materials share the following characteristics:

- Durable

- Moisture-resistant

- Leak-proof

- Easy to seal

- Easy to label

- Able to prevent food from absorbing other flavors or odors

- Able to withstand cold temperatures without becoming brittle or breaking

COOL TIP

The larger the container of food, the slower it freezes. To hasten freezing time and prevent large ice crystals and freezer burn from forming, package large quantities of food in several smaller containers instead of one big one.

Stocking Up on Packaging

Keep your disposable packaging supply stash as stocked as your pantry, and you'll always be prepared to store and freeze your culinary creations for future use.

Have the following on hand and you'll be ready to pack most anything:

- Zipper-lock plastic freezer bags in 1-quart and 1-gallon sizes
- Heavy-duty aluminum foil
- Plastic freezer wrap
- Waxed paper
- Freezer paper
- Freezer tape and markers
- A variety of lidded food storage containers in sizes that meet your family's needs
- Disposable aluminum baking pans and pie tins in sizes that meet your family's needs

Serious freezer cooks should check out restaurant supply stores and buy containers used for to-go orders. You'll find a huge variety of inexpensive packaging options that can go directly from freezer to oven or microwave.

When you're choosing containers, be sure to keep in mind the size of the container versus the amount of food you'll be able to pack in it. You want to leave enough *headspace* at the top of the container for the food to expand if necessary.

TABLE TALK

Headspace is the space between the food and the top of the container. Many high-liquid-content foods destined for the freezer require an inch or so of air at the top to allow for expansion during freezing. Exceptions to the rule are loosely packed vegetables, raw meats, and baked goods.

Many baking dishes can go from freezer to oven, especially if they're metal or glass. Several retail cookware lines offer cookware designed specifically to handle these extremes. When using glass, be sure it's oven-safe glass because regular glass containers can crack during freezing.

Portion Control Made Easy

Portion control is continually cited as one of the biggest challenges facing anyone trying to live a healthy lifestyle. By packaging foods in the proper portion sizes before you freeze them, it's easy to avoid overeating.

After all, there are no leftovers waiting in the kitchen to tempt you to have seconds. And in order to get more, you have to heat another meal.

Label, Label, Label

Unless you enjoy playing meal roulette, it's imperative that you label the packages of food before you store them in your freezer. Be sure to include not only what's in the package but when it was frozen. That way, you're sure to use older items first.

Keep permanent markers on hand to write directly onto freezer paper, aluminum foil, plastic wrap, and plastic freezer bags. If you close packages with freezer tape, whose adhesive is specially designed to stick even in cold moist conditions, you can label directly onto the tape. Tape is also handy for labeling packages you'll reuse for another purpose later. Wax pencils are a great temporary labeling option.

COOL TIP

As your freezer begins to fill with the fruits of your kitchen labors, it can get difficult to determine exactly what's in there and in what quantities. An easy solution is to keep an inventory list right on the freezer. Pick up a small magnet-backed dry erase board at an office supply store, and use it to keep a list of the dishes in your freezer and how many of each is in there. When you remove a dish, reduce the number on the inventory list. Teach the kids to do the same, and you'll always have an accurate count of how many freezer meals are on ice.

Packing a Small Freezer

You'd be amazed at how much food can fit into the freezer compartment of a standard refrigerator/freezer. Some foods, like bone-in meats, take up a lot of space and there's nothing you can do about it. Many other foods, however, can be manipulated to maximize available space.

Soups, sauces, foods in sauces, and just about any other flexible food can be packed in zipper-lock plastic freezer bags to save space. Squeeze out the extra air, be sure the bags are well sealed, and freeze flat. Once they're frozen, you can easily stack the bags or line them up side by side, bookcase style, to make the best use of the space available.

The Least You Need to Know

- For maximum efficiency and lifespan, keep your refrigerator/freezer's coils dusted and the interior frost free.
- Food processors and slow cookers can save you tons of time in the kitchen.
- For best results, wrap foods well, label accurately, and freeze as quickly as possible.
- You can save space in small freezers by freezing foods flat in zipper-lock plastic freezer storage bags.

Shopping and Cooking Strategies

In This Chapter

- Determining your freezer cooking style
- Maximizing your grocery budget
- Plans for cooking small, medium, and large
- Holiday and special dinner strategies

You're probably chomping at the bit to start filling your freezer with delicious, heat-and-eat meals. In this chapter, I show you how to do just that—efficiently, economically, and in a way that suits your cooking style.

The plans outlined in this chapter will appeal to different types of cooks, yet they all share one common goal: to stock your freezer with a variety of foods you can pull out, heat, and enjoy. You can accomplish that goal in any way that suits you, but no matter which plan you choose, you'll be cooking more than your family will consume at any one sitting, so you'll be constantly adding to your frozen meal collection. Over time, as you build up a surplus, you'll spend less time cooking and have more nights off as you rely on your own personal chef, your freezer!

A Well-Stocked Pantry

Next to a freezer full of prepared meals, a well-stocked pantry is the busy cook's best friend. Making freezer food won't save you much time if you have to constantly run to the store for forgotten ingredients.

Keep a reliable supply of staples like sugar, flour, rice, canned tomatoes, beans, pastas, stocks, herbs, spices, flavoring sauces (soy sauce, Worcestershire sauce, etc.), and any other ingredients you regularly use. (See Appendix C for a checklist for stocking your pantry.)

Save money by buying staples in bulk when you find them on sale or at a warehouse store, and you'll always be ready for a spontaneous cooking session should the mood strike you.

A Well-Stocked Kitchen

The pots, pans, bowls, and utensils you probably already have in your kitchen are all you need to create easy freezer meals. But depending on your family's needs, you may be doubling or tripling the recipes and, likewise, making more food in a single session than you normally would. It's a good idea to read through the recipe you plan on preparing before you ever begin to cook and determine that you have everything you need to prepare and package the recipe in the quantity you want to make.

As long as you clean as you go, you can get away with a minimal amount of pots, pans, and mixing bowls. Baking dishes, on the other hand, are often in short supply in many kitchens. Rather than purchasing more baking dishes, you could use disposable aluminum foil baking pans instead. These are available in a wide variety of shapes and sizes at many supermarkets.

COOL TIP

Just because the label says "disposable" doesn't mean you can't wash and reuse an aluminum pan or plastic freezer container several times before it wears out. Save the planet—and your wallet—and reuse and recycle.

Low- and No-Plan Plans

Some people are natural planners. Others prefer a more free-form approach, taking life as it comes. If you fall into the latter category, you probably cook the same way. After all, how can you plan meals a week or more in advance when you don't know what you'll feel like eating or what culinary treasures you'll find at the market?

If you consider yourself a last-minute cook, try these easy no- and low-planning techniques.

Make More, Cook Less

With this easy no-plan plan, you cook exactly the way you do now, with one important difference—you double or triple the recipes and freeze the extra food for future meals. In fact, unless you're a single person living alone, you should think about making extra each and every time you cook for the freezer.

Aside from buying more of the ingredients you already intended to purchase, no extra planning goes into this cooking method. If you already have the ingredients on hand, making several dishes of the same recipe takes almost no extra time, and you'll only have to clean the kitchen and do the dishes once. Package the cooled extras in the freezer containers of your choice (see Chapter 2), and store for future meals.

This "make more" strategy works well with any of the recipes in this book, but don't limit yourself to just these. Get well acquainted with Chapter 1, where you learn which foods do and do not freeze well. Chances are, many of your family's favorite foods are already freezer friendly or can be altered a bit to make them so.

Anytime you set out to prepare a meal, stop and ask yourself if the recipe will work as freezer food. If it does, make more. Even if the entire meal you're already planning won't freeze well, perhaps the side dish or another component will. So make more of that. Do this every time you cook, and your freezer will soon be filled with a variety of tasty foods, and you won't have to cook as often.

> **COOL TIP**
>
> When cooking for the freezer, it's perfectly fine to use frozen vegetables. After all, the veggies are going to end up in the freezer anyway. When using frozen fruits or vegetables, you don't need to bother blanching them because the manufacturer already did it. Add frozen produce toward the end of cooking. It won't need as much time as fresh to cook.

Pick Two or Three

If you want to get only slightly more ambitious than no plan at all, choose two recipes—or even three if you really want to go wild. You don't have to actually prepare the two or three recipes on the same night, but have the ingredients on hand to make a few meals without having to go shopping again. You'll not only save time but also money on the fuel it takes to go back and forth to the store.

Choose this strategy when you know you'll have time over the next 5 or so days to make the meals and use the ingredients before they spoil. Don't stress too much over this. If your week suddenly gets busy, you can always freeze the most perishable ingredients, like meats, until later when you're ready to cook with them.

The Smart Shopper's Plan

Want to see how far you can really stretch your grocery budget? Then let the market decide your menu, and take full advantage of sales and bargains in a way you probably never have before. By grouping similar recipes together, you can buy ingredients in bulk and on sale and really rack up the savings.

To begin, check out the sale flyers for your local supermarkets. (If you don't get a newspaper, log on to the grocery store's website for the same information.) See what's on sale and then pick three or four recipes that use those *loss leader* foods as a main ingredient.

> **TABLE TALK**
>
> A **loss leader** is a sale item at a grocery store with a price so low the store technically takes a loss on it. Great examples include the low- or no-cost turkeys and hams available at Thanksgiving and Easter. Why would a business do this? Because it bets that while you're at the store buying the low-priced item, you'll do the rest of your shopping there, too. For freezer cooks buying in bulk, loss leaders can provide some of the best ways to fill your freezer with inexpensive meals.

The first time you try this strategy, you might find yourself intimidated at the thought of buying such large amounts. You might easily buy 10 pounds or more of meat. Don't worry! Remember that you have a plan to use it all.

When you return home from the market or big-box store, you can opt to spend a few hours cooking all the recipes on your list at once, or choose to spread out the cooking any way that fits your schedule. Make one per night for the next four nights, or perhaps make two dishes on each of the next two nights. It's up to you. Just be sure that if you get busy and are unable to cook it all in the next few days, pop any uncooked meat in the freezer. You can defrost it and proceed with your plan later.

Regardless of whether you intend to make all the recipes on your shopping list in one session, you can still prep for all of them as much as possible after you return from the market.

Taking a half hour or so after shopping streamlines your cooking later. For instance, if several recipes call for chopped onions, chop all the onions at once and store them in a zipper-lock plastic bag in the refrigerator until you're ready to use them. Read through the recipes you want to make to see if they have any other ingredients or techniques you can do now, while the chopping board and food processor are out.

Each recipe in this plan adds two or more entrées to your freezer's larder, so you don't have to cook this way very often before you can start taking it easy. Until then, pick another key ingredient on sale, choose some recipes that put it to good use, and repeat the process.

The Once-a-Week Plan

With this plan, you choose one day a week when you have a few uninterrupted hours to accomplish an entire week's worth of cooking. Your family will enjoy delicious, home-cooked meals from Sunday through Saturday, but all you'll need to do most nights is pull something out of the freezer, reheat, and perhaps toss in a fresh salad.

If cooking once a week sounds appealing, just wait, it gets better! The amount of work you'll need to do on your single cooking day decreases with each passing week. Every week, you'll store more meals in the freezer than your family can consume during that period. The first week you begin, you'll probably want to cook seven different main courses because you'll be starting with nothing in the freezer. Of course, you'll make two or three portions of each of these seven entrées, meaning you'll now have seven or more dinners waiting in the freezer.

The following week, you may opt to make five different entrées and use some of the first week's surplus for the remaining 2 days. On the third week, you'll have even more dishes squirreled away, so you may choose to take off 3 days. Your stockpile grows quickly, as long as you keep making more portions than you need every time you cook. By the fourth week, you may only need to make two or three recipes and still have a week's worth of different dinners in the freezer.

The key to success with once-a-week cooking, as with any cook-ahead method, is menu planning. This needn't be complicated, time-consuming, or inflexible. Just because you make a plan doesn't mean you have to rigidly stick to it. If something comes up and you find yourself eating out, just move your menu plan a day forward and continue. Consider it a head-start on next week's menu!

I give you a menu-planning worksheet in Appendix D. Fill in the blanks with recipes and meals you plan to serve during the upcoming week. Some you'll make; others will come from your freezer inventory sheet (remember that from Chapter 2?). Depending on your family's morning and afternoon habits and needs, you may or may not opt to plan as far as breakfasts, lunches, and snacks.

When you have your plan, make your shopping list for the items you intend to make that week.

Once you get the hang of it, planning a week's menu only takes 15 to 20 minutes, but it saves you from eating unhealthy fast-food or take-out meals because you neglected to plan for dinner. As the menu plan helps build your shopping list, you also avoid having to run to the store for forgotten ingredients.

> **COOL TIP**
>
> Do you have a busy family that regularly eats at different times? Package meals individually and include cooking instructions so each family member can access an easy homemade hot meal whenever they need it.

Make It a Party!

Why cook alone when you can do it with two or three friends?

Try it, and you'll discover that the weekly chore of cooking becomes an opportunity to catch up with friends and have fun while simultaneously preparing meals for everyone's families to enjoy later.

The easiest way to casually cook together is for each person in the group to choose a recipe or two and prepare the ingredients for those recipes. On cooking day, each person shows up with everything necessary to assemble their dish or dishes in a large enough quantity to satisfy the group's needs, and the session largely becomes a matter of assembly.

Rotate whose kitchen you use each time you get together—unless one person in the group has a larger or better-equipped space and they don't mind hosting.

The expenses of each recipe will likely differ, so save receipts and figure out how much it costs to make each recipe. Divide the cost by the number of portioned meals you make. Even if group members need different amounts, it will be easy to figure out how much each person owes by the number of portions they take home at the end of the day.

> **FREEZER BURN**
>
> It's so easy to get wrapped up shopping for food that you forget about packing supplies. The problem of dealing with a kitchen full of prepared foods and nowhere to put them is multiplied when cooking with friends. Don't forget, before you get together, that you need enough materials to package the foods everyone makes. It's most economical to purchase these in bulk at a restaurant supply or warehouse store. When cooking with friends, elect someone to make the purchase for everyone and then split the cost later.

Hybrid Cooking Plans

Freezer cooking can and should be all about you: what works for your schedule, your budget, and your family's tastes and dietary needs. When freezer cooking, you can be as aggressive or as lazy as you want at any given moment.

After you've been using any of the plans in this chapter for a while and have built up a substantial inventory in the freezer, it's easy to move back and forth among them. For example, knowing you have a freezer full of backup meals gives you the luxury to cook if and when you feel like it, as in the simple plan.

Or if you've been using the once-a-week plan for a while and have a good variety of foods stashed, you could supplement the collection while saving some bucks by switching to the smart shopper's plan.

Regardless of how you've set about stocking your freezer, if you're not starting completely from scratch, the once-a-month plan I introduce you to in Chapter 4 isn't nearly as intimidating or time-consuming. You might even be able to do an entire month's worth of shopping and cooking in a single day because you'll already have a substantial head-start in the freezer.

Special Events and Socializing

Having a freezer full of prepared food can take away massive amounts of entertaining and holiday stress. You can prepare days, weeks, even months in advance. When the big day comes, you'll be ready, and your family and friends will puzzle at how you did it all. Guests will watch in wonder as you serve the perfect dinner or homemade hors d'oeuvres yet still have time to mingle. Everyone will marvel at your seemingly effortless ability to be the perfect host or hostess. Only you need know the secret!

Give yourself plenty of time and plan for special occasions long before things get hectic and crazy. Try making a holiday recipe or two whenever you find some spare time. Or try to piggyback party prep, a little at a time, into your regularly scheduled cooking sessions. When the big day arrives, not only will the cooking be done, you'll be starting with a clean kitchen!

Big Formal Dinners

You may not want every part of your holiday meal to come out of the freezer, but a whole lot of it can, leaving substantially less work for you to do at the last minute. By preparing in advance, all you'll have to do is pop a turkey, ham, or roast in the oven; toss a salad; and heat up the rest of the meal.

Sure, you technically could prepare the main course in advance, too, but just because you *can* do something doesn't mean you *should*. For the most part, holiday entrées don't take much work, just time in the oven. For a presentation and taste that makes everyone *ooh* and *ahh*, make these on the big day itself.

As for the rest of the meal? Nobody needs to know you made the appetizers, soups, side dishes, and desserts days, weeks, or even months in advance.

Casual and Cocktail Parties

Cocktail party time is anytime when you have all the snacks ready and waiting.

As soon as you start thinking about hosting a party, begin squirreling away appetizers in the freezer. Or simply keep the freezer filled with snacks and finger foods during the entire holiday season.

Providing you keep the bar equally well stocked, you'll be ready for informal gatherings whenever they happen.

Postholiday Help

The freezer can help you out just as much after a holiday as it can before. Instead of listening to the family whine about having to eat turkey or ham *yet again*, freeze the leftovers and bring them out for dinners or sandwiches later, when they'll look forward to those foods again.

The day after the holiday is also a good time to look for ways to transform holiday leftovers into new dishes you can freeze. You'll find a nice variety of recipes using cooked ham or turkey in this book—and don't forget you can substitute cooked turkey in any recipe calling for cooked chicken. Treat your leftovers like a sharp shopper's session: plan in advance how to use leftover holiday food, and you'll be sure not to waste a bit.

COLD FACT

Cooked meats turn tough and dry when frozen. To keep moisture in leftover holiday meats like cooked turkey or ham, cover the cooked meat with gravy or sauce before freezing.

The Least You Need to Know

- A little bit of planning can save you a lot of time and money.
- The more you fill your freezer, the more days off from kitchen chores you can take.
- You can easily adapt meal plans to accommodate life's unexpected occurrences.
- Cooking with friends can save everyone time and money—and make kitchen time fun.
- Freezer cooking can help reduce holiday and entertaining stress.

Cook for a Weekend, Eat for a Month

In This Chapter

- Planning for "cooking large"
- Maximizing kitchen efficiency
- Cooking large with a friend

Is it really possible to spend two days cooking and then not have to do it again for an entire month? Absolutely! But "cooking large" like this takes careful planning and organization to pull off.

The more you organize the project and prepare in advance, the easier your marathon cooking weekend will go. I'm not going to sugarcoat it: you will put in long, exhausting hours, and by the end of it, you'll be more than ready to put your feet up. But when you think of all the free time you'll enjoy later because you don't have to think about planning or preparing meals again for an entire month, I think you'll agree that it's more than worth it!

The Essential Planning Session

Planning a month's worth of menus is much the same as planning for weekly cooking sessions, except you're planning for four weeks at a time. It might sound overwhelming at first, but it's really not once you get the hang of it.

Spread four menu-planning worksheets (see Appendix D) in front of you, and start filling in the blanks. Looking at all four sheets at once keeps you from repeating too many dishes too close to each other. It's handy to keep your current freezer inventory list nearby when planning so you can fill in some of the blanks with what's on hand if possible.

Even if you don't have a single meal banked in the freezer, you don't necessarily need to make 28 different meals or more. Fill in the end of the month with some of the dishes you make at the start, and give yourself a break. Most people won't get bored if a meal is repeated twice in a month.

Your planning session shouldn't stop with menu planning because the more organized you are now, the smoother cooking day is likely to go. Make lists of chores you can bundle, necessary cookware and supplies, and what packaging materials you need.

Now is also the time to make a master shopping list as well as decide the recipe cooking order so you know exactly where to start on the big day.

Don't get discouraged if the planning session for your first attempt at monthly cooking takes several hours. It gets easier each time you do it, and with time and experience, you'll be able to get it down to about an hour.

After your planning session, you should have the following lists or plans prepared:

- A list of 12 to 20 recipes you'll prepare in a single day. The closer you are to 12, the more realistic the goal. If you're heading toward 20, be sure most are quick to prepare and prep ingredients ahead of time if you want to finish in a single session.

- A shopping list of all the ingredients you need. You can refine the list before the big day, but prepare a basic list to start. If you think you might already have an item, place a question mark next to it on the list and check it out later.

- A list of chores you can bundle or do ahead of time.

- A list of the necessary pots, pans, and cooking tools to accomplish the day's plan.

- A list of the necessary packaging materials needed to wrap and freeze the dishes you'll be making.

If you plan on cooking with a partner (more on this later in the chapter), you'll also want to have a list that specifies each person's responsibilities and the items he or she needs to bring to the cooking session.

Preshopping Prep

Before heading out to the store, it's imperative that you take some time to ready your kitchen. You'll be coming home from the market with massive amounts of groceries.

The time to think about where you're going to put them all is now, *before* you go to the store.

Start by cleaning out your refrigerator. Not only will you clear space, you'll also be able to take an inventory of the foods in there to determine if any fit into your current cooking plans. If so, scratch them off your shopping list.

COOL TIP

If you think you'll need extra refrigerator space while preparing your month's worth of meals, fill a large cooler with ice. As long as you keep the ice supply steady, you'll have a great short-term place to store extra food.

Be sure you have room in the freezer for all the dishes coming its way. While you're preparing for this month's cooking marathon, you can eat up most of last month's stash so you have more space in the freezer.

Clean off the counters and table tops to make as much space as possible before you leave to shop. If you need more counter space and the weather is nice, consider placing a table outside near an electrical outlet so extra appliances like deep fryers, slow cookers, or portable toaster or convection ovens can do their thing outside. You'll save space and cut down on the heat in your kitchen.

You may also opt to have cutting boards, colanders, the food processor, and other kitchen prep implements out and ready for when you return. That way, you can save time by prepping ingredients for recipes as you put them away.

Shopping Large

It's here—the big shopping day! Before you step one foot out the door to go shopping for your cooking session, your master shopping list must be complete and ready to go. The upcoming cooking time is going to be busy enough as it is. You don't want to have to stop and make extra trips to the grocery store because you forgot key ingredients.

You put together a list earlier, when you planned your month's worth of menus. Take out that list again, and let's have a look at it. It helps if your list is organized in sections for like items such as meats, dairy, fresh produce, canned goods, frozen foods, herbs and spices, pantry staples (like flours and sugars), grains and pastas, miscellaneous items, and packaging materials.

If you need the same item for several recipes, keep track of the total amount you need in pounds, packages, items, or whatever quantifier makes sense for that particular item, and note that on your shopping list.

Take an inventory of what ingredients you already have on hand, and compare that to your shopping list. Can you cross off any items from your list?

Go through the pantry checklist in Appendix C, compare it to your shopping list, and be sure anything missing from your list is updated.

Finally, check your inventory of foil, plastic wrap, freezer paper, freezer containers, and anything else you need to package the meals you'll be making; then add to your list any items you need to pick up. After a hard day's work, you don't want to deal with having a kitchen full of prepared foods and nowhere to put them.

If you'll be shopping at more than one store, it helps to make a separate list for each store.

FREEZER BURN

When you cook large, you also spend large. Instead of spreading the grocery bill over several shopping trips, you pay it all at once. You may be saving money overall, but your single trip expenditure will be substantial. Budget accordingly if you need to so you're not faced with a surprise in the checkout line.

When you're at the store, don't be afraid to talk to the employees. You can sometimes negotiate discount prices at meat and produce markets when you're buying in large quantities. And sometimes grocers will waive quantity limits if you're buying in large amounts. It never hurts to ask!

You'll be facing the checkout line with a huge amount of groceries. Save yourself and your fellow shoppers some time and do your large shopping at off-peak hours. And try to shop early the day before you plan to cook so you have plenty of time to prepare ingredients in advance. If possible, save yourself some stress and leave the kids at home.

When shopping during warm weather, keep a cooler with ice in your car for meats and other perishables.

Kitchen Efficiency

A little extra planning and organizing before attempting to cook a month's worth of meals in a single session can make the difference between it being a challenging yet fun and rewarding experience, to one you never want to repeat again.

Instead of looking at just the individual recipes you'll be preparing, try to see the bigger picture of the task as a whole.

Once you actually start cooking, be sure to clean as you go as much as possible. This helps free counter space, and you won't run out of mixing bowls or pots and pans when you need them most. You'll also have far less of a mess to contend with at the end of the day when you'll be tired.

Bundle Your Chores

Several days before beginning a marathon cooking session, read through all the recipes you intend to make and write out a list of all the chores they have in common. When it comes time to prepare, bundle those chores together and save loads of time.

For example, if you're making six different dishes that all call for chopped mushrooms or peeled apples, total the amount of each ingredient you need and then make them at once. (Using a food processor, it only takes seconds!) Keep the prepped ingredients in zipper-lock plastic bags until you're ready to use them.

COOL TIP

Multitasking comes in really handy when you're cooking large. If you have the food processor out, do all the food processor chores back to back. A quick rinse of the processor between foods, and you're back in business. If you're chopping garlic for one dish, chop it for all the dishes you plan to make at once. Be sure to chop milder-flavored ingredients like carrots and apples before stronger ones like garlic and onions to avoid any flavor contamination. What other ways can you multitask?

Blanching (see Chapter 1) is another time-consuming chore that makes sense to bundle. List all the vegetables and fruits that need to be blanched before going into your freezer-friendly recipes. Bring a large pot of water to a simmer over medium heat. Some cookware comes with a steamer basket you can use to get the veggies in and out of the pot without the necessity of dumping out the hot water, and if you have this useful accessory, use it. Otherwise, a large slotted spoon can help get produce in and out of the pot without the necessity of dumping out the water each time to drain. Be sure to blanch delicately flavored and colored produce before those with stronger tastes or pigments to avoid flavor and color contamination. Don't hesitate to start over with fresh water if the color or flavor becomes too strong during batch blanching.

Blanch each vegetable variety separately. Use a separate pot of water to blanch fruit. Keep chilled blanched produce in zipper-lock bags in the refrigerator until ready for use in recipes.

Set Up a Logical Order

Look at all the recipes in your plan and determine the best order to prepare them. If you think about this strategically instead of just randomly cooking, you can maximize your time and energy as well as use space and appliances more efficiently.

When deciding the best order to prepare dishes for a month's worth of meals, try to pick at least one recipe you can make in a slow cooker and get that started early in the day. The dish will slowly cook as you prepare the rest of your month's menu, and by the time you're finished you'll have a well-deserved hot meal to look forward to before you package up the rest for freezing.

Also consider the recipes that need to be baked in the oven before you cool and freeze them. It's usually a good idea to start with the one that cooks at the lowest oven temperature. That way, you just keep bumping up the temperature for each succeeding dish you prepare.

Prepare recipes that cook on the stovetop while those in the oven bake. Assemble recipes that don't need any cooking before freezing while others are baking.

Schedule any recipes that require extra time for earlier in the session. For instance, start with long-simmered or slow-baked dishes or yeast doughs that require time to rise.

If you plan on making recipes that require counter space, such as pizzas that need to be rolled out or fussy little appetizers that require lots of assembly, schedule them last. You'll already have other items out of the way.

Sharing the Cooking

Why take on a marathon cooking session all by yourself? Especially when getting together with a friend or family member shares the expense, the work, and the rewards? If you have a large kitchen, you may be able to include three people in your cooking group, but because you'll be making so much food, I don't recommend any more than that. Two people are plenty if you have a small kitchen. Otherwise, things can get too crowded. You'll each need work space, and you don't want to be tripping over each other, especially when sharp knives are involved.

FREEZER BURN

Bacteria grow most rapidly between 40°F to 140°F, the so-called "danger zone," so it's important to keep foods either hotter or colder than that range. When cooking at a friend's house, be sure to bring along a cooler and ice so you can safely pack and transport the food back home to your freezer.

Choosing a Cooking Partner

Not all cooking partners are created equal. Before you invite someone to your marathon cooking party, ask yourself some questions.

Do you two have similar taste in food? If you don't like the recipes your partner chooses and vice versa, you'll both be eating foods you don't like for at least half a month.

Do you need the same amount of food? This isn't absolutely essential, but it does make it easier to divide workload and expenses if you and your cooking partner have similar-size families.

Is your partner reliable? Do not attempt to cook with folks who regularly flake out on obligations unless you're prepared to take on the cooking by yourself when they remain true to old patterns.

Are you and your partner compatible? Even if everything else lines up, if the person you're cooking with has habits or mannerisms that drive you crazy—even if you love him or her—you'll make yourself miserable trying to undertake such a large project with them. Do yourself a favor and save interactions with this person for short-term socializing.

Dividing the Duties

Try to get together with your partner a week or so before you plan on cooking to discuss how many recipes you need to make and in what quantities.

Everyone will benefit by incorporating elements of the smart shopper's plan in Chapter 3. You'll be buying a lot of groceries, and by tailoring menu plans around what's on sale, you can save a bundle of money.

How you divide the duties and the bills depends on your needs. If two people get together and they both have the same-size family, it's easy to split everything down the middle. If one party needs more portions than another, you'll have to do a little more math.

You may opt to go on a group shopping trip, but it's often more effective to elect one person to shop for everyone and split the costs later. Rotate the shopper each month so one person doesn't take on too much work.

Alternatively, each person can claim certain recipes they will be "responsible for," meaning they show up on cooking day with the ingredients necessary to assemble that dish in a large-enough quantity to satisfy the collective needs of the partners. Whether that person also brings packaging materials and the necessary pots, pans, bowls, and utensils depends on whether the group bought packing supplies together in advance, and how much cookware the host kitchen has on hand. Be sure to discuss these issues in advance.

To divide expenses when each partner needs a different amount, keep the receipts and total what it costs to make the entire recipe. Divide by the number of portions, and have each person pay for the number of portions they take home. If some of the items came from the pantry as opposed to the store, you can estimate their cost or look it up on your local supermarket's website.

The Least You Need to Know

- Cooking a month's worth of meals at once takes planning and organization.
- Prepare for the influx of food coming your kitchen's way by cleaning and preparing it before you go shopping.
- Cut grocery costs by planning menus according to current sales.
- Share the work and reward of freezer cooking, and get more done in less time.

From-the-Freezer Morning Meals

Nutritionists and moms alike tout breakfast as the most important meal of the day. But busy people know it's the most challenging meal to fit in a busy weekday morning. After all, who has time to prepare breakfast, sit down and eat it, and still get to school or work on time?

Let your freezer take away that morning-meal stress! By preparing breakfasts later in the day, when you're awake and not rushed, you'll save time (and maybe a little sanity) in the mornings.

Your freezer can help you avoid morning boredom. Whether you crave traditional fare like bacon, sausage, eggs, and pancakes or are seeking more creative ways to wake up your taste buds, the recipes in Part 2 fit the bill. You'll find fare for special occasion brunches and leisurely weekend mornings. You can even surprise a special someone with breakfast in bed, without messing up the kitchen!

Traditional Breakfasts

In This Chapter

- Freezing eggs and egg dishes
- Breakfast meats and the freezer
- Delicious breakfasts your family will love

There's nothing like the smell of bacon or sausage cooking to wake up the senses. But who has time on a busy morning to stop and cook a traditional breakfast of eggs and their usual accompaniments?

With help from your freezer and the recipes in this chapter, time in the morning to cook a traditional breakfast is no longer an issue.

Freezing Eggs

When thinking about egg dishes that might freeze well, focus on recipes in which the yolks don't remain runny. The freezer tends to transform runny egg yolks, whether cooked or raw, into a thick, unusable, gelatinous goo. On the other hand, mix yolks and egg whites together, and the resulting dish should freeze beautifully. You can freeze raw eggs this way, too. Remove from the shell, whisk until whites and yolks are well combined, and freeze for future use. Egg whites alone freeze beautifully.

These measurement equivalents will help you when using thawed frozen eggs in recipes:

> 2 tablespoons thawed egg white or 1 ounce/28 grams thawed egg white by weight = 1 large fresh egg white
>
> 3 tablespoons thawed scrambled eggs = 1 large fresh egg

Freezing Breakfast Meats

Unlike meats with a lot of connective tissue (think: steaks and chops), cooked breakfast meats freeze without much compromise. Cook sausage patties or links or strips of bacon, wrap well, and freeze. Then simply reheat for a minute or so in the microwave for a quick breakfast.

Take advantage of sales on sausage and bacon, and freeze the meat raw. Because of their high fat content, these meats conveniently thaw quicker than most.

Don't store raw bacon or sausage more than a month or so because fat can still turn rancid in the freezer. The salt in cured meats hastens the process.

Breakfast Burritos

All your favorite breakfast flavors are here—spicy sausage, home-fried potatoes, and eggs—all wrapped in a neat little package you can take with you on busy mornings.

Yield:	Prep time:	Initial cook time:	Reheat time:	Serving size:
16 burritos	50 minutes	35 minutes	2½ minutes	1 burrito

5 or 6 medium potatoes, diced

1 TB. plus 2 tsp. olive oil

Salt

Black pepper

1 large onion, diced

1 (7-oz.) can diced green chiles, drained

1 lb. bulk lite breakfast sausage

16 large eggs

1 tsp. butter or margarine

16 (8-in.) flour tortillas

2 cups shredded Jack or cheddar cheese

1. Bring a large pot of water to a boil over high heat.

2. Add potatoes to boiling water, and *parboil* for 10 minutes. Drain.

3. In a large skillet over medium-high heat, heat 1 tablespoon olive oil. Add potatoes, and sauté, stirring occasionally, for about 10 minutes or until potatoes are browned and almost cooked through. (Depending on the size of your skillet, you may need to do this in two batches to avoid overcrowding.) Season with salt and pepper, remove from pan to a large bowl, and set aside.

4. In the same skillet over medium-high heat, heat remaining 2 teaspoons olive oil. Add onion and fresh green chiles (if using fresh), and sauté for about 5 minutes or until softened and onions are just beginning to brown. Add sausage, and cook, stirring frequently to break sausage into crumbles, for about 6 minutes or until sausage is cooked through. Stir in the canned green chiles (if using canned), remove to a separate bowl, and set aside.

5. In a medium bowl, whisk eggs.

6. In the same skillet over medium heat, heat 1 teaspoon butter. Add eggs and cook, stirring and turning eggs constantly, for about 3 or 4 minutes or until eggs are just cooked. Remove from heat.

7. Center 1 tortilla on a 12-inch piece of waxed paper. Place ingredients down the center of each tortilla, leaving a $\frac{1}{2}$-inch border at the top and bottom. For each tortilla, use $\frac{1}{3}$ cup cooked potatoes, $\frac{1}{4}$ cup sausage mixture, $\frac{1}{4}$ cup egg, and 2 tablespoons shredded Jack cheese. Fold in top and bottom of tortilla and then roll tightly.

8. Wrap filled burritos tightly in the waxed paper, store wrapped burritos in a large zipper-lock plastic bag, label, and freeze.

To reheat after freezing:

1. Unwrap burrito from the waxed paper, and place on a paper towel–lined plate. Microwave on high for about $2\frac{1}{2}$ minutes or until heated through, stopping to turn once during cooking.

2. Serve with your favorite hot sauce (optional).

TABLE TALK

Similar to blanching with a longer cooking time, **parboiling** involves partially cooking foods in boiling water.

English Muffin Breakfast Sandwiches

These sandwiches contain the classic flavors of egg and ham, just like a traditional diner's plate breakfast, accented by a creamy melt of cheddar cheese.

Yield:	Prep time:	Initial cook time:	Reheat time:	Serving size:
12 sandwiches	10 minutes	10 minutes	40 minutes oven/ 1½ minutes microwave	1 sandwich

12 English muffins, any variety

6 slices cheddar cheese

12 slices *Canadian bacon*

12 large eggs

2 tsp. butter or margarine

1. Split English muffins in ½ and arrange in a single layer on a cutting board or baking sheet. Cover ½ of each English muffin with ½ slice cheddar cheese. Top cheese with 1 slice Canadian bacon.

2. In a medium bowl, whisk eggs.

3. In a large skillet over medium-high heat, heat butter. Add eggs, and cook for about 1½ minutes or until just set but still runny. Using a spatula, flip eggs over and cook for about 1½ to 2 more minutes or until just set. Do not overcook and let the eggs turn hard!

4. Divide eggs into 12 portions, and place 1 cooked egg portion on top of Canadian bacon, folding egg patty to fit if necessary. Top with second muffin ½, and allow to cool completely.

5. Wrap each sandwich in aluminum foil or plastic wrap, label, and freeze wrapped sandwiches in large zipper-lock plastic freezer bags.

To reheat after freezing:

1. Preheat oven or toaster oven to 375°F. Bake frozen, foil-wrapped sandwich for 40 minutes, or until heated through and cheese is melted. (Open a corner and peek in to check.) Alternatively, remove sandwich from foil or plastic wrap, and place on a folded paper towel on a plate. Microwave for about 1½ minutes or until heated through.

Variation: This sandwich is easy to adapt. Swap the Canadian bacon for a cooked breakfast sausage patty, a vegetarian sausage patty, or a couple slices cooked bacon. A little chopped onion and bell peppers added to the cooking eggs gives the dish a boost of flavor and nutrition. You can experiment with different types of cheeses, too.

TABLE TALK

Canadian bacon, or "back bacon" to Canadians, is made from lean smoked eye of loin. It's closer in taste and texture to ham than traditional bacon. It usually comes packaged and presliced and is always precooked, so it only needs an optional reheating to serve.

Biscuit Breakfast Sandwiches

Flaky buttermilk biscuits encase scrambled eggs and smoky bacon in this Southern-inspired breakfast favorite.

Yield:	Prep time:	Initial cook time:	Reheat time:	Serving size:
14 biscuit sandwiches	25 minutes	35 minutes	45 minutes oven/1 minute, 20 seconds microwave	1 sandwich

3 cups all-purpose flour	14 slices bacon
1 TB. baking powder	16 eggs
1 tsp. salt	2 tsp. butter or margarine
1 TB. sugar	1 TB. water
¾ cup vegetable shortening	14 slices cheddar cheese
1⅓ cups buttermilk	

1. Preheat the oven to 425°F. Grease a large baking sheet with vegetable shortening, spray with cooking spray, or line with a sheet of parchment paper.

2. In a food processor, combine all-purpose flour, baking powder, salt, sugar, and vegetable shortening. Pulse 10 to 20 times or until well combined. Take care not to overprocess; mixture should be crumbly when ready. If it turns pasty, you've gone too far. Alternatively, use a pastry blender to cut shortening into dry ingredients until you have a coarse crumbly mixture.

3. Add buttermilk, and pulse machine briefly 3 or 4 times until dough just comes together.

4. Turn dough out onto a lightly floured surface, and roll to a 1-inch thickness. Use a 3-inch round cookie cutter (or the bottom of a small drinking glass) to cut dough into 14 circles, rerolling scraps when necessary. Place dough circles close together on the greased baking sheet. Beat remaining 2 eggs with 1 tablespoon water until well combined. Lightly brush tops of biscuits with egg mixture. Bake for about 25 minutes or until beginning to turn golden. Cool on a wire rack.

5. Lower the oven temperature to 400°F. Place bacon slices on a broiler pan, and bake for about 10 minutes or until cooked and crispy.

6. In a medium bowl, whisk eggs.

7. In a large skillet over medium-high heat, heat butter. Add eggs, and cook, stirring gently, for $1\frac{1}{2}$ minutes or until eggs are just set. Use a spatula to flip eggs over and cook for about a minute or so more until just set. Remove from heat.

8. Split each biscuit in $\frac{1}{2}$. Place 1 slice cheddar cheese on $\frac{1}{2}$ of each biscuit, tearing cheese to fit neatly on biscuit. Top with a portion of scrambled egg. Cut a slice of bacon in $\frac{1}{2}$ and cross halves on top of egg before topping with second biscuit $\frac{1}{2}$.

9. Wrap sandwiches in plastic wrap, freezer paper, or foil. Place cooled wrapped sandwiches in a zipper-lock plastic freezer bag, label, and freeze.

To reheat after freezing:

1. Remove wrapping from frozen sandwich and rewrap in a slightly dampened paper towel. Microwave for about 1 minute, 20 seconds. Alternatively, heat foil-wrapped sandwich in a 375°F oven or toaster oven for about 45 minutes or until heated through.

COOL TIP

With sandwiches like this one and the previous one, you sometimes run into the problem of the cheese melting at a different rate than the rest of the sandwich. If you find the cheese turning to liquid before the rest of the sandwich reheats, freeze the sandwiches with the cheese on the side, and add it during the last 30 seconds or so of microwave heating time or the last 10 minutes of oven cooking time.

Home-Fry Breakfast Potatoes

Crispy pan-fried potatoes, accented with the flavors of onion, bell pepper, and garlic, make a perfect side dish to a traditional American-style fried egg breakfast.

Yield:	Prep time:	Initial cook time:	Reheat time:	Serving size:
6½ cups	15 minutes	20 minutes	12 minutes	½ cup

6 medium russet potatoes	2 TB. olive oil
2 medium yellow onions, diced	Salt
2 small red and/or green bell peppers, ribs and seeds removed, and chopped	Black pepper

1. Bring a large pot of water to a boil over high heat.

2. While water heats, slice washed, skin-on potatoes lengthwise into 3 or 4 planks each. Stack several planks on top of one another, and slice into 3 or 4 long strips. Gather strips together, and chop into small, ½-inch cubes.

3. Add potatoes to boiling water, and parboil for 10 minutes. Add onions and bell peppers during the last 3 minutes of cooking. Drain.

4. In a large skillet over medium-high heat, heat olive oil. Add potatoes, onions, and peppers, and cook, turning occasionally, for about 10 minutes or until beginning to brown and crisp. Season with salt and pepper, and cool completely.

5. Freeze in a single layer on a waxed paper–lined baking sheet. Remove frozen potatoes to a zipper-lock plastic freezer bag, label, and freeze.

To reheat after freezing:

1. In a large skillet (be sure it's large enough to hold potatoes without overcrowding) over medium-high heat, heat 1 to 3 teaspoons olive oil (depending on how much potatoes you're making).

2. Remove as much potatoes as you like from the bag, and add to the skillet. Use caution and stand back anytime you add frozen food to a hot pan with oil—it can and will splatter! Cook potatoes, breaking up pieces with a spatula and turning occasionally, for 10 to 12 minutes or until brown, crisp, and heated

through. Season with salt and pepper, and serve as a side dish or top with 1 or 2 sunny-side-up fried eggs.

COOL TIP

If you happen to be baking potatoes for another meal, or have the oven on for whatever reason, you can skip step 1 of this recipe and bake the potatoes instead of parboiling them. Remove them from the oven when they are ¾ cooked, let cool, dice, and proceed.

Cinnamon Swirl French Toast

Cinnamon, both in the bread and in the batter, gives this sweet French toast a double dose of cinnamon-y goodness.

Yield:	Prep time:	Initial cook time:	Reheat time:	Serving size:
24 slices	5 minutes	20 minutes	3 minutes toaster/ 30 seconds microwave	2 slices

7 large eggs

¾ cup whole milk

2 tsp. vanilla extract

2 TB. sugar

1 tsp. ground cinnamon

⅛ tsp. salt

24 slices cinnamon raisin bread

1. Preheat a griddle or large skillet over medium heat.

2. In a large, shallow bowl, whisk together eggs, whole milk, vanilla extract, sugar, ground cinnamon, and salt.

3. Spray the griddle or skillet with cooking spray or coat with a thin layer of cooking oil mixed with a small amount of melted butter.

4. Dip 1 slice of bread in egg mixture, turning to coat both sides. Be careful not to soak bread too long, especially if it's fresh, or it'll fall apart. Place coated bread on the prepared griddle or skillet. Repeat with more bread until cooking space is filled. (You will have to batter and cook in batches.)

5. Cook for 1 or 2 minutes or until golden brown. (Use a spatula to lift up a corner for a peek.) Flip over and cook for about 1½ more minutes or until golden brown on the other side.

6. Stack cooked slices on plates and allow to cool completely before placing in a zipper-lock plastic freezer bag, labeling, and freezing.

To reheat after freezing:

1. Toast in the toaster or toaster oven, on the dark setting, as you would any other slice of bread (preferred method). Alternatively, microwave for about 30 seconds per slice.

2. Serve with butter and maple or fruit syrup.

Buttermilk Pancakes

Buttermilk makes these traditional pancakes light, fluffy, and tender, with a delicate, sweet flavor.

Yield:	Prep time:	Initial cook time:	Reheat time:	Serving size:
36 pancakes	10 minutes	25 minutes	10 minutes oven/ 3 minutes toaster/ 30 seconds microwave	3 pancakes

3 cups all-purpose flour	1 tsp. baking soda
¼ cup sugar	4 large eggs
½ tsp. salt	3¼ cups buttermilk
2 tsp. baking powder	1 tsp. vanilla extract

1. Preheat a griddle or large skillet over medium heat.

2. In a large bowl, whisk together all-purpose flour, sugar, salt, baking powder, and baking soda until well combined. Add eggs, buttermilk, and vanilla extract, and whisk until just combined and no lumps remain. Do not overmix.

3. Coat the griddle or skillet with a thin coat of cooking oil or cooking spray. Spoon ⅓ cup batter onto the cooking surface for each pancake. Cook for about 1½ minutes, or until bubbles begin to dot surface of pancake. Use a spatula to flip over pancakes, and cook for 1 more minute or so or until golden brown on the second side.

4. Cool pancakes completely on plates or baking sheets, stack in a zipper-lock plastic freezer bag, label, and freeze.

To reheat after freezing:

1. Place frozen pancakes on a baking sheet coated with cooking spray in a preheated 350°F oven or toaster oven for 10 minutes (preferred method). For a crispier pancake, place frozen pancake in the toaster on the dark setting, just as you would a slice of bread. Alternatively, microwave for about 20 to 30 seconds per single pancake. Watch carefully because the pancakes will get tough if they spend too long in the microwave.

2. Serve with butter and maple or fruit syrup

Variation: To create a whole new taste sensation, add fresh blueberries or raspberries; raisins or dried, sweetened cranberries; finely chopped dried fruit such as dates, peaches, mangoes, or pineapple; finely chopped fresh fruit such as bananas, apples, peaches, strawberries, etc.; chopped toasted nuts or coconut; crisp cooked bacon bits; or chocolate chips, peanut butter chips, or toffee chips.

COOL TIP

To test to see if the griddle is hot enough, flick a few drops of water onto it. If they sputter and bounce before evaporating, it's hot enough.

Malted Waffles

If you've ever had a waffle that had an indescribably good flavor you couldn't quite identify, *malted milk powder* was probably responsible, as it is in this recipe. The same powder that gives malted milkshakes their character does the same for waffles.

Yield:	Prep time:	Initial cook time:	Reheat time:	Serving size:
8 large waffles	10 minutes	20 minutes	3 minutes	1 waffle

1½ cups all-purpose flour

1½ tsp. baking powder

1 TB. sugar

½ tsp. salt

¼ cup malted milk powder

2 large eggs

1¼ cups milk

5 TB. unsalted butter or margarine, melted

1. Preheat a waffle iron according to manufacturer's instructions.

2. In a large bowl, mix all-purpose flour, baking powder, sugar, salt, and malted milk powder. Add eggs and milk, and whisk well. Whisk in melted butter until well blended. Do not overmix.

3. Spray waffle iron surfaces with cooking spray. Spoon on enough batter so it will spread and cover the surface without spilling out over the edges. (The amount will vary from waffle iron to waffle iron. Check the instructions that came with yours.) Cook for about 4 minutes per waffle or until browned.

4. Cool waffles completely on plates or baking sheets, stack in a zipper-lock plastic freezer bag, label, and freeze.

To reheat after freezing:

1. Reheat in the toaster on the dark setting just as you would any piece of bread. Serve with butter and maple or fruit syrup.

Variation: For **Malted Pecan Waffles,** add ½ cup finely chopped toasted pecans to the batter.

TABLE TALK

Malted milk powder is made from a mixture of malted barley and wheat mixed with whole milk and then evaporated into a powder. Some brands also add sugar. Either kind works in this recipe.

Irish-Style Oatmeal with Cranberries

Irish or *steel-cut oats* have a chewier texture and higher fiber content than old-fashioned or quick-cooking oats. Sweetened dried cranberries provide a perfect counterpart to the whole-grain steel-cut oats' naturally nutty flavor.

Yield:	Prep time:	Initial cook time:	Reheat time:	Serving size:
3 cups	5 minutes	20 minutes	5 minutes	1 cup

4 cups water	¾ cup sweetened dried cranberries
1 cup steel-cut or Irish oats	¼ tsp. ground cinnamon

1. In a medium saucepan over high heat, bring water to a boil.

2. Sprinkle oats over boiling water, and stir to mix well. Add sweetened dried cranberries and ground cinnamon, and stir well.

3. Reduce heat to low and simmer, uncovered, for about 20 minutes or until most of liquid is absorbed and oatmeal is a little runny. (Putting the prepared oats into the freezer slightly undercooked ensures they come out perfect upon reheating.)

4. Cool completely. Stir well, package in rigid freezer containers, label, and freeze.

To reheat after freezing:

1. Reheat in the microwave. The time depends on the size of the portion. A frozen 1 cup portion takes about 5 minutes to heat completely. Stop and stir once during that time.

2. Traditional Irish oatmeal is served with buttermilk, but you can also serve with milk, cream, or butter. Add additional sugar if needed.

Variation: If you're not a cranberry fan, substitute raisins or dried currants instead.

TABLE TALK

Besides great flavor and texture, **steel-cut** or **Irish oats** also have more nutritional value than rolled oats, which are steamed, rolled, resteamed, and toasted. Whole-grain steel-cut oats go through none of this processing, so they retain their naturally high fiber content and levels of B vitamins, calcium, and protein.

Outside-the-Box Breakfasts

In This Chapter

- Indulgent ways to start the day
- Sweet and savory muffins
- Casseroles and dishes to feed a crowd

Eggs, bacon, sausage, pancakes, French toast—there's something to be said for these traditional breakfast favorites. But there's so much more you can start your day off with! Break your breakfast routines with recipes that use old favorites in new ways or go beyond the breakfast basics.

In this chapter, I give you sweet A.M. indulgences, portable muffins and banana bread, as well as breakfast casseroles that feed a hungry crowd.

The recipes in this chapter might inspire you to further think outside the breakfast box. Look in other chapters of this book to see what recipes you can adapt as breakfast. How about a breakfast version of pizza (recipes in Chapter 15)? The Mini Quiche Lorraine appetizers in Chapter 7 contain traditional breakfast flavors in a new form, or you can vary the recipe however you like.

Use your imagination when it comes to breakfast, and you'll be surprised at the creative culinary ways your freezer can help you start the day!

Cheese Blintzes

These delicate, creamy stuffed crepes taste like the height of decadence but are actually a relatively light treat you can enjoy any morning or use to wow guests at brunch. They take a little time to make, but they aren't difficult and you'll be well rewarded for your effort.

Yield:	Prep time:	Initial cook time:	Reheat time:	Serving size:
30 blintzes	1 hour	30 minutes	20 minutes	2 blintzes

8 large eggs

3 cups whole or reduced-fat milk

4 TB. unsalted butter, melted

¾ tsp. salt

1 TB. plus ¼ cup sugar

1½ cups plus 3 TB. all-purpose flour

1 (32-oz.) pkg. plus 1 (15-oz.) pkg. ricotta cheese (whole milk or part skim)

2 tsp. vanilla extract

1 batch Blueberry Compote (recipe in Chapter 18)

1. In a medium bowl, and using an electric mixer on medium speed, blend 6 eggs, whole milk, melted butter, ½ teaspoon salt, 1 tablespoon sugar, and 1½ cups all-purpose flour. (Alternatively, you can use a blender to mix.) Let batter rest for 5 minutes.

2. Heat an 8-inch nonstick sauté pan over medium heat. Spray lightly with cooking spray, and pour in a scant ¼ cup batter. Immediately begin to tilt the pan in all directions to coat the entire bottom of the pan and slightly up the sides with a paper-thin coating of batter.

3. Cook over medium heat until top of crepe is set and you can easily lift edge with the corner of a plastic heat-proof spatula. Watch carefully because with a properly heated skillet, the whole process only takes about 30 seconds. As much as possible, avoid browning crepes. As a beginner, you'll probably waste a few, but you'll soon be a pro.

4. Turn cooked crepe onto a plate. (If it's properly set, there's no need to flip it and cook the other side.) Repeat with remaining batter, stacking cooked crepes between layers of waxed paper.

5. In a medium bowl, mix together ricotta cheese, remaining 2 eggs, remaining ¼ cup sugar, vanilla extract, remaining ¼ teaspoon salt, and remaining 3 tablespoons all-purpose flour.

6. To fill crepes, place about 3 tablespoons filling in a line down the center of each crepe, leaving about a 1-inch margin at top and bottom. Fold in top and bottom of crepe. Fold one side over top of filling and continue rolling until you have a small oblong shape.

7. Freeze filled blintzes individually on a waxed paper–lined baking sheet or platter. Once frozen, store in a rigid freezer container or zipper-lock plastic freezer bag, label, and freeze.

To reheat after freezing:

1. Heat a skillet large enough to hold the number of blintzes you intend to cook over medium-low heat. Add 1 teaspoon cooking oil and 1 teaspoon butter. Add frozen blintzes, and fry for about 8 or 9 minutes per side, turning at least twice during cooking, until browned and beginning to crisp. (Be careful of the temperature—if it's too high, blintzes will burn before filling warms all the way through.) An easy way around this is to microwave frozen blintzes for 1 or 2 minutes, depending on how many you're making, to slightly defrost them before adding to the skillet. Serve topped with 1 or 2 tablespoons Blueberry Compote and 1 dollop sour cream or plain yogurt.

COOL TIP

You can fill crepes with all kinds of sweet or savory ingredients, which makes them a handy recipe component to keep on hand. Freeze stacks of cooked unfilled crepes with a layer of waxed paper between each, wrapped tightly in foil, and placed in a plastic zipper-lock freezer bag. Pull out just the number you need to use, thaw, fill, and enjoy!

Cinnamon Rolls

There's nothing like the aroma of freshly baking cinnamon rolls to get folks out of bed in the morning. Trouble was, someone used to have to get up very early to make these sweet treats. No more, thanks to these rolls, which go straight from the freezer to the oven.

Yield:	Prep time:	Reheat time:	Serving size:
44 rolls	8 hours	45 minutes	1 roll

1 (18.25-oz.) box yellow cake mix

5¾ cups all-purpose flour

4½ tsp. dry yeast (2 envelopes)

¾ tsp. salt

5½ cups very warm water (100°F to 110°F)

¾ cup sugar

1 TB. ground cinnamon

½ cup unsalted butter, melted

1 batch Cream Cheese Frosting (recipe in Chapter 18; optional)

1. In a large bowl, stir together yellow cake mix, all-purpose flour, and dry yeast. Add very warm water, and salt and stir until everything is well combined. (Dough will be sticky.) Cover with a clean kitchen towel and let rise in a warm place, free from drafts, for 1½ hours. Dough will be not quite doubled.

2. In a small bowl, combine sugar and ground cinnamon. Set aside.

3. Grease baking pans with butter or vegetable shortening—enough to hold 44 (3-inch) rolls, in whatever quantities you want to freeze them in to suit your family's needs. I often freeze two small rolls in a small pie pan. That's just enough for two people to have a small treat.

4. Turn out dough onto a floured surface. Divide in ½, and roll out 1 portion to an approximately 13×9-inch rectangle.

5. Brush rolled dough with ½ of melted butter, and sprinkle ½ of cinnamon-sugar mixture over top.

6. Roll up dough, starting at the long end, into a log. Cut crosswise into 1-inch slices, and place slices onto prepared baking sheets, just touching each other, but not overcrowding. Repeat with remaining dough. Cover baking pans with foil, and refrigerate for at least 6 hours.

7. Remove chilled, foil-covered rolls from the refrigerator, label, and freeze.

To bake after freezing:

1. Preheat the oven to 350°F. Bake uncovered frozen rolls in their baking pan for 45 minutes or until golden brown. Top slightly cooled rolls with Cream Cheese Frosting (if desired).

Variation: Add ½ cup chopped toasted nuts and/or raisins to the cinnamon-sugar mixture.

COLD FACT

Most "cinnamon" sold in the United States is actually cassia, the dried bark of a tree in the Laurel family. Actual cinnamon comes from the bark of an evergreen tree. No worries whether or not your cinnamon is "genuine" because the two are virtually indistinguishable in recipes.

Orange Blueberry Muffins

Tart blueberries are underscored by the subtle flavor of orange in these low-fat muffins kept moist thanks to tangy yogurt.

Yield:	Prep time:	Initial cook time:	Reheat time:	Serving size:
24 muffins	10 minutes	25 minutes	30 seconds	1 muffin

4 cups all-purpose flour

1 cup plus 2 TB. sugar

2 tsp. baking powder

2 tsp. baking soda

½ tsp. salt

½ cup frozen orange juice concentrate, thawed

2 tsp. vanilla extract

⅛ cup vegetable oil

3 cups (24 oz.) vanilla low-fat yogurt

2 large eggs

2 cups fresh or frozen blueberries, not defrosted

1. Preheat the oven to 400°F. Spray 24 (3-inch) muffin cups with cooking spray, or grease with vegetable shortening.

2. In a large bowl, stir together all-purpose flour, 1 cup sugar, baking powder, baking soda, and salt.

3. In a small bowl, whisk together orange juice concentrate, vanilla extract, vegetable oil, vanilla low-fat yogurt, and eggs. Stir into dry ingredients, and mix until just mixed. Fold in blueberries.

4. Divide batter among the 24 prepared muffin cups, sprinkle 2 tablespoons sugar over tops, and bake for about 25 minutes or until tops are beginning to turn golden. Let muffins cool in the pan for 5 minutes before removing to a wire rack to cool completely.

5. Place cooled muffins in a zipper-lock plastic freezer bag, label, and freeze.

To reheat after freezing:

1. Thaw the number of muffins you want at room temperature, and enjoy. Alternatively, microwave frozen muffin for about 30 seconds or just until thawed and warmed.

Carrot Zucchini Muffins

These lightly spicy, not-too-sweet, raisin-studded muffins hold a secret—they're filled with vegetables! Carrots and zucchini boost the nutritional value while keeping the muffins moist without any added oil or fat.

Yield:	Prep time:	Initial cook time:	Reheat time:	Serving size:
16 muffins	25 minutes	20 minutes	30 seconds	1 muffin

2 medium carrots (about 1½ cups shredded)

2 small zucchini (about 1½ cups shredded)

1 cup all-purpose flour

1 cup whole-wheat flour

½ cup plus 2 TB. raw sugar or firmly packed brown sugar

1 TB. baking powder

½ tsp. salt

2 tsp. ground cinnamon

1½ tsp. ground ginger

¼ tsp. ground nutmeg

1 cup whole milk

2 large eggs

2 tsp. vanilla extract

1 cup raisins

1. Preheat the oven to 425°F. Grease 16 (3-inch) muffin cups with butter or vegetable shortening. (Because most muffin tins contain 6 or 12 cups, you'll most likely be leaving some cups in one tin ungreased.)

2. Peel carrots. Using a large box grater, shred carrots and zucchini. (If you have a food processor with a grating attachment, you can use it and significantly reduce the prep time.) Set shredded vegetables aside.

3. In a large bowl, combine all-purpose flour, whole-wheat flour, ½ cup raw sugar, baking powder, salt, ground cinnamon, ground ginger, and ground nutmeg.

4. In a small bowl, whisk together whole milk, eggs, and vanilla extract.

5. Pour milk mixture into dry ingredients all at once, and stir until just combined.

6. Stir in shredded carrots, shredded zucchini, and raisins just until everything is incorporated.

7. Fill each greased muffin cup about ⅔ full. Sprinkle tops of muffins with remaining 2 tablespoons raw sugar, and bake for about 20 minutes or until muffins are set and tops are beginning to turn golden.

8. Let muffins cool in the pan for 5 minutes before removing to a wire rack to cool completely. Place cooled muffins in a zipper-lock plastic freezer bag, label, and freeze.

To reheat after freezing:

1. Thaw the number of muffins you want at room temperature, and enjoy. Alternatively, microwave a frozen muffin for about 30 seconds and enjoy.

> **COOL TIP**
>
> You'll notice this healthy muffin recipe contains no oil, butter, or other added fat. The carrots and zucchini keep the muffins moist. Fruits can do the same. Try substituting part or all of the oil or fat in baking recipes with applesauce or prune purée. You'll be amazed at the moist results.

Banana Bread

Use up your extra-ripe sweet bananas in this breakfast bread you can augment with nuts or chocolate chips.

Yield:	Prep time:	Initial cook time:	Serving size:
4 (3½×7½-inch) loaves	15 minutes	1 hour	1¼-inch slice

6 cups all-purpose flour

¾ cup sugar

1½ cups firmly packed brown sugar

1 tsp. salt

2 tsp. baking powder

1½ tsp. baking soda

1 tsp. ground cinnamon

¾ tsp. ground nutmeg

8 medium extra-ripe bananas, peeled and mashed (3 cups)

¾ cup buttermilk

3 large eggs

¾ cup butter, melted

2 tsp. vanilla extract

1. Preheat the oven to 350°F. Spray 4 (3½×7½-inch) loaf pans or grease with vegetable shortening or butter.

2. In a medium bowl, combine all-purpose flour, sugar, brown sugar, salt, baking powder, baking soda, ground cinnamon, and ground nutmeg.

3. In a large bowl, and using an electric mixer on medium speed, blend bananas, buttermilk, eggs, melted butter, and vanilla extract. Add dry ingredients, and stir with a wooden spoon until just combined.

4. Fill prepared pans ⅔ full and bake for about 50 minutes or until a wooden toothpick inserted into the center comes out clean. Cool loaves in the pans for 10 minutes before inverting onto a wire rack to cool completely.

5. Wrap in foil, label, and freeze.

To eat after freezing:

1. Thaw at room temperature, and enjoy.

Variation: This bread is very open to adaptation. Try adding about 2 cups of any of the following to the batter before baking: toasted nuts, chocolate chips, peanut butter chips, raisins, or dried sweetened cranberries.

Southern Cheese Grits Casserole

Dressed up with sharp cheddar cheese and butter, these rich grits are anything but bland.

Yield:	Prep time:	Initial cook time:	Reheat time:	Serving size:
6 cups	5 minutes	10 minutes	40 minutes	½ cup

4 cups water

¾ tsp. salt

1 cup regular grits (not quick-cook)

3 TB. unsalted butter

1½ cups grated sharp or extra-sharp cheddar cheese

½ tsp. hot sauce, or to taste (optional)

2 large eggs

Salt

Black pepper

1. In a large saucepan over high heat, bring water and salt to a boil. Whisk in grits until mixture is smooth. Reduce heat to low, and simmer, stirring frequently, for about 10 minutes.

2. Remove from heat and stir in butter and grated cheddar cheese until melted and combined. Stir in hot sauce (if using).

3. In a small bowl, whisk eggs. Add to grits mixture and stir well. Season grits with salt and pepper, and pour into one large or several smaller baking dishes.

4. Cool completely, cover with foil, label, and freeze.

To bake after freezing:

1. Preheat the oven to 400°F. Bake grits for 40 minutes or until heated through and top is starting to brown.

Variation: To make **Shrimp and Cheese Grits,** in a large skillet over medium-high heat, heat 1 tablespoon olive oil. Add ½ cup chopped green onions and ⅓ pound diced ham, and sauté for about 5 minutes, stirring frequently, until just beginning to brown. Add 1 pound medium peeled shrimp, and cook, stirring often, for about 3 or 4 minutes or until shrimp are pink and not quite fully cooked. Stir shrimp mixture into the prepared cheese grits, and season with salt and pepper. Cool, package, and bake as directed.

Ban-Apple French Toast Casserole

Sweet bananas and tart apples meld with a custardy bread pudding in this casserole version of French toast that makes it easy to feed a crowd an elegant breakfast.

Yield:	Prep time:	Reheat time:	Serving size:
2 (8-inch) square pans	20 minutes	1 hour	1-inch square piece

1 large Granny Smith apple	2¾ cups whole milk or half-and-half
1 large banana	
1 (1-lb.) loaf French bread, cut into 1-in. chunks	1 tsp. ground cinnamon
	⅛ tsp. ground nutmeg
1 (8-oz.) pkg. regular or low-fat cream cheese, cut into ½-in. chunks	⅓ cup sugar
	2 tsp. vanilla extract
8 large eggs	

1. Bring a medium pot of water to a boil over high heat.

2. While water heats, peel and core Granny Smith apple and dice into small, ¼-inch chunks. Peel and finely dice banana. Blanch apple and banana chunks in boiling water for 2 minutes. Drain, rinse with cold water, and drain again. Set aside.

3. Butter 2 (8-inch) square baking dishes. Layer ½ of bread cubes in the bottom of the prepared baking pans. Sprinkle ½ of cream cheese cubes over bread, followed by ½ of blanched fruit. Top with remaining bread cubes.

4. In a medium bowl, whisk together eggs, whole milk, ground cinnamon, ground nutmeg, sugar, and vanilla extract until well combined. Pour ½ of mixture over each baking pan, soaking bread. Cover with aluminum foil, label, and refrigerate for 2 to 6 hours before freezing.

5. If you want to freeze separate servings, bake casserole at 375°F for 40 minutes or until puffed and golden brown. Store cooled, wrapped pieces in a labeled zipper-lock plastic freezer bag or rigid freezer container. If you want to freeze the entire casserole, cover it tightly with aluminum foil, label, and freeze before baking.

To bake or reheat after freezing:

1. To reheat a portion that's been previously baked, cook in a 375°F oven or toaster oven for about 45 minutes. Alternatively, microwave for about 3 or 4 minutes per portion.

   To cook a whole casserole that's been frozen in an unbaked state, place uncovered frozen casserole in a 375°F oven for about 1 hour or until puffed and golden brown. This method takes a little more time, but it yields a crispy-crusted perfectly puffed casserole exactly the same quality as if it had been baked fresh.

2. Serve with maple or fruit syrup.

COOL TIP

Bananas don't keep long, and your grocer knows it. If your store has an abundance of bananas teetering on the edge of over-ripeness, ask for a discount. You'll probably get it, especially if you're buying a lot. You can also freeze bananas for later use in smoothies or baking. Peel, place in plastic freezer bags, and freeze.

Savory Breakfast Strata

This rich breakfast bread pudding blends the traditional flavors of sausage and cheese with meaty mushrooms, onions, and sweet bell peppers. Chewy French bread, softened by an eggy batter, brings it all together for a hearty make-ahead breakfast or brunch entrée.

Yield:	Prep time:	Reheat time:	Serving size:
1 (9×13-inch) pan	30 minutes	1 hour	3×4-inch square

1 lb. bulk lite breakfast sausage	2 cups grated Gruyère cheese
2 tsp. olive oil	8 large eggs
1 large yellow onion, diced	2¾ cups whole or reduced-fat milk
1 large red, green, yellow, or orange bell pepper, ribs and seeds removed, and diced	2 TB. all-purpose flour
	2 tsp. dry mustard powder
8 oz. white or cremini mushrooms, sliced	2 tsp. dried Italian seasoning
	½ tsp. salt
1 tsp. minced garlic	¼ tsp. black pepper
1 (1-lb.) loaf French bread, cut into 1-in. cubes	2 TB. unsalted butter or margarine, melted

1. Butter a 13×9-inch deep baking dish.

2. Heat a large skillet over medium-high heat. Spray with cooking spray. Add sausage and cook, stirring frequently to break up large pieces, for 6 minutes, or until browned. Remove sausage to a large bowl, and set aside.

3. In the same skillet over medium-high heat, heat olive oil. Add onion, cook for 3 minutes, and stir. Add bell pepper and mushrooms, and cook, stirring occasionally, for about 6 more minutes or until vegetables are tender. Add garlic, and cook for about 2 more minutes. Add cooked vegetables to cooked sausage, and mix well.

4. Layer ½ of cubed bread in the bottom of the greased baking dish. Layer ½ of sausage mixture on top, followed by ½ of Gruyère cheese. Repeat layers, ending with cheese on top.

5. In a separate large bowl, whisk together eggs, whole milk, all-purpose flour, dry mustard powder, dried Italian seasoning, salt, pepper, and melted butter. Pour into the baking dish, coating layers. Cover with aluminum foil, label, and refrigerate for at least 4 hours or up to overnight.

6. If you want to freeze separate servings, bake strata at 375°F for 40 minutes or until puffed and golden brown. Store cooled, wrapped pieces in a labeled zipper-lock plastic freezer bag. If you want to freeze entire casserole, cover tightly with aluminum foil, label, and freeze before baking.

To bake after freezing:

1. To reheat a portion that's been previously baked, cook in a 375°F oven or toaster oven for about 45 minutes. Alternatively, microwave for about 3 or 4 minutes per portion.

   To cook a whole strata that's been frozen in an unbaked state, place uncovered frozen casserole in a 375°F oven for about 1 hour or until puffed and golden brown. This method takes a little more time, but it yields a crispy-crusted perfectly puffed strata exactly the same quality as if it had been baked fresh.

Variations: What goes into the layers of your breakfast strata is up to you. This recipe is a great guideline, but you can substitute the sausage, cheese, seasonings, and veggies for those you prefer. How about a Swiss cheese and asparagus version for springtime? Or a Southwestern version with roasted green chiles and chorizo? A ham and veggie strata makes a great way to use up holiday dinner leftovers.

COLD FACT

This dish takes its name from the geological term *strata,* which refers to the visible layers of the earth. A culinary strata layers ingredients.

Lunches, Appetizers, and Snacks

Check out the smaller side of freezer cooking. You'll never be without a lunch that's the envy of your co-workers. If you have access to a freezer and microwave oven at work or school, so much the better, but you'll also find recipes that can be prepared and packed in a lunchbox for midday meals.

After-school snacks become something special with your freezer's help, and your house suddenly becomes the one where all the kids want to hang out … which may or may not be a good thing!

Your freezer is a fabulous friend to have when you feel like entertaining. Spontaneous parties can occur quickly and easily when you stock your freezer with elegant appetizers and casual finger foods. Stressful holiday dinners are a lot less stressful when you start the day with a clean kitchen and most of the work done ahead of time.

Start stockpiling the recipes in Part 3, invite some friends over, and get ready to have some fun!

Appealing Appetizers

In This Chapter

- A party in your freezer
- Entertaining made easy
- Finger foods and elegant bites

By keeping a variety of appetizers and finger foods stashed in your freezer, you're always minutes away from successful entertaining. Drop-in guests no longer induce stress, and celebrations and events are prepared for well in advance of the big day.

Your freezer can make you the life of the party, so get ready to ramp up your social life with the recipes in this chapter that make it easy to entertain guests, especially unexpected ones!

When you allow your freezer to act as your caterer, on the day of the party, you'll have plenty of time to attend to details other than food like organizing the house, getting dressed, and relaxing. When guests arrive you'll be calm, looking fabulous, and ready for fun!

Shrimp and Pork Pot Stickers

Savory pork blends perfectly with sweet shrimp in these tasty little packets served pan-fried with a dipping sauce.

Yield:	Prep time:	Reheat time:	Serving size:
64 pot stickers	1 hour	8 minutes	4 pot stickers

1 lb. ground pork

1 lb. tiny cooked shrimp, or 1 lb. larger cooked shrimp, finely chopped

1 large egg

3 green onions, minced

1 (1-in.) piece fresh ginger, peeled and grated

½ tsp. minced garlic

2 tsp. sesame oil

1 TB. rice vinegar

1 TB. soy sauce or reduced-sodium soy sauce

1 tsp. black or white pepper

64 wonton wrappers

1. In a large bowl, combine pork, shrimp, egg, green onions, ginger, garlic, sesame oil, rice vinegar, soy sauce, and pepper. Using your hands, mix everything together until it's completely combined.

2. Place about 1 teaspoon filling in the center of each wonton wrapper. Use a pastry brush to wet edges of wrapper, and fold diagonally to form a triangle. Pinch edges well to seal. Bring two side points to meet in center, add a dab of water, and pinch together. Repeat with remaining filling.

3. Place prepared dumplings on a waxed paper–lined baking sheet, and freeze in a single layer. Once frozen, remove to a rigid freezer container or a zipper-top plastic freezer bag, label, and freeze.

To cook after freezing:

1. In a large skillet (be sure it's large enough to hold the number of pot stickers you want to cook without overcrowding) over medium-high heat, heat a small amount of vegetable or canola oil. Carefully (oil may splatter) add frozen pot stickers to the skillet and cook for 3 minutes without moving or until bottoms are browned. Carefully turn over pot stickers. Add ½ cup water to the hot skillet and immediately cover. Reduce heat to medium, and let dumplings steam for 4 or 5 minutes or until cooked through. Serve with additional soy sauce for dipping.

Variation: These pot stickers are also terrific in soup. To make **Wonton Soup,** bring 1 quart Poultry Stock (recipe in Chapter 10) to a boil, add 12 frozen uncooked pot stickers, 2 minced green onions, ½ cup thinly sliced bok choy, 8 medium cooked shrimp, and 4 thin slices cooked Chinese-Style Pork Tenderloin (recipe in Chapter 11). Bring to a boil, lower heat to medium-low, and simmer for 6 to 8 minutes. Divide among 4 bowls to serve.

FREEZER BURN

The world is filled with variations on the stuffed dumpling, but whether they are pot stickers, pierogis, empanadas, or samosas, they all share one thing: their success depends on completely and firmly sealing the edges. Even a tiny millimeter of unsealed edge is enough to cause filling to leak out. Take extra care and be sure the edges are completely sealed, and you'll always be rewarded with perfect dumplings.

Swedish Meatballs

Savory little meatballs mix with a subtly spiced creamy sauce for a tasty appetizer. I've lowered the fat content in this recipe by replacing the traditional heavy cream with evaporated milk, which freezes beautifully.

Yield:	Prep time:	Initial cook time:	Reheat time:	Serving size:
44 meatballs	10 minutes	25 minutes	10 minutes	3 meatballs

1 (12-oz.) can evaporated milk	1 tsp. butter or margarine
1 small yellow onion, finely diced	3 cups beef broth
⅓ cup dry breadcrumbs	¼ cup all-purpose flour
1 tsp. salt	¼ tsp. ground nutmeg
1 tsp. black pepper	¼ tsp. allspice
1 lb. lean ground beef	1 TB. lemon juice

1. In a medium bowl, combine ½ cup evaporated milk, diced onion, breadcrumbs, salt, pepper, and lean ground beef. Using your hands, mix until well combined. Shape meat into small meatballs using about 1 tablespoon meat mixture per ball.

2. In a large skillet over medium heat, heat butter. Add meatballs, and cook, turning every minute or so, for 6 minutes or until brown on all sides. Remove meatballs from the skillet and drain excess fat from the pan.

3. Return meatballs to the skillet, and pour in 2½ cups beef broth. Cover and simmer for 10 minutes.

4. Meanwhile, whisk together remaining ½ cup beef broth with flour until well combined and free of lumps. Set aside.

5. Remove meatballs from the skillet with a slotted spoon, reserving juices in the pan. Using a spoon, skim off any excess fat from the pan juices. Pour in remaining 1 cup evaporated milk, flour mixture, nutmeg, and allspice, stirring until combined and smooth. Return meatballs to the skillet. Cook, uncovered and stirring occasionally, for about 5 minutes or until sauce thickens. Stir in lemon juice, and season with more salt and pepper.

6. Let cool completely, package in rigid freezer containers, label, and freeze.

To reheat after freezing:

1. In a saucepan over medium heat, heat frozen meatballs and sauce. Cook, stirring frequently to prevent scorching on the bottom, for 10 minutes or until sauce is simmering and meatballs are heated through.

   Alternatively, place frozen meatballs and sauce in a microwave-safe container. Cover loosely with a paper towel to prevent splattering, and microwave on high for 3 to 6 minutes, depending on portion size, or until heated through. Stop and stir every minute or so during cooking. Serve with crusty bread for soaking up sauce.

COOL TIP

A chafing dish or a slow cooker set on the warm setting is a handy way to keep the meatballs and sauce hot during a party. Turn this appetizer into an entrée by serving meatballs and sauce over cooked egg noodles.

Crab-Stuffed Mushrooms

Sweet crab fills savory mushroom caps in these little creamy-cheesy party bites.

Yield:	Prep time:	Initial cook time:	Reheat time:	Serving size:
about 24 pieces	20 minutes	5 minutes	20 minutes	2 to 3 pieces

2 (8-oz.) pkg. large white or cremini
  mushrooms

¼ cup chopped fresh Italian parsley

2 green onions, chopped

½ tsp. minced garlic

½ (8-oz.) pkg. cream cheese

¼ tsp. dried tarragon

¼ tsp. cayenne (optional)

¼ cup grated Parmesan cheese

8 oz. pkg. cooked lump crabmeat,
  drained

Salt

Black pepper

⅓ cup dried breadcrumbs

1. Bring a large pot of water with a steamer basket to a boil over high heat.

2. While water heats, wash mushrooms. Carefully pull off and discard stems. Add mushrooms to the steamer basket, and steam for 5 minutes. Drain and cool completely.

3. In a food processor bowl, combine Italian parsley, green onions, and garlic, and process until finely minced. Add cream cheese, tarragon, cayenne (if using), and Parmesan cheese, and process until smooth. Add drained crabmeat, and process until just combined. Season with salt and pepper.

4. Generously stuff each mushroom cap with filling. Lightly sprinkle top of stuffed caps with breadcrumbs, and place on a waxed paper–lined baking sheet.

5. Freeze in a single layer. Once frozen, remove mushrooms to a rigid freezer container, label, and freeze.

To bake after freezing:

1. Spray a baking sheet with cooking spray, and place desired number of frozen stuffed mushrooms on it. Heat in a 375°F oven or toaster oven for 20 minutes or until heated through and tops are bubbly and beginning to brown.

COLD FACT

It takes 85 days to grow a crop of commercial mushrooms. Once they reach the flowering or "pining" stage of growth, a mushroom can double in size every 24 hours!

Honey-Baked Brie en Croûte

Flaky puff pastry encases creamy Brie cheese topped with sweet honey and piney rosemary for an impressive appetizer that always wows guests.

Yield:	Prep time:	Reheat time:	Serving size:
1 (10-inch) baked Brie	5 minutes	40 to 45 minutes	⅙ of 1 Brie

10 sheets frozen phyllo pastry dough, thawed	1 TB. finely chopped fresh rosemary leaves
¼ cup olive oil	¼ cup toasted walnuts, chopped
1 (10-oz.) wheel Brie cheese	1 tsp. black pepper
3 TB. honey	

1. Spread a large piece of waxed paper on the countertop and top with 1 sheet phyllo dough. Brush lightly with olive oil. Stack next layer of dough on top of first, brush with oil, and repeat with remaining dough.

2. Carefully cut top rind off Brie, and place in center of prepared phyllo dough. Spread honey over top of Brie, and sprinkle with chopped fresh rosemary, walnuts, and black pepper. Carefully fold pastry up sides and over top, encasing Brie, honey, and rosemary inside. Brush top with olive oil.

3. Wrap in foil or plastic wrap, label, and freeze.

To bake after freezing:

1. Place frozen, wrapped Brie on a baking sheet sprayed with cooking spray. Bake in a 375°F oven for about 40 to 45 minutes or until pastry is golden brown. Serve with crusty bread or crackers.

COOL TIP

It's easy to toast nuts or seeds, and the resulting flavor is well worth it. Place raw nuts or seeds in an ungreased cast-iron or nonstick skillet over medium-high heat. Stir frequently and keep a close eye on what you're doing because it only takes a minute or so before they start to turn brown. Depending on the size of the nuts or seeds, they can go from brown to burnt in a matter of seconds. You can alternately toast nuts on an ungreased baking sheet in a 400°F oven, stirring after a minute or so. It should only take about 5 or 6 minutes total.

Mini Samosas

Exotic curry spices these elegant little edible packets, perfect for passing at parties with sweet and spicy Mango Chutney (recipe in Chapter 16). Using wonton wrappers makes these easy and fuss-free to assemble.

Yield:	Prep time:	Reheat time:	Serving size:
64 samosas	15 minutes microwave/ 45 minutes oven	4 minutes	3 to 4 samosas

2½ lb. baking potatoes

2 TB. olive oil

2 large yellow onions, diced

1 TB. minced garlic

2 medium jalapeño or serrano chiles, seeds and ribs removed and minced

1 TB. minced fresh ginger

1¼ cups frozen peas

1½ tsp. ground dried coriander seeds

1 TB. *curry powder*

1 tsp. sugar

2 tsp. salt

1½ tsp. black pepper

64 wonton wrappers

Vegetable oil for frying

1. Wash potatoes, poke each with a fork a couple times, and bake in the microwave for 5 to 10 minutes (depending on size) or in a 350°F oven for 45 to 60 minutes or until tender. Let cool until you're able to handle. Split potatoes in ½, scoop out flesh into a large bowl, and discard skins. Set flesh aside.

2. In a large skillet over medium-high heat, heat olive oil. Add onions, and cook, stirring occasionally, for about 3 minutes or until translucent and just starting to brown. Add garlic, jalapeños, ginger, and peas, and cook, stirring, for 2 minutes.

3. Add coriander, curry powder, sugar, salt, pepper, and contents of the skillet to the bowl with potatoes. Using a large spoon, stir until everything is combined.

4. Place 1 wonton wrapper on a clean surface, and lightly wet the 4 edges. Place 1 tablespoon filling in a diagonal line down the middle. Pick up a corner and fold in to the center, so it looks like you're beginning to fold a paper airplane. Now start rolling, shaping potato filling into the cone shape you're forming by rolling as you go. Hold the cone in your hand, and push filling down. Moisten top flap and fold down, sealing all edges. You should be left with what looks like a flat-topped ice-cream cone.

5. Freeze samosas flat on a waxed paper–lined baking sheet. Once frozen, remove to a rigid freezer container or a zipper-lock plastic freezer bag, label, and freeze.

To cook after freezing:

1. Heat vegetable oil in a deep-fat fryer to 350°F, or heat enough oil to cover samosas in a deep pot or skillet. Add the number of samosas you want, and fry for about 2 minutes. Turn and fry for 2 more minutes or until golden brown and heated through. Serve with Mango Chutney (recipe in Chapter 16).

TABLE TALK

Curry powder is a combination of rich, flavorful spices. Most curry powders include black pepper, chile pepper, cloves, coriander, fenugreek, cinnamon, cardamom, cumin, ginger, turmeric, and nutmeg. You can mix your own according to your tastes, or buy it already mixed in the spice aisle of your grocery store.

Wonton Shrimp

Party guests will never guess just how easy these impressive crunchy little shrimp bites are to make. You assemble, freeze, and fry them fresh in minutes!

Yield:	Prep time:	Reheat time:	Serving size:
24 pieces	15 minutes	4 minutes	3 pieces

24 wonton wrappers

Vegetable oil for frying

24 medium to large frozen shrimp, peeled, and with tails on

1. Place 1 wonton wrapper on a clean surface. Place 1 shrimp in center of wrapper with tail hanging over edge. Gather up wrapper edges to meet just below tail's shell portion, and pinch tightly closed. You can use a drop or two of water to help seal.

2. Freeze wonton-wrapped shrimp in a single layer on a waxed paper–covered baking sheet. Once frozen, move to a zipper-lock plastic freezer storage bag, label, and freeze.

To cook after freezing:

1. Heat vegetable oil in a deep-fat fryer to 350°F, or heat enough oil to cover shrimp in a deep pot or skillet. Add the number of shrimp you want, and fry for about 4 minutes or until golden brown and cooked through. Serve with Pineapple Sweet and Sour Dipping Sauce or Mango Chutney (recipes in Chapter 16).

COOL TIP

Unless your spouse owns a shrimp boat and he's just brought in the harvest, there's no need to get fresh shrimp for this recipe. They're headed to the freezer anyway, so wrap fully frozen shrimp in wonton wrappers and get a head-start on the chill process!

Mini Quiche Lorraines

This elegant little retro appetizer is rich with flavor from eggs, smoky bacon, and nutty Swiss cheese.

Yield:	Prep time:	Initial cook time:	Reheat time:	Serving size:
48 mini quiches	45 minutes	40 minutes	25 minutes oven/ 30 seconds microwave	3 mini quiches

4 TB. butter or margarine	4 large eggs
4 TB. vegetable shortening	1½ cups half-and-half
1⅓ cups all-purpose flour	½ tsp. salt
4 TB. milk	½ tsp. black pepper
½ lb. bacon	¼ tsp. ground nutmeg
¾ cup (6 oz.) shredded Swiss cheese	

1. Add butter, vegetable shortening, and all-purpose flour to the bowl of a food processor, and pulse 8 to 10 times or until well combined. (Alternatively, you can use 2 butter knives or a pastry blender to do this, but be prepared to spend more time at it.)

2. Add milk to the processor and pulse a few times until just combined, or stir in milk until dough just holds together. Gather into a ball, flatten into a disc, and refrigerate for at least 30 minutes.

3. Meanwhile, preheat the oven to 400°F.

4. Place bacon slices on a broiler pan, and bake for about 10 minutes or until bacon is cooked and crispy. Let cool and crumble. Reduce the oven temperature to 375°F.

5. Turn out chilled dough onto a lightly floured surface. Divide dough in ½, and roll out crust to ⅛ inch thick. Use a 2½-inch round cookie cutter or a small glass with an opening about that size to cut 24 dough circles, rerolling as necessary. Press each circle into a mini-muffin cup—dough should cover bottom and sides with no overhang. Repeat with remaining dough and muffin cups.

6. Sprinkle cooked and crumbled bacon into bottom of each dough-lined cup, about ½ teaspoon per cup. Sprinkle about ¾ teaspoon Swiss cheese into each cup on top of bacon.

7. In a medium bowl, whisk together eggs, half-and-half, salt, pepper, and ground nutmeg until well combined. Pour egg mixture into muffin cups until just filled. Bake for about 40 minutes or until quiches are set and tops are golden brown. Cool for 5 minutes before removing from pans and cooling completely on a wire rack.

8. Stack cooled quiches, with waxed paper between layers, in a rigid freezer container or containers, label, and freeze.

To reheat after freezing:

1. Place frozen quiches on a baking sheet sprayed with cooking spray, and bake in a 375°F oven for 20 to 25 minutes. Alternatively, microwave 2 frozen quiches for about 30 seconds or until heated through.

Variation: Instead of appetizers, turn this recipe into a brunch or lunch entrée by making one big 9-inch pie instead of mini quiches. You can also substitute diced cooked ham for the bacon.

COOL TIP

Quiche is another one of those dishes that is open to endless interpretation. The sky's the limit when it comes to fillings and seasonings. Try adding your favorite combinations of cheeses, vegetables, meats, and seafood, and come up with your own unique quiche creations.

Hot Artichoke Dip

The unique flavor of tangy artichokes blends beautifully with cream cheese in this classic warm party dip that's delicious when served with crusty bread.

Yield:	Prep time:	Reheat time:	Serving size:
2¼ cups	20 minutes	45 minutes	¼ cup

1 or 2 medium jalapeño peppers, ribs and seeds removed

2 whole green onions

¼ tsp. minced garlic

½ (8-oz.) pkg. cream cheese

¾ cup grated Parmesan cheese

¼ cup mayonnaise

1 tsp. lemon juice

Salt

Black pepper

¼ tsp. cayenne (optional)

2 tsp. soy sauce

1 (14-oz.) can water-packed artichoke hearts, drained

1. Bring a medium pot of water to boil over high heat.

2. Add jalapeños and green onions, and blanch for 3 minutes. Drain, rinse with cold water, and drain completely.

3. In a food processor, combine blanched jalapeños and green onions with garlic, and process until finely chopped. Add cream cheese, ½ cup Parmesan cheese, mayonnaise, lemon juice, salt, pepper, cayenne (if using), and soy sauce, and process until smooth. Add drained artichoke hearts, and process until coarsely chopped.

4. Scoop into a small baking dish, or if preferred, a number of smaller baking dishes. (Ramekins work well.) Sprinkle remaining ¼ cup Parmesan cheese over top, cover with aluminum foil, label, and freeze.

To bake after freezing:

1. Bake frozen dip in a 375°F oven for about 45 minutes to 1 hour (timing depends on portion size) or until bubbly and top is beginning to brown. Serve with crusty bread for dipping.

COLD FACT

Virtually all commercially grown artichokes grown in the United States are grown in California, and 75 percent of these come from the town of Castroville, the self-proclaimed "Artichoke Capital of the World."

Crab Cakes with Pesto Aioli

There's not much to distract from the sweet, delicate flavor of the crab in these delicious crab cakes. I adapted the recipe for the freezer from one given to me years ago by the chef of California's famed Santa Anita racetrack.

Yield:	Prep time:	Initial cook time:	Reheat time:	Serving size:
8 crab cakes	25 minutes	11 minutes	8 minutes	1 crab cake

2 TB. finely minced red bell pepper

2 TB. finely minced green bell pepper

3 TB. finely minced green onion

1 cup heavy cream

1 lb. cooked lump crabmeat

4 tsp. plus ½ cup mayonnaise

½ tsp. Dijon mustard

½ tsp. Old Bay seasoning

3 TB. plus 2 cups panko breadcrumbs

Salt

Black pepper

1 cup all-purpose flour

2 large eggs

Canola or vegetable oil

2 tsp. Pesto (recipe in Chapter 16)

½ tsp. lemon juice

⅛ tsp. cayenne, or to taste

1. Bring a medium pot of water to boil over high heat.

2. Add minced red and green bell pepper and green onion, and blanch for 1 minute. Drain, rinse with cold water, and drain completely. Set aside.

3. In a small saucepan over medium heat, bring heavy cream to a simmer. Simmer for about 10 minutes or until reduced to ⅔ cup. Cool slightly.

4. Place crabmeat in a medium bowl. Add blanched and cooled vegetables, cooled cream, 4 teaspoons mayonnaise, Dijon mustard, Old Bay seasoning, 3 tablespoons panko breadcrumbs, salt, and pepper. Mix gently to avoid breaking up lumps of crab too much. Place the bowl in the freezer to chill for about 10 minutes.

5. Form chilled crab mixture into 8 equal-size patties of about ⅓ cup each. Place patties on a waxed paper–covered baking sheet, and return to the freezer for another 5 minutes.

6. Place all-purpose flour and remaining 2 cups panko breadcrumbs on 2 large plates. In a small, shallow bowl, beat eggs with a fork until combined. Gently coat each crab cake in flour, dip in egg, and coat completely in panko breadcrumbs. Place on a waxed paper–covered sheet.

7. You can cook crab cakes before or after freezing. If you prefer to cook later (best option), freeze on baking sheet before wrapping individual cakes tightly in plastic wrap. To cook first so you can just reheat later, heat about 1 inch canola oil in a skillet over medium-high heat, or heat oil in a deep fryer to 325°F. Fry cakes, turning once if using skillet, for about 2½ minutes per side or until golden brown on both sides. Drain on a wire rack. Let cool completely, wrap tightly, label, and freeze.

To cook or reheat after freezing:

1. To reheat crab cakes that have been cooked before freezing, cook in a 375°F oven or toaster oven for about 30 minutes or until heated through. For frozen uncooked crab cakes, follow directions for frying in step 7, allowing about an extra 1½ to 2 minutes cooking time.

2. To make pesto aioli, in a small bowl, whisk together remaining ½ cup mayonnaise, Pesto, lemon juice, and cayenne until well blended. Drizzle on crab cakes just before serving. (Mayonnaise does not freeze well, so make this fresh.)

COOL TIP

Use a gentle touch when breading the crab cakes. There's not a lot of filler ingredients holding these cakes together. Should they start to fall apart, just squeeze them firmly back together.

Satisfying Snacks

In This Chapter

- After-school hunger-tamers
- Family friendly finger foods
- Casual snacks for all occasions

Grocery store freezers are full of all kinds of snack items, but it's far more economical—and tasty!—to make your own. It's also far more environmentally friendly. Commercially prepared frozen foods that need extensive packaging and shipping in refrigerated trucks and in-store storage in freezers create one of the grocery world's biggest carbon footprints.

This chapter contains a variety of casual snacks perfect for noshing on while watching a game on TV, family movie nights, kid's parties, or just about any occasion when you need a small, satisfying bite. Many of the recipes can even join the appetizers in Chapter 7 as fare at more formal events. Some recipes you can simply heat and eat; others cook up fresh in minutes for an instant end to snack cravings.

Buffalo-Style Hot Wings

Sharp, vinegar-based hot sauce gives these savory chicken wings their unique—and addictive!—flavor.

Yield:	Prep time:	Initial cook time:	Reheat time:	Serving size:
24 pieces	10 minutes	10 minutes	8 minutes	4 pieces

3 lb. chicken wings (about 24 to 30 wings)

1 cup all-purpose flour

1 tsp. salt

1½ tsp. black pepper

1½ tsp. garlic powder

1 tsp. paprika

¼ tsp. cayenne, or to taste

Peanut or vegetable oil for frying

½ cup butter or margarine

½ cup vinegar-based hot sauce, such as Tabasco

1. Turn chicken wings into "drummettes" by using poultry shears or a sharp knife to cut off wing tip at the first joint and then cut the wing at the elbow joint. (Reserve tips for making Poultry Stock; see Chapter 10.)

2. In a medium bowl, combine all-purpose flour, salt, 1 teaspoon pepper, 1 teaspoon garlic powder, paprika, and ¼ teaspoon cayenne. Using tongs, dip wings into flour mixture to coat. Set aside on a wire rack, and let rest for 5 minutes.

3. Heat peanut oil in a deep fryer to 350°F or heat enough oil to cover wings in a large, deep skillet over medium-high heat. Fry coated wings, in batches to avoid overcrowding, for about 10 minutes or until golden brown and meat is cooked through. Drain on a wire rack set over a baking sheet.

4. In a large skillet over medium heat, melt butter. Stir in hot sauce, remaining ½ teaspoon garlic powder, and remaining ½ teaspoon pepper. Add fried chicken wings, and toss to coat in sauce. Let cool completely.

5. Package wings and sauce in a zipper-lock plastic freezer bag, label, and freeze.

Variation: Instead of frying, you can grill wings over a medium-hot fire, turning once, for about 7 minutes per side or until browned and cooked through, or bake in a 400°F oven for about 20 minutes or until browned and cooked through. Proceed with the rest of the recipe as directed.

To reheat after freezing:

1. Place frozen wings and sauce in a large skillet over medium heat. Cook, stirring frequently, for about 6 to 8 minutes or until heated through. The hot sauce may lose a little of its "bite" during the freezing process. Taste the wings and add another splash during reheating if needed.

COLD FACT

Buffalo wings are named after Buffalo, New York, where they were created at the Anchor Bar. Culinary legend has it that the proprietors' college-age son and friends came in late one night and the now-famous snack was improvised from what was on hand. The traditional accompaniment of celery sticks and blue cheese dressing came about the same way. The hungry students went away well fed, and the hot wings were so popular, they became a staple at the bar and later throughout the country.

Teriyaki Wings

Classic sweet-and-salty teriyaki sauce adorns these easy grilled or baked snacks.

Yield:	Prep time:	Reheat time:	Serving size:
24 pieces	10 minutes	20 minutes	4 pieces

3 lb. chicken wings (about 24 to 30 wings)

1 cup soy sauce

½ cup firmly packed brown sugar

¼ cup rice vinegar

2 tsp. sesame oil

2 tsp. minced garlic

1 TB. minced fresh ginger

1 to 2 tsp. sriracha hot sauce (optional)

1. Turn chicken wings into "drummettes" by using poultry shears or a sharp knife to cut off wing tip at first joint and then cut the wing at the elbow joint. (Reserve tips for making Poultry Stock; see Chapter 10.) Place wings in a zipper-lock plastic freezer bag.

2. In a small bowl, combine soy sauce, brown sugar, rice vinegar, sesame oil, garlic, ginger, and hot sauce (if using).

3. Pour marinade over wings in the bag, and squeeze the bag to mix and coat wings completely. Remove air from the bag, seal, label, and freeze.

To cook after freezing:

1. Thaw wings in marinade in the refrigerator or on the defrost cycle in the microwave.

2. Bake wings on a baking sheet coated with cooking spray in a 400°F oven for about 20 minutes or until browned and cooked through. Alternatively, grill thawed wings over a medium-hot fire, turning once, for about 7 minutes per side or until browned and cooked through.

COOL TIP

When brown sugar is called for in a recipe, unless it says otherwise, you should always measure it firmly packed.

Classic Sliders

There's no need to run out for a midnight fast-food fix when you've got the flavor of classic sliders in the freezer. I suggest doubling or tripling the recipe.

Yield:	Prep time:	Initial cook time:	Reheat time:	Serving size:
16 sliders	30 minutes	10 minutes	1 minute, 10 seconds	2 sliders

1 medium yellow or white onion, chopped

1 lb. lean ground beef

16 dinner rolls

2 TB. ketchup

16 slices American cheese

1. Bring a small pot of water to boil over high heat.

2. Add onion, and blanch for 1 minute. Drain and set aside.

3. Divide beef into 16 equal portions. Press each portion into a very thin, round patty slightly larger than the circumference of the dinner roll to allow for shrinkage during cooking. Stack patties between sheets of waxed paper.

4. Open dinner rolls, and spread each ½ with a very thin smear of ketchup. Top ½ of each roll with 1 slice American cheese. Top cheese with a sprinkling of blanched onions.

5. Heat a large skillet or griddle over medium-high heat and spray with cooking spray. Add burger patties, and cook for about 30 seconds per side or until just cooked through. Place cooked burger patty on roll, cover with second ½ of roll, and wrap, 2 to a package, in plastic wrap.

6. Place cooled wrapped sliders in a large zipper-lock plastic freezer bag, label, and freeze.

To reheat after freezing:

1. Remove plastic wrap and place 2 sliders on a paper towel on a plate. Microwave for about 1 minute, 10 seconds or until heated through. Watch carefully, so you don't overcook.

COLD FACT

Sliders, as they eventually came to be known, were invented in 1921 at the world's first White Castle restaurant in Wichita, Kansas, where the tiny hamburgers originally sold for 5¢ each.

Mozzarella Sticks

Served with Chunky Marinara Sauce (recipe in Chapter 16), these snacks have the flavor and melted-cheese satisfaction that comes with pizza, minus the crust. Traditionally served fried, you can also bake the sticks for a lower-fat alternative.

Yield:	Prep time:	Reheat time:	Serving size:
24 sticks	25 minutes	4 minutes	1 stick

4 large eggs

1½ cups all-purpose flour

3½ cups Italian-seasoned breadcrumbs

24 (4½×½-in.) sticks mozzarella or string cheese

Vegetable oil for frying (optional)

2 cups Chunky Marinara Sauce (recipe in Chapter 16)

1. In a small bowl, beat 2 eggs with a fork.

2. Place all-purpose flour on a large plate.

3. Pour Italian-seasoned breadcrumbs into a large plastic bag.

4. Prepare a baking sheet by covering it with a piece of waxed paper.

5. Using tongs, dip 1 cheese stick in egg and then roll in flour to coat. Dip stick back into egg and shake in seasoned breadcrumbs to coat again. Place coated cheese stick on the paper-covered baking sheet, and repeat with remaining cheese sticks. Add remaining eggs to the bowl as you need them.

6. Freeze mozzarella sticks on the baking sheet. Once frozen, transfer them to a rigid freezer container or a zipper-lock plastic freezer bag, label, and freeze.

To cook after freezing:

1. Heat vegetable oil in a deep fryer to 350°F or heat enough oil to cover cheese sticks in a wok or deep skillet over medium-high heat. Fry frozen cheese sticks for 4 minutes or until golden brown. Alternatively, bake frozen cheese sticks in a 400°F oven for about 8 minutes or until heated through. Allow to set for minute before serving with Chunky Marinara Sauce on the side for dipping.

Pizza Bites

Tangy tomato sauce, spicy pepperoni, and creamy mozzarella mix in these delicious little snack bites.

Yield:	Prep time:	Reheat time:	Serving size:
50 pieces	1¼ hours	4 minutes	3 pieces

3½ cups Chunky Marinara Sauce (recipe in Chapter 16)

3 cups shredded mozzarella cheese

50 wonton wrappers

50 slices pepperoni (optional)

Vegetable oil for frying

Freshly grated Parmesan cheese for serving (optional)

1. In a large bowl, stir together Chunky Marinara Sauce and shredded mozzarella cheese.

2. Place 1 wonton wrapper on a clean surface. Place 1 slice pepperoni (if using) and 2 teaspoons sauce-cheese mixture in center. Lightly wet 4 sides of wrapper, and fold on a diagonal to form a small triangle. Seal edges. Repeat with remaining ingredients.

3. Freeze in a single layer on a waxed paper–lined baking sheet. Once frozen, remove to lidded freezer container or a zipper-lock plastic freezer bag, label, and freeze.

To cook after freezing:

1. Heat vegetable oil in a deep fryer to 350°F, or heat enough oil to cover in a wok or deep skillet over medium-high heat. Fry frozen pizza bites for 4 minutes or until golden brown and heated through. Garnish with freshly grated Parmesan cheese (if using).

COOL TIP

Wonton wrappers are an extremely versatile staple ingredient that can cross cultural boundaries with ease. Use your imagination, and you can come up with all kinds of things to stuff the delicate pastry wrappers with, both sweet and savory.

Crispy Chicken Strips

Marinating chicken in buttermilk before coating in crunchy *panko* breadcrumbs keeps this family favorite moist and tender, whether you opt to bake or fry.

Yield:	Prep time:	Reheat time:	Serving size:
12 pieces	4 hours	5 minutes	2 pieces

2 lb. boneless, skinless chicken breasts	2 tsp. Cajun seasoning
1 cup buttermilk	3 tsp. salt
2 TB. Dijon mustard	3 tsp. black pepper
2 tsp. hot sauce	1½ cups panko breadcrumbs
	Vegetable or canola oil for frying

1. Cut chicken breasts into strips about ½ inch wide.

2. In a small bowl, whisk together buttermilk, Dijon mustard, hot sauce, Cajun seasoning, 1 teaspoon salt, and 1 teaspoon pepper. Pour buttermilk marinade into a zipper-lock plastic bag, add chicken strips, and refrigerate for 4 to 12 hours.

3. In a large plastic bag, combine panko breadcrumbs, remaining 2 teaspoons salt, and remaining 2 teaspoons pepper. Shake to combine.

4. Drain chicken, and discard marinade. Shake chicken strips, 2 or 3 at a time, in panko mixture to coat well.

5. Freeze in a single layer on a waxed paper–lined baking sheet. Once frozen, remove to a zipper-lock plastic freezer bag, label, and freeze.

To cook after freezing:

1. Heat vegetable oil in a deep fryer, or about 2 inches oil in a large skillet over medium heat. Fry frozen chicken breasts for about 4 or 5 minutes, turning once, or until golden brown and cooked through. Alternatively, spray a baking sheet with cooking spray, and place chicken strips on sheet. Spray top of chicken with cooking spray. Bake in a 400°F oven for about 30 minutes or until golden brown and cooked through.

TABLE TALK

Lighter and coarser than ordinary breadcrumbs, Japanese **panko** crumbs create a wonderful crunchy coating for fried foods. You can find panko in Asian markets and in the Asian food sections of well-stocked supermarkets.

Garlic Cheese Bread

This recipe takes already-delicious garlic bread to a whole new level with the addition of flavorful Parmesan cheese and a creamy melt of mozzarella. This is a perfect anytime snack or a great side dish for an Italian-style pasta dinner.

Yield:	Prep time:	Initial cook time:	Reheat time:	Serving size:
2 (½-lb.) loaves	10 minutes	3 minutes	18 minutes	3-inch slice

2 TB. unsalted butter

2 TB. olive oil

1 tsp. minced garlic

¼ cup grated Parmesan cheese

½ cup shredded whole or part-skim mozzarella cheese

1 (1-lb.) loaf French or Italian bread

2 tsp. *Italian seasoning*

1. In a small saucepan over medium-low heat or in the microwave, heat butter and olive oil together with garlic until just melted.

2. In a small bowl, mix together Parmesan cheese and mozzarella cheese.

3. Cut loaf of bread lengthwise down the center. Using a pastry brush, apply butter mixture liberally to both cut surfaces. Sprinkle with Italian seasoning and cheese mixture.

4. Wrap each half separately in foil, label, and freeze.

To reheat after freezing:

1. Unwrap bread and bake in a 375°F oven for about 18 to 20 minutes or until cheese is melted and starting to brown and bread is toasted.

TABLE TALK

Italian seasoning is an herb blend consisting of basil, oregano, rosemary, thyme, and sometimes parsley and other dried herbs.

Pecan-Crusted Jalapeño Poppers

Fiery hot jalapeño peppers stuffed with a cooling cream cheese filling are perfectly accented by a crispy toasted pecan crust in these amazing little snack bites.

Yield:	Prep time:	Initial cook time:	Reheat time:	Serving size:
24 poppers	1 hour	8 minutes	4 minutes	1 popper

1½ cups shelled pecans

24 small jalapeño peppers

1 (8-oz.) pkg. plus 1 (3-oz.) pkg. cream cheese

2 cups shredded extra-sharp cheddar cheese

3 large eggs

⅓ cup milk

1½ cups all-purpose flour

2 tsp. salt

1 tsp. black pepper

1½ cups panko breadcrumbs

Vegetable oil for frying

1. In an ungreased cast-iron or nonstick skillet over medium heat, add pecans. Toast, stirring occasionally, for about 5 minutes or until lightly browned. Alternatively, toast pecans on an ungreased baking sheet in a 360°F oven for about 10 minutes or until browned. Use a food processor to coarsely chop toasted pecans, and set aside.

2. Bring a large pot of water to boil over high heat.

3. Wearing plastic gloves, cut off the top stem portion from jalapeños. Then, using a knife, carefully remove seeds and core, leaving pepper intact. Blanch prepared jalapeños in boiling water for 3 minutes. Rinse with cold water, drain, and set aside.

4. In a medium bowl, and using an electric mixer on high speed, beat cream cheese for 2 or 3 minutes or until light and fluffy. Stir in shredded cheddar cheese.

5. Stuff each pepper with about 2 teaspoons cheese mixture.

6. In a small bowl, beat eggs with milk.

7. On a shallow plate, mix all-purpose flour, salt, and pepper.

8. On another shallow plate, mix chopped toasted pecans with panko breadcrumbs.

9. Cover a baking sheet with waxed paper.

10. Using tongs, dip 1 stuffed pepper in egg mixture to moisten and then roll in flour mixture to coat. Repeat with remaining peppers. Dip floured pepper back in egg mixture and then in pecan-panko mixture to completely coat. Place coated pepper on the waxed paper–covered baking sheet, and repeat with remaining peppers.

11. Freeze in a single layer on the baking sheet. Once frozen, transfer them to a rigid freezer container, placing waxed paper between layers, label, and freeze.

To cook after freezing:

1. Heat vegetable oil to 350°F in a deep fryer, or heat enough oil to cover peppers in a wok or deep skillet over medium-high heat. Fry frozen stuffed jalapeños for about 4 minutes or until golden brown. Alternatively, bake poppers on a baking sheet sprayed with cooking spray in a 375°F oven for about 10 minutes.

FREEZER BURN

To prevent your fingers from burning for hours after handling the jalapeños, always wear gloves when working with them, especially when you'll be handling them as much as you do in this recipe. Keep your gloved hands away from your face because you can burn the delicate tissue around your eyes, nose, and mouth with the chile oils on the gloves—no laughing matter if you've ever done it. Contrary to popular belief, a chile pepper's heat is held in its inner membranes, not the seeds. If you want your finished dish to be less spicy, take care to remove all the white inner membrane from your chiles.

Vegetable Egg Rolls

Gingery seasoned vegetables encased in a crispy fried wrapper make a fabulous starter for an Asian-inspired meal or anytime snack.

Yield:	Prep time:	Reheat time:	Serving size:
18 egg rolls	1 hour	5 minutes	1 egg roll

1 cup finely chopped carrots (about 2 large)

2 celery ribs, finely chopped

3 whole green onions, minced

6 cups packed shredded napa cabbage

1 cup bean sprouts

2 cloves garlic, minced

2 tsp. minced fresh ginger

18 egg roll wrappers

Vegetable oil for frying

1. Bring a large pot of water to boil over high heat.

2. Add carrots, celery, onions, napa cabbage, and bean sprouts, and blanch for 1 minute. Drain, rinse with cold water, and let drain well.

3. Mix cooled drained vegetables with garlic and ginger, and stir until well combined.

4. Place 1 egg roll wrapper on a clean surface, and use a pastry brush to wet all 4 edges. Place ¼ cup filling near bottom edge about 1 inch from border, and spread to within ¾ inch of the left and right edges. Fold in left and right edges over filling and then fold up the bottom edge over filling and sides of wrapper. Begin rolling, tucking in the sides to encase any escaping filling as necessary, until you have a tight cylinder. Seal seam with a little water.

5. Freeze in a single layer on a waxed paper–lined baking sheet. Once frozen, remove to a rigid freezer container or a zipper-lock plastic freezer bag, label, and freeze.

To cook after freezing:

1. Heat enough vegetable oil to cover egg rolls to 375°F in a deep fat fryer, or in a wok or a deep skillet over medium-high heat. Carefully add frozen rolls to hot oil—use caution because oil may spit and splatter, so stand back. Fry for about 5 minutes or until egg rolls are golden brown. Serve with Pineapple Sweet and Sour Dipping Sauce (recipe in Chapter 16) or hot Chinese mustard.

Variations: Add 2 cups cooked chopped shrimp to the filling mixture for **Shrimp Egg Rolls**, or 2 cups cooked finely diced Chinese-Style Pork Tenderloin (recipe in Chapter 11) for **Pork Egg Rolls.** You'll need 8 extra wrappers, which increases the yield of the recipe to 26 egg rolls.

COOL TIP

The secret to success with frozen egg rolls is to get the filling ingredients as dry as possible before filling and freezing. Use clean hands to squeeze out excess water, and blot with paper towels to get as much moisture out as possible. Take this extra step, and the finished egg rolls will be every bit as good as those freshly made.

Scotch Eggs

Spicy sausage envelops hard-boiled eggs in this classic British pub snack.

Yield:	Prep time:	Initial cook time:	Reheat time:	Serving size:
6 eggs	10 minutes	10 to 12 minutes	40 minutes	½ egg

6 large eggs

1 cup dried breadcrumbs

1 tsp. salt

1 tsp. black pepper

1 tsp. paprika

1 lb. bulk lite breakfast sausage

Vegetable or canola oil for frying

1. Put eggs in a single layer in a large pot, and cover with cold water. Set over high heat, and as soon as water comes to a full boil, remove the pot from the heat and let eggs sit in hot water for about 20 minutes. Rinse under cold water, and peel eggs.

2. In a medium bowl, mix breadcrumbs with salt, pepper, and paprika.

3. Divide sausage into 6 equal portions. Using your hands, flatten 1 portion into a large patty. Place peeled hard-boiled egg in center of patty, and use your hands to mold sausage around egg, encasing egg completely. Roll coated egg in bread-crumb mixture to coat on all sides, and place on a waxed paper–covered plate. Repeat with remaining eggs.

4. Heat vegetable oil in a deep fryer, or heat about 2 inches oil in a large skillet over medium heat. Add eggs, and fry, turning frequently with tongs if using a skillet to brown all sides, for about 3 or 4 minutes or until sausage is just cooked. Cool completely.

5. Freeze in a single layer on a waxed paper–lined baking sheet. Once frozen, remove to a zipper-lock plastic freezer bag, label, and freeze.

To reheat after freezing:

1. Heat frozen eggs on a baking sheet in a 375°F oven for about 40 minutes or until heated through.

COOL TIP

Scotch eggs are usually eaten cold in Britain, making them great lunchbox and picnic fare. If you don't want to reheat, just thaw completely in the refrigerator and eat!

Let's Do Lunch!

In This Chapter

- Sandwiches on call
- Brown-bag specials
- Lunches for every occasion

You could fill up on vending machine junk food or a quick dash to the nearest fast-food drive-thru for lunch, but with easy freezer meals, that's no longer necessary! With your freezer's help, you can pack your lunchbox with delicious dishes that would have been too time-consuming or too much trouble to prepare in the middle of the day. Now they're totally accessible!

Midday Meal Strategies

If you tote your lunch to school or work and have access to a microwave oven, you're home free. Just grab whatever you're craving from the freezer on your way out the door. And there's no need to limit yourself to the recipes in this lunch chapter, either. This works for nearly any freezer meal.

Even if you don't have access to a microwave, the freezer can still send you on your way with a good lunch. Make a week's worth of cold sandwiches; add meat, cheese, and condiments like butter or mustard; individually package; and store in the freezer. Throw on mayo, lettuce, and tomato after thawing, and you've got a quick and easy lunch.

Don't forget that a cooler can keep things hot as well as cold. Wrap hot dishes or foil-wrapped baked sandwiches in a heavy towel and pack in a cooler. They'll still be hot at lunchtime.

Meaty Stuffed Sandwich Melts

Sweet onions and peppers mix with meaty mushrooms and ground beef, and melted provolone cheese brings it all together in this hearty, open-faced sandwich perfect to satisfy big appetites.

Yield:	Prep time:	Initial cook time:	Reheat time:	Serving size:
4 open-faced sandwiches	10 minutes	20 minutes	30 minutes	1/3 sandwich

2 tsp. olive oil

1½ lb. lean ground beef

1 TB. soy sauce

1 TB. Worcestershire sauce

2 medium white, yellow, or sweet onions, finely diced

2 medium green, orange, red, or yellow bell peppers, ribs and seeds removed, and finely diced

8 oz. sliced white or cremini mushrooms

3 cloves garlic

1¾ cups grated Provolone cheese

½ cup mayonnaise

Salt

Black pepper

2 (1-lb.) loaves French bread

1. In a large skillet over medium-high heat, heat 1 teaspoon olive oil. Add ground beef and cook, stirring constantly to break up chunks, for about 6 or 7 minutes or until just cooked through. Remove meat from the pan, and drain in a colander to remove any excess fat. Place cooked meat in a large bowl, and set aside.

2. Heat remaining 1 teaspoon olive oil in the same skillet over medium-high heat. Add diced onions and bell peppers, and cook, stirring frequently, for about 5 minutes or until softened and beginning to brown. Add mushrooms and cook, stirring occasionally, for about 5 more minutes. Add garlic, stir, cook for 2 minutes, and remove to the colander to drain.

3. Mix drained cooked vegetables with ground beef. Add grated Provolone cheese and mayonnaise, and stir until well combined. Season with salt and pepper.

4. Cut bread loaves in ½ lengthwise, and remove some of the inner bread to make a hollowed-out shell. Divide filling mixture among 4 hollowed-bread shells. Let cool completely. Wrap in a generously sized sheet of aluminum foil, label, and freeze.

To reheat after freezing:

1. Preheat the oven to 350°F. Bake frozen wrapped sandwiches for about 20 minutes. Unwrap top of foil and bake for 6 to 10 more minutes or until cheese is melted and filling is heated through.

FREEZER BURN

To prevent the melting cheese from sticking to the foil while this sandwich (and the next) cooks, carefully unwrap the top of the sandwich and rewrap, leaving a small amount of space between the top of the cheese-covered bread and the foil.

Vegetable-Stuffed Sandwich Melts

This satisfying open-faced melt sandwich has lots of great flavors going on, including tangy tomatoes, artichoke hearts, and briny black olives, all brought together with a melting of mozzarella.

Yield:	Prep time:	Initial cook time:	Reheat time:	Serving size:
6 open-faced sandwiches	15 minutes	7 minutes	30 minutes	⅓ sandwich

2 tsp. olive oil

8 oz. sliced white or cremini mushrooms

1 small white, yellow, or sweet onion, diced

2 tsp. minced garlic

2 (14-oz.) cans water-packed artichoke hearts, drained

2 (14.5-oz.) can fire-roasted crushed tomatoes, drained

⅔ cup chopped black olives

4 cups shredded mozzarella cheese

1 cup grated Parmesan cheese

1 TB. Italian seasoning

Black pepper

2 tsp. crushed red pepper, or to taste (optional)

3 (1-lb.) loaves French bread

1. In a large skillet over medium-high heat, heat olive oil. Add mushrooms and onion and sauté, stirring frequently, for about 5 minutes or until softened and mushrooms have lost most of their water. Add garlic and cook, stirring, for another 2 minutes.

2. Squeeze out any excess liquid from drained artichoke hearts, and chop.

3. In a large bowl, stir together drained artichoke hearts, tomatoes, black olives, 3 cups mozzarella cheese, Parmesan cheese, Italian seasoning, pepper, and crushed red pepper (if using). Add cooked mushroom mixture, and stir until well combined.

4. Cut bread loaves in ½ lengthwise, and scoop out some inner bread to make a hollowed-out shell. Spread ⅙ of vegetable-cheese mixture on each hollowed-out shell. Divide remaining 1 cup shredded mozzarella over tops of bread.

5. Freeze on a baking sheet. Once frozen, wrap each piece in aluminum foil, place in a zipper-lock plastic freezer bag, label, and freeze.

To cook after freezing:

1. Preheat the oven to 350°F. Bake frozen foil-wrapped sandwich for about 20 minutes. Unwrap top of foil and bake for 6 to 10 more minutes or until cheese is melted.

COOL TIP

Don't throw out the scooped-out bread! Use it to make breadcrumbs, or cut into small cubes and toss with 2 or 3 tablespoons olive oil and (if desired) 1 teaspoon minced garlic. Spread in a single layer on a baking sheet and place in a 275°F oven for 10 minutes. Stir, toss, and cook for 10 more minutes. Cool and keep in an airtight container.

Submarine Sandwiches

The briny olive spread on this classic sub sandwich gives it a unique and unforgettable flavor.

Yield:	Prep time:	Initial cook time:	Serving size:
3 large sandwiches	30 minutes	3 minutes	¼ sandwich

1 small red bell pepper, ribs and
    seeds removed, and cut into
    large chunks

1 small yellow onion, cut into large
    chunks

2 celery ribs, cut into large chunks

1 small carrot, peeled and cut into
    large chunks

¼ cup fresh Italian parsley, minced

¾ tsp. minced garlic

½ cup kalamata or other brine-
    cured black olives, pitted

½ cup green olives, pitted

¼ cup olive oil

1 tsp. black pepper

2 tsp. lemon juice

3 (1-lb.) loaves French bread

1 lb. thinly sliced salami

1 lb. thinly sliced mortadella

1 lb. sliced provolone cheese

1. Bring a medium pot of water to a boil over high heat.

2. Add red bell pepper, onion, celery, and carrot, and blanch for 3 minutes, adding Italian parsley during last minute of blanching. Drain vegetables, rinse with cold water to stop the cooking process, and drain well.

3. In the bowl of food processor, combine garlic, kalamata olives, green olives, and blanched vegetables with Italian parsley, olive oil, pepper, and lemon juice, and pulse until well combined and finely chopped.

4. Slice loaves of bread lengthwise down the center. Spread each bottom bread ½ with olive spread. Divide salami, mortadella, and provolone among 3 sandwiches. Top with remaining bread ½, wrap tightly in foil, label, and freeze.

To eat after freezing:

1. No heating necessary. Simply thaw and eat. You can add sliced fresh tomato and lettuce after thawing if you like.

Bean and Cheese Burritos

Hearty beans combine with slightly spicy Spanish rice and melted Jack cheese for a fabulous portable lunch.

Yield:	Prep time:	Initial cook time:	Reheat time:	Serving size:
20 burritos	15 minutes	20 minutes	3 minutes	1 burrito

2 TB. corn or vegetable oil	1 cup prepared salsa
1 small yellow onion, chopped	20 (8-in.) flour tortillas
2 cups uncooked white or brown rice	2 (15-oz.) cans black or pinto beans, rinsed and drained
2½ cups vegetable or chicken stock	5 cups shredded Jack cheese

1. In a large saucepan over medium heat, heat corn oil. Add onion, and cook for about 5 minutes or until softened and translucent.

2. Mix in rice. Cook, stirring often, for about 3 minutes or until rice begins to brown. Stir in vegetable stock and salsa. Reduce heat to low, cover, and simmer for 20 minutes or until liquid has been absorbed.

3. Center 1 tortilla on a piece of waxed paper, parchment paper, or freezer paper. Leaving about a 1-inch margin on the bottom, layer a line of ingredients down the center: ¼ cup black beans, ¼ cup rice, and ¼ cup shredded Jack cheese. Fold up bottom of burrito, fold one side over the other, and roll tightly.

4. Wrap rolled burritos tightly in the paper, place in a large zipper-lock plastic freezer bag, label, and freeze.

To reheat after freezing:

1. Remove burritos from paper and place on a paper towel–lined plate. Microwave for about 2½ to 3 minutes or until heated through.

Variations: This recipe is easy to customize. Add additional protein with cooked diced chicken, beef, pork, shrimp, fish, or tofu. Chopped grilled vegetables like onions, peppers, mushrooms, and squash make tasty and healthful additions. (Follow the vegetable grilling instructions in the Grilled Vegetable Couscous recipe in Chapter 15.)

Bacon and Veggie–Stuffed Potatoes

Fluffy baked potatoes stuffed to capacity with fresh vegetables and smoky bacon bits are hearty enough to make a satisfying midday meal.

Yield:	Prep time:	Initial cook time:	Reheat time:	Serving size:
4 stuffed potatoes	15 minutes	1 hour	65 minutes	1 potato

4 large baking potatoes

4 slices bacon

¼ cup finely chopped whole green onions

2½ cups mixed vegetables (carrots, zucchini, broccoli, green beans, asparagus, etc.), diced

2 tsp. olive oil

1 tsp. minced garlic

½ cup sour cream or low-fat sour cream

4 cups shredded sharp cheddar cheese

Salt

Black pepper

1. Scrub potatoes and prick the tops with a fork. Bake in a 375°F oven for about 1 hour or until tender when pierced with a fork.

2. Meanwhile, in a large skillet over medium heat, cook bacon, turning to brown on both sides, for about 6 minutes or until crisp. Allow to cool slightly, and chop into small bits.

3. Bring a large pot of water to boil over high heat. Add green onions and diced vegetables, and blanch for 2 minutes. Remove from heat, rinse in cold water, and drain.

4. In the large skillet over medium-high heat, heat olive oil. Add blanched vegetables, and sauté for about 3 to 5 minutes or until beginning to brown. Stir in minced garlic, and cook, stirring, for 1 more minute. Remove from heat, and stir in bacon bits.

5. Allow potatoes to cool slightly, until you're able to handle them. Cut off tops of potatoes, and scoop out most of flesh into a large bowl, leaving a shell of about ¼ inch all the way around. Add sour cream and sharp cheddar cheese to potato flesh, and mash until as smooth as you like. Season with salt and pepper.

6. Mound ⅓ of mashed potatoes into hollowed-out shells. Divide vegetable-bacon mixture among shells, and top with remaining mashed potatoes. Sprinkle tops with remaining cheese. Cool completely, wrap in foil, label, and freeze.

To bake after freezing:

1. Preheat the oven to 400°F. Bake frozen foil-wrapped potato for 15 minutes. Lower oven temp to 350°F, and bake for about 50 minutes or until cooked through. Open foil during the last 15 minutes of cooking.

COOL TIP

You can save time when preparing this recipe by baking the potatoes in the microwave the first time. Scrub the potatoes and prick several times with the tines of a fork. Microwave on high for 5 minutes. Turn potato, and cook for 4 or 5 more minutes or until cooked through and soft when pierced with a fork.

Italian Stromboli

Salami and ham, accented by onions, sweet bell peppers, and tangy tomatoes, combine with creamy melted provolone in this sandwich that's equally great hot out of the oven or cold the next day.

Yield:	Prep time:	Initial cook time:	Reheat time:	Serving size:
2 (8-inch) sandwiches	2 hours	40 minutes	1 minute	⅓ sandwich

1¼ cups very warm water

2¼ tsp. dried yeast (1 pkg.)

1 tsp. sugar

2 TB. olive oil

1 tsp. salt

3 cups *bread flour*

1 medium yellow onion, thinly sliced

1 medium red or green bell pepper, ribs and seeds removed, and thinly sliced

5 medium Roma tomatoes, sliced

½ lb. sliced provolone cheese

½ lb. sliced salami

½ lb. sliced ham

⅓ cup chopped kalamata olives (optional)

1 egg, beaten

1 TB. sesame seeds or poppy seeds

1. In a food processor, combine very warm water, dried yeast, sugar, and olive oil. Pulse to combine, and allow to rest for 5 minutes. Add salt and bread flour, and process until a ball of dough starts to form. Continue to process for about 3 minutes or until dough is smooth and elastic.

2. Shape dough into a ball, and place in a large, oiled bowl. Cover with a clean towel, and let rise in a warm, draft-free spot for about 1 hour or until doubled. (If you want to keep extra dough in the freezer, you can chill dough in the refrigerator at this point for 2 hours and then freeze for later use.)

3. While dough is rising, bring a large pot of water to a simmer over medium-high heat. Add onion and red bell pepper, and blanch for about 2 minutes. Drain, rinse gently with cold water to stop the cooking process, and set aside to cool and drain completely. Add sliced Roma tomatoes, and blanch for about 30 seconds. Drain, rinse gently with cold water to stop the cooking process, and set aside to cool and drain completely.

4. Preheat the oven to 375°F. Spray a large baking sheet with cooking spray. (Skip the baking sheet if you have a baking stone in your oven.)

5. Punch down dough, and cut in ½. On a lightly floured surface, roll each ½ into an approximate 8×6-inch rectangle. Leaving a ½-inch border all the way around, place provolone cheese slices side by side over dough. Repeat with salami and ham. Divide blanched vegetables among sandwiches. Sprinkle with chopped kalamata olives (if using).

6. Roll dough, starting at one long end, as you would a jelly roll, encasing fillings inside as you roll. Pinch ends closed and tuck under. Moisten a finger and pinch all seams closed to prevent fillings from leaking out during baking.

7. Carefully transfer filled sandwich to the prepared baking sheet (or a pizza peel dusted with cornmeal if using a baking stone). Brush top with beaten egg and sprinkle with sesame seeds. Use a sharp knife to cut 3 long diagonal slashes along top of loaf.

8. Bake for about 40 minutes or until golden brown. Let cool completely, slice if desired, wrap, label, and freeze.

To reheat after freezing:

1. Heat frozen stromboli slices in the microwave for about 1 minute or until heated through.

Variation: You can also freeze the stromboli unbaked and then bake it fresh later. Place unwrapped frozen stromboli on a baking sheet that's been sprayed with cooking spray. Bake in a 375°F oven for about 1 hour, 10 minutes or until golden brown on top and heated through. You'll also begin to see cheese melting out of the slashes on top.

TABLE TALK

Bread flour contains higher levels of gluten-forming proteins and helps give the dough its chewy texture. The recipe will still work with all-purpose flour, but it's better with bread flour.

Tomato and Zucchini Quiche

Ripe tomatoes mix with garden-fresh zucchini and tangy cheddar cheese in this fabulous lunch or brunch pie that looks as great as it tastes.

Yield:	Prep time:	Initial cook time:	Reheat time:	Serving size:
1 (9-inch) quiche	30 minutes	55 minutes	1 hour, 10 minutes oven/ 3 minutes microwave	⅙ quiche

4 TB. butter or margarine

4 TB. vegetable shortening

1⅓ cups all-purpose flour

4 TB. milk

2 tsp. olive oil

2 medium zucchini, diced

1 medium yellow onion, chopped

½ tsp. minced garlic

4 large eggs

1 (12-oz.) can evaporated milk

1 tsp. dry mustard powder

1 tsp. Italian seasoning

Salt

Black pepper

¾ cup grated cheddar cheese

3 medium Roma tomatoes, sliced

¼ cup grated Parmesan cheese

1. In a food processor, combine butter, vegetable shortening, and all-purpose flour. Pulse 8 to 10 times or until well combined. Alternatively, you can use a pastry blender to do this, but it'll take longer.

2. Transfer mixture to a large bowl, and stir in milk until dough just holds together. Gather dough into a ball, flatten into a disc, and refrigerate for at least 30 minutes.

3. Preheat the oven to 375°F.

4. In a large skillet over medium-high heat, heat olive oil. Add diced zucchini and onion, and cook, stirring frequently, for about 5 minutes or until softened. Add garlic, and cook, stirring, for 1 more minute. Remove from heat.

5. Roll out crust on a lightly floured surface to approximately 11 inches in diameter. Ease dough into pie pan, and crimp edges to form a rim. Set aside.

6. In a medium bowl, whisk eggs with evaporated milk, dry mustard powder, Italian seasoning, salt, and pepper.

7. Sprinkle cheddar cheese over bottom of crust. Spread zucchini mixture evenly over cheese. Pour egg mixture into crust. Carefully float a layer of sliced tomatoes on top, and sprinkle with Parmesan cheese.

8. Bake for about 50 minutes or until a knife inserted into center of quiche comes out clean. Cool completely, wrap in foil, label, and freeze. Or cut quiche and freeze in individual portions.

To reheat after freezing:

1. Preheat the oven to 375°F. Heat quiche, covered in foil, for 1 hour. Unwrap and bake for about 10 more minutes or until heated through. Alternatively, microwave single portions for about 2½ to 3 minutes.

Variations: Substitute almost any other sautéed vegetable for the zucchini. Try cauliflower, broccoli, asparagus, or spinach. Be sure to drain the vegetable well after sautéing and before adding to quiche. Or instead of making one large quiche for a lunch or brunch entrée, you can make appetizer-size mini quiches. Follow the assembly directions for the Mini Quiche Lorraines in Chapter 7.

COLD FACT

The French region of Lorraine, the birthplace of quiche, was originally under German rule. The word *quiche* is derived from *kuchen,* the German word for cake.

Meatballs in Marinara

Classic Italian tomato sauce envelops savory meatballs for a lunchtime staple you can enjoy over spaghetti or on an Italian roll with melted cheese.

Yield:	Prep time:	Initial cook time:	Reheat time:	Serving size:
12 cups meatballs and sauce	30 minutes	25 minutes	10 minutes	1 cup

1 lb. ground pork	1 tsp. black pepper
1 lb. lean ground beef	4 TB. olive oil
1 small yellow onion plus 1 large yellow onion, diced	2 (28-oz.) cans plum tomatoes, with juice
1 TB. plus 1 tsp. minced garlic	1 (6-oz.) can tomato paste
2 large eggs	1 bay leaf
½ cup dry breadcrumbs	4 tsp. Italian seasoning
¼ cup chopped fresh *Italian parsley* or 2 TB. dried	1 tsp. crushed red pepper (optional)
1½ tsp. salt	

1. In a large bowl, combine ground pork, ground beef, 1 small diced onion, 1 tablespoon minced garlic, eggs, breadcrumbs, Italian parsley, salt, and pepper. Using your hands, mix until everything is well combined. Roll mixture into small balls about 2 tablespoons each.

2. In a large skillet over medium-high heat, heat 2 tablespoons olive oil. Add meatballs, and sauté for about 6 to 7 minutes, turning to brown on all sides, until golden brown but not quite cooked through. Remove from the pan using a slotted spoon, and drain any excess fat.

3. In a large saucepan over medium heat, heat remaining 2 tablespoons olive oil. Add remaining 1 large diced onion and remaining 1 teaspoon minced garlic, and cook, stirring frequently, for about 3 minutes or until soft.

4. In a food processor, purée tomatoes and their juice with tomato paste. Stir into the saucepan with onion and garlic.

5. Add bay leaf, Italian seasoning, and crushed red pepper (if using), and season with salt and pepper. Bring to a simmer, add meatballs, and simmer for about 15 more minutes or until meatballs are cooked through and sauce is thickened. Cool completely, and remove bay leaf. Package in zipper-lock plastic bags, label, and freeze flat.

To reheat after freezing:

1. Remove frozen meatballs and sauce from the bag and place on a microwave-safe dish. Cook, covered and stopping to stir every minute or so, until heated through. Cook time will depend on portion size. Alternatively, heat (thawed or frozen), covered, in a saucepan over medium heat until heated through. Stir frequently to prevent scorching on the bottom, and serve over cooked spaghetti.

Variation: For a **Hot Meatball Sub,** spoon warm meatballs and sauce into a split Italian roll, top with mozzarella cheese, and cook under the broiler until cheese melts.

TABLE TALK

Also known as flat leaf parsley, **Italian parsley** is more flavorful than the curly edged variety usually used as a garnish.

Grilled Sausage Sandwiches

Spicy or sweet Italian sausage teams up with grilled onions and peppers in a crusty roll for a satisfying lunch.

Yield:	Prep time:	Initial cook time:	Reheat time:	Serving size:
6 sandwiches	10 minutes	15 minutes	10 minutes	1 sandwich

2 tsp. olive oil	½ tsp. minced garlic
2 large yellow onions, thinly sliced	6 links sweet or hot Italian sausage
2 large red or green bell peppers, ribs and seeds removed, and thinly sliced	6 sub sandwich rolls

1. In a large skillet over medium-high heat, heat olive oil. Add onions and bell peppers, and cook, stirring frequently, for about 5 minutes or until vegetables begin to brown. Stir in garlic, and cook for 2 more minutes. Remove onions and peppers from the skillet and set aside.

2. Spray the skillet with cooking spray, and add sausage. Cook, turning frequently, for about 6 or 7 minutes or until sausage is browned on all sides and cooked through. Cool vegetables and sausages completely, package in a zipper-lock plastic freezer bag, label, and freeze. Package and freeze rolls in a separate plastic bag.

To reheat after freezing:

1. Thaw sausage and vegetable mixture in the refrigerator or in the microwave (timing will depend on portion size). Heat 1 teaspoon or so olive oil in a skillet over medium-high heat, add thawed sausage and vegetables, and sauté for about 10 minutes or until heated through. Alternately, heat in the microwave until mixture is heated through (again, timing will depend on portion size).

2. To thaw rolls, heat in a toaster oven for 5 minutes, if desired. Stuff with sausage mixture and serve.

FREEZER BURN

Take care when thawing or heating bread in a microwave. A few seconds too long will turn it tough and dry.

French Dip Sandwiches with Au Jus Dipping Sauce

Meaty sandwiches are dipped in a savory beefy broth, given additional flavor by the addition of beer, for a lunchtime classic.

Yield:	Prep time:	Initial cook time:	Reheat time:	Serving size:
8 cups meat and sauce	10 minutes	55 minutes	10 minutes	1 cup

1 (3-lb.) boneless round, rump, or pot roast

1 TB. olive oil

2 medium onions, sliced into rings

1 TB. minced garlic

1 (12-oz.) can or bottle beer

2 cups beef stock

1 (1-oz.) pkg. dried onion soup mix

8 French rolls

1. If possible, ask the butcher at the meat counter to slice roast into thin slices. If not, use a large sharp or serrated knife to slice meat thinly. This is easiest to do with a partially frozen roast.

2. In a medium pot over medium-high heat, heat olive oil. Add onions, and cook, stirring occasionally, for about 10 minutes or until they begin to caramelize and small brown bits cling to the bottom of the pot. Add garlic, and cook, stirring, for 1 more minute.

3. Add beer, and stir to scrape up any brown bits from the bottom of the pot. Stir in beef stock and onion soup mix.

4. Using tongs, add meat slices to the pan. Bring to a boil, reduce heat to low, cover, and simmer for about 45 minutes or until meat is cooked through and tender. Cool completely, package in zipper-lock plastic freezer bags or rigid freezer containers, label, and freeze. Package and freeze rolls in a separate plastic bag.

To reheat after freezing:

1. Thaw rolls at room temperature or in a toaster oven. Toast rolls if desired.

2. Add frozen meat and au jus sauce to a saucepan and heat over medium-high heat until mixture comes to a simmer. Split roll and use tongs to mound beef on roll. Serve with a small cup of hot au jus on the side for dipping.

COOL TIP

You can vary the flavor of the au jus by using different types of beer. Dark beer—or even stout—gives a deeper, robust flavor with a slightly bitter under-tone that's beautifully offset by the caramelized onions. Using a lager brings a more subtle flavor that allows the beef and onion flavors to shine.

Soups and Stews

In This Chapter

- Basic all-purpose soup stocks
- The secrets to perfect soups
- Soups and stews for all occasions

There's nothing like a steaming bowl of soup to nourish both body and soul. With your freezer's help, that comfort can now be available anytime!

Most soups freeze well, so don't stop with the recipes in this chapter. Let your inner soup-maker run wild and have fun experimenting. Keep basic poultry, meat, and vegetable stocks on hand (and that's easy thanks to the recipes in this chapter), and you'll be ready for any kind of soup-making adventure.

Soup Tips and Strategies

The heart of any good soup is a good stock. Sure, you can buy canned stock, but it's easy (and more frugal) to make your own. Homemade stock brings a better flavor than canned, and you'll also be able to control the amount of sodium.

When making chicken, meat, or vegetable stocks to store in the freezer, consider *reducing* them to make a concentrate. After making stock, strain and *defat* (if necessary), and return stock to the stove over medium heat. Boil until the stock is reduced by at least ½ or up to ¾ of the original volume. The remaining stock will have intense flavor but will take up significantly less room in the freezer. When you're ready to use the stock in recipes, add enough water to achieve a flavor balance you like.

TABLE TALK

To **reduce** is to boil or simmer a broth or sauce to remove some of the water content, resulting in more concentrated flavor and color. The easiest way to **defat,** or remove all the fat from the stock, is to refrigerate the stock until the fat rises to the top and hardens. Using a spoon or knife, you can then easily skim off the hardened layer of fat. You're now ready to either freeze or further reduce the stock.

An easy and fuss-free way to make most any soup or stock recipe is in the slow cooker. Do any browning or sautéing the recipe calls for on the stovetop, add the ingredients to the slow cooker, cover, and let the appliance do the rest. Most soups can cook on high for at least 6 hours and on low for 8 hours or more—all while you do something else!

Poultry Stock

Use this flavor-rich poultry stock in any recipes calling for chicken or poultry broth or stock.

Yield:	Prep time:	Initial cook time:	Reheat time:	Serving size:
10 cups reduced stock	5 minutes	4 hours	varies	varies

1 head garlic

6 lb. chicken or turkey parts (necks, backs, wings, or anything else on sale)

2 yellow large onions, cut into large chunks

6 large carrots, peeled and cut into chunks

5 large celery stalks, cut in chunks

½ bunch fresh parsley, stems and leaves

1. Separate cloves of garlic and remove as much of the outer white papery skin as you can with your fingers. Use the broad side of a knife to crush cloves. You don't have to peel them.

2. Place poultry in a large stockpot along with garlic, onions, carrots, celery, and parsley. Add about 1½ gallons water or enough to cover ingredients by at least 2 inches, whichever is greater. Bring to a simmer over medium-high heat; this will take almost an hour.

3. Skim off any surface scum as it forms with a small strainer. Cook stock at a low simmer for about 3 more hours.

4. Strain stock. Skim fat from the top of hot stock or refrigerate in order to easily remove all fat. Return defatted stock to the stockpot, and boil over medium heat for about 30 minutes or until reduced by half. Cool completely; package in zipper-lock plastic freezer bags, rigid freezer containers, or ice cube trays; label; and freeze.

To use after freezing:

1. Heat frozen stock in a saucepan over high heat, stirring frequently, until heated through. Alternatively, microwave stock on high, stopping to stir every minute or so, until heated through. Use as directed in recipes.

Variation: To make a richer-flavored, darker-colored **Roasted Poultry Stock,** place poultry parts and bones in a baking pan. Roast in a 425°F oven for about 40 minutes or until deep brown. Proceed with the recipe as directed.

COOL TIP

If you don't want to buy fresh poultry, you could save up bones and carcasses from roasted or rotisserie chicken and turkey in the freezer until you have about 6 pounds. For that matter, you can save meat bones and veggie scraps for making those stocks as well.

Meat Stock

Here's a rich, meaty base for those recipes calling for beef, pork, or another meat stock.

Yield:	Prep time:	Initial cook time:	Reheat time:	Serving size:
12 cups reduced stock	10 minutes	4 hours	varies	varies

½ head garlic

8 lb. beef and/or pork soup bones (necks, shanks, knuckles, or oxtails), cut into 2-in. pieces

4 large yellow onions, cut into chunks

3 large carrots, peeled and cut into chunks

3 large celery ribs, cut into chunks

2 large tomatoes, quartered

2 bay leaves

1 cup water

½ bunch fresh parsley, stems and leaves

1. Preheat the oven to 450°F.

2. Separate cloves of garlic and remove as much of the outer white papery skin as you can with your fingers. Use the broad side of a knife to crush cloves. You don't have to peel them.

3. Arrange soup bones in a single layer in a baking pan, leaving a little space around each. Roast for about 20 minutes. Remove baking sheets from the oven, and stir bones. Scatter garlic cloves, onions, carrots, celery, and tomatoes around bones, and roast for 20 more minutes. Transfer roasted meat and veggies to a large stockpot.

4. *Deglaze* the baking sheets by pouring water onto them while still hot and using a spatula to scrape up any brown bits. Pour bits and water into the stockpot.

5. Add bay leaves and parsley to the stockpot along with enough water to cover everything by about 2 inches. Bring to a simmer over medium-high heat; this will take almost an hour.

6. Skim off any surface scum as it forms with a small strainer. Cook stock at a low simmer for about 3 more hours.

7. Strain stock. Skim fat from the top of hot stock or refrigerate in order to easily remove all fat. Return defatted stock to the stockpot, and boil over medium heat for about 30 minutes or until reduced by half. Remove bay leaf. Cool completely; package in zipper-lock plastic freezer bags, rigid freezer containers, or ice cube trays; label; and freeze.

To use after freezing:

1. Heat frozen stock in a saucepan over high heat, stirring frequently, until heated through. Alternatively, microwave stock on high, stopping to stir every minute or so, until heated through. Use as directed in recipes.

TABLE TALK

Deglazing is a cooking technique used after meats and/or vegetables have been browned in a pan. A liquid, usually wine or stock, is added to the pan over high heat, and the richly colored remains of the meat and vegetables are gently scraped away with a wooden spoon. The combination of liquid and food particles makes for a rich flavor. You may want to pour off any excess fat before deglazing.

Vegetable Stock

This lightly flavored vegetable stock makes a good stand-in for chicken stock in vegetarian dishes.

Yield:	Prep time:	Initial cook time:	Reheat time:	Serving size:
8 cups reduced stock	10 minutes	1½ hours	varies	varies

½ head garlic

5 large yellow onions, cut into chunks

4 large celery stalks, cut into chunks

4 large carrots, peeled and cut into chunks

3 large tomatoes, cut into large chunks

2 medium parsnips, peeled and cut into chunks

1 medium bulb *fennel,* quartered

8 oz. white or cremini mushrooms and stems

1 bunch fresh Italian parsley, leaves and stems

2 bay leaves

½ tsp. whole black peppercorns

5 qt. water

1. Separate cloves of garlic and remove as much of the outer white papery skin as you can with your fingers. Use the broad side of a knife to crush cloves. You don't have to peel them.

2. In a large stockpot over medium-high heat, combine crushed garlic with onions, celery, carrots, tomatoes, parsnips, fennel, mushrooms, parsley, bay leaves, peppercorns, and water. Bring to a boil, reduce heat to low, and simmer for at least 1 hour.

3. Strain stock and return to the pot. Boil over medium heat for 25 minutes or until reduced by half. Cool completely; remove bay leaf; package in zipper-lock plastic freezer bags, rigid freezer containers, or ice cube trays; label; and freeze.

To use after freezing:

1. Heat frozen stock in a saucepan over high heat, stirring frequently, until heated through. Alternatively, microwave stock on high, stopping to stir every minute or so, until heated through. Use as directed in recipes.

Variation: To make a richer-flavored, darker-colored **Roasted Vegetable Stock,** place the vegetables in a baking pan and lightly drizzle with olive oil. Roast in a 425°F oven for about 45 minutes or until well browned. Add vegetables and any brown bits from the pans to the stockpot, and proceed with the recipe as directed.

TABLE TALK

Fennel is a fragrant vegetable with a mild licorice flavor. The edible bulb and stalks can be used like celery, and the seeds can be used for seasoning. (Fennel seeds are available dried in the spice section of the market.) To prepare fresh fennel for cooking, cut off the green stalks (save the leaves to use for seasoning at a later time), and peel away the tough outer leaves until the almost white heart is exposed. Cut the bulb in half and remove the core. Slice the halves according to your needs.

Old-Fashioned Chicken Noodle Soup

The ultimate homemade comfort food of chicken, carrots, and celery floating in a rich broth and accompanied by egg noodles can now be ready in minutes, straight from the freezer.

Yield:	Prep time:	Initial cook time:	Reheat time:	Serving size:
20 cups	10 minutes	1 hour, 15 minutes	15 minutes	1 cup

3 lb. chicken parts

16 cups chicken stock

5 medium carrots, peeled and sliced into ½-in.-thick rounds

3 large celery stalks, chopped into ½-in. pieces

1 large yellow onion, coarsely chopped

1 tsp. minced garlic

1 tsp. dried thyme

⅓ cup chopped fresh Italian parsley

2 bay leaves

Salt

Black pepper

1 (12-oz.) pkg. cooked egg noodles

1. In a large stockpot over medium-high heat, add chicken parts and chicken stock. Bring to a boil, reduce heat to medium-low, partially cover (leave the lid slightly ajar), and simmer for 1 hour. Skim off any surface scum with a strainer, and pour soup through a strainer into another pot, retaining chicken pieces.

2. Add carrots, celery, onion, minced garlic, dried thyme, Italian parsley, bay leaves, salt, and pepper to the pot. Simmer for about 15 minutes or until vegetables are just tender.

3. While vegetables are cooking, remove skin from chicken and remove meat from bones. Discard skin and bones, chop chicken meat into small pieces or shred, and add to soup. Cook for about 5 minutes or until heated through.

4. Cool soup, remove bay leaf, and refrigerate for at least 8 hours. Skim off surface fat. Package in zipper-lock plastic freezer bags or rigid freezer containers, label, and freeze.

To reheat after freezing:

1. Heat frozen or thawed soup in a saucepan over medium-high heat, stirring frequently, until heated through.

2. Cook egg noodles in a separate pot according to package instructions, and add noodles to soup bowls just before serving. If you like your noodles ultra soft, you can add uncooked noodles to the soup just before freezing. Reheat in the same manner. (If there's a way to keep pasta *al dente* in soup after freezing and thawing, I haven't found it, so I usually recommend adding pasta when reheating.)

COOL TIP

Save money when making chicken soups by buying inexpensive cuts like wings. If you buy whole chickens and cut them up for parts, save a bag for necks and backs which also make great soup. If you plan on making either of the chicken wing recipes in Chapter 8, be sure to add the wing tips to your soup-making stockpile. If turkey parts happen to be on sale, you can substitute them for the chicken in this soup.

Curried Butternut Squash Soup

Here's a sophisticated soup with a sweet, ever-so-slightly spicy flavor.

Yield:	Prep time:	Initial cook time:	Reheat time:	Serving size:
8 cups	15 minutes	45 minutes	15 minutes	1 cup

1 (2½-lb.) butternut squash	5 cups chicken or vegetable stock
1 TB. unsalted butter	½ tsp. dried coriander
1 TB. olive oil	2 tsp. curry powder
1 medium yellow onion, diced	⅛ tsp. cayenne, or to taste
1 tsp. minced garlic	Salt
½ cup orange juice, preferably fresh squeezed	Black pepper

1. Using a large chef's knife, cut butternut squash in ½. Scoop out seeds with a spoon, and peel off squash's outer yellow layer with a vegetable peeler. Cut peeled squash into 1-inch chunks.

2. In a large stockpot over medium-high heat, heat unsalted butter and olive oil. Add onion and garlic, and sauté for 1 minute. Add cubed squash, and cook, stirring frequently, for 3 minutes. Add orange juice, stir, and cook for 2 more minutes.

3. Stir in chicken stock, dried coriander, curry powder, and cayenne. Stir to blend, and season with salt and pepper. Bring mixture to a boil, reduce heat to low, cover, and simmer for about 45 minutes, stirring occasionally, or until squash is very tender. Remove from heat, and let cool slightly.

4. Using an immersion blender, purée soup. Alternatively, transfer soup, in batches, to a blender or food processor to purée. Cool completely, package in zipper-lock plastic freezer bags or rigid freezer containers, label, and freeze.

To reheat after freezing:

1. Heat frozen soup in a stockpot over medium heat, stirring frequently, until heated through. Alternatively, microwave soup on high, stopping to stir every minute or so, until heated through.

Variations: For **Cream of Butternut Squash Soup,** stir in ½ cup heavy cream or half-and-half just before serving. Or you can substitute acorn, kabocha, or other yellow or orange winter squash for the butternut squash.

FREEZER BURN

Exercise caution anytime you put hot liquid in a blender or food processor. Never fill the appliance more than half full, and always use the lid to prevent the liquid from shooting out the top and causing burns.

Tomato Soup with Pesto

Make this simple soup with garden fresh tomatoes, and you preserve that fabulous flavor of summer all year round. A swirl of pesto brings in the flavor of fresh basil.

Yield:	Prep time:	Initial cook time:	Reheat time:	Serving size:
10 cups	15 minutes	25 minutes	15 minutes	1 cup

1 TB. butter or margarine	⅛ cup all-purpose flour
1 TB. olive oil	½ tsp. sugar
1 large yellow onion, diced	Salt
½ tsp. minced garlic	Black pepper
5 lb. (about 15 medium) chopped fresh tomatoes (7½ cups)	5 tsp. Pesto (recipe in Chapter 16), ½ tsp. per serving (optional)
2 tsp. balsamic vinegar	
3 cups Vegetable Stock or Poultry Stock (recipes earlier in this chapter)	

1. In a large stockpot over medium heat, heat butter and olive oil. Add onion and minced garlic, and cook, stirring, for about 5 minutes or until onions are soft but not browned. Add chopped tomatoes and balsamic vinegar, and stir to mix.

2. In a small bowl, combine ½ cup Vegetable Stock with flour, and beat until no lumps remain. Stir into tomato mixture, followed by remaining 2½ cups Vegetable Stock and sugar. Season with salt and pepper. Increase heat to high, and bring mixture to a boil. Reduce heat to medium-low, and cook for 20 minutes. Remove from heat.

3. Using an immersion blender, purée soup. Alternatively, transfer soup, in batches, to a blender or food processor to purée. Use a strainer to remove most of seeds and tomato skin solids, and return soup to the pot.

4. Return soup to heat, and bring to a boil. Remove from heat, and cool completely. Package in zipper-lock plastic freezer bags or rigid freezer containers, label, and freeze.

To reheat after freezing:

1. Heat frozen soup in a stockpot over medium heat, stirring frequently, until heated through. Alternatively, microwave soup on high, stopping to stir every minute or so, until heated through. Top with a dollop of Pesto just before serving, if desired.

Variation: For **Cream of Tomato Soup,** stir 1 cup heavy cream into finished heated Tomato Soup just before serving.

FREEZER BURN

When adding milk or cream to soups, always do so just before serving and only cook until heated. The acidic ingredients in the soup will curdle dairy products if they cook too long.

Southwest Tortilla Soup

This favorite restaurant soup is a fiesta of intense flavors, thanks to the chiles, corn tortillas, chicken, and tart lime.

Yield:	Prep time:	Initial cook time:	Reheat time:	Serving size:
8 cups	10 minutes	30 minutes	15 minutes	1 cup

5 (5½-in.) corn tortillas

1 TB. olive oil

1 large yellow onion, finely diced

1 TB. minced garlic

1 (15-oz.) can crushed tomatoes, with juice

1 (6-oz.) can diced green chiles, with juices

6 cups chicken stock

1 bay leaf

½ tsp. cumin

1 tsp. dried oregano

1 TB. chili powder

½ cup finely chopped fresh cilantro

1 cup cooked shredded chicken

Juice of 1 lime (about 1 TB.)

Salt

Black pepper

1. Preheat the oven or a toaster oven to 300°F.

2. Cut tortillas in ¼s, arrange in a single layer on a baking sheet, and toast for about 15 minutes or until hard and just beginning to brown. Alternatively, toast tortillas in a dry cast-iron skillet over medium heat, turning once. Crush toasted tortillas to a powder in a blender or food processor, and set aside.

3. In a large stockpot over medium-high heat, heat olive oil. Add onion and garlic, and sauté for about 4 minutes or until softened. Add tomatoes and their juice and green chiles, and stir with a wooden spoon to combine.

4. Add chicken stock, bay leaf, cumin, oregano, and chili powder. Increase heat to high, and bring to a boil. Stir in crushed tortillas. Reduce heat to medium-low, and simmer for 15 minutes. Stir in cilantro, season with salt and pepper, and remove bay leaf.

5. Using an immersion blender, purée soup. Alternatively, transfer soup, in batches, to a blender or food processor to purée.

6. Return soup to the pot, and stir in cooked shredded chicken and lime juice. Cool completely, package in zipper-lock plastic freezer bags or rigid freezer containers, label, and freeze.

To reheat after freezing:

1. Heat frozen soup in a stockpot over medium heat, stirring frequently, until heated through. Alternatively, microwave soup on high, stopping to stir every minute or so, until heated through.

COOL TIP

While bay leaves add terrific flavor to dishes, their tough exterior makes them unappetizing to actually eat, so always remove them from the dish before serving.

Dairy-Free Creamy Corn Soup

It's hard to believe this creamy corn soup contains no dairy products. Make and freeze it when summer's corn is at the peak of sweetness, and you can enjoy that unbelievable flavor year round.

Yield:	Prep time:	Initial cook time:	Reheat time:	Serving size:
8 cups	25 minutes	30 minutes	15 minutes	1 cup

8 large ears fresh corn	½ tsp. minced garlic
2 tsp. butter or margarine	¼ tsp. celery seeds
2 tsp. olive oil	1 tsp. dried basil
3 whole green onions, minced	1 qt. vegetable or chicken stock
2 medium yellow onions, chopped	Salt
3 medium celery ribs, finely chopped	Black pepper

1. Place the largest bowl you can find on the counter, and use a box grater to grate peeled corn into it. You'll end up with roughly 8 cups corn kernels and their accompanying milky pulp if you grate corn all the way down to cobs.

2. In a stockpot over medium-high heat, heat butter and olive oil. Add green onions, onions, celery, and garlic, and cook, stirring frequently, for about 5 minutes or until vegetables begin to soften.

3. Stir in celery seeds, basil, vegetable stock, and corn and its juices. Bring to a boil, reduce heat, partially cover, and simmer for about 15 minutes. Season with salt and pepper.

4. If you like your soup chunky, leave it as is. Otherwise, using an immersion blender, purée soup. Alternatively, transfer soup, in batches, to a blender or food processor to purée. Cool soup completely, package in zipper-lock plastic freezer bags or rigid freezer containers, label, and freeze.

To reheat after freezing:

1. Heat frozen soup in a stockpot over medium heat, stirring frequently, until heated through. Alternatively, microwave soup on high, stopping to stir every minute or so, until heated through.

Cuban Pork and Black Bean Soup

Black beans never tasted as good as when accompanied by meaty pieces of pork and smoky ham in this hearty soup.

Yield:	Prep time:	Initial cook time:	Reheat time:	Serving size:
18 cups	6 hours	90 minutes	15 minutes	1 cup

1 lb. dried black beans

3 lb. boneless pork shoulder (butt)

Salt

Black pepper

2 TB. olive oil

2 large yellow onions, diced

2 TB. minced garlic

1 (28-oz.) can diced tomatoes, with juice

2 tsp. cumin

4 cups chicken stock

4 cups water

1½ cups diced cooked ham

18 lime wedges

1. Place beans in a large pot and cover with cold water. Let soak 6 hours or as long as overnight. Rinse and drain.

2. Trim as much visible fat from pork as possible and cut into 1-inch pieces. Season with salt and pepper.

3. In a large stockpot over medium-high heat, heat olive oil. Add pork, and cook, stirring frequently, for about 8 minutes or until browned on all sides. Using a slotted spoon, remove pork from the pot and set aside. Remove all but 1 tablespoon fat from the pot.

4. Add onions and garlic to the pot, and sauté for about 2 minutes or until softened. Add tomatoes and their juice, cumin, and drained beans, and stir to combine.

5. Add chicken stock, water, and diced ham. Stir, increase heat to high, and bring to a boil. Reduce heat to medium-low, cover, and simmer, stirring occasionally, for 1½ hours or until beans are tender. Cool completely, package in zipper-lock plastic freezer bags or rigid freezer containers, label, and freeze.

To reheat after freezing:

1. Heat frozen soup in a saucepan over high heat, stirring frequently, until heated through. Alternatively, microwave soup on high, stopping to stir every minute or so, until heated through. Serve each portion garnished with a fresh lime wedge.

COLD FACT

Although dried beans last indefinitely, fresher beans will cook faster, have better flavor, and have more nutrients than older ones. Use bean cooking times as a general guideline. Taste beans for tenderness early and often during the cooking process.

Best-Ever Pea Soup

Make this hearty pea soup the day after a ham dinner, as a meaty ham bone helps give it its smoky flavor.

Yield:	Prep time:	Initial cook time:	Reheat time:	Serving size:
9 cups	15 minutes	90 minutes	15 minutes	1 cup

2 TB. olive oil

1 large yellow onion, finely diced

2 large ribs celery, finely diced

2 medium carrots, peeled and finely diced

1½ tsp. minced garlic

1 meaty ham bone

8 cups water

1 lb. dried green split peas

1 tsp. salt

1 tsp. black pepper

2 bay leaves

2 tsp. dried thyme

1 cup diced cooked ham (optional)

1. In a large stockpot over medium-high heat, heat olive oil. Add onion, celery, carrots, and garlic, and cook, stirring, for about 5 minutes or until softened.

2. Add ham bone, water, peas, salt, pepper, bay leaves, and thyme, and mix well. Increase heat to high and bring to a boil. Reduce heat to low, cover, and simmer gently, stirring occasionally, for about 1½ hours or until peas have turned to mush.

3. Remove ham bone and bay leaf. When cool enough to handle, remove meat from bone. Discard bone, chop meat, and add to soup. Add diced cooked ham (if using), and stir to blend. Cool completely. Package in zipper-lock plastic freezer bags or rigid freezer containers, label, and freeze.

To reheat after freezing:

1. Heat frozen soup in a saucepan over high heat, stirring frequently, until simmering. Alternatively, microwave soup on high, stopping to stir every minute or so, until heated through.

COOL TIP

Rather than peeling and dicing the onion, celery, and carrots by hand, you can save time by using a food processor. Peel the necessary veggies, and pop them in the food processor.

Albondigas (Mexican Meatball Stew)

Mint adds a subtle yet unforgettable flavor to savory meatballs floating in slightly spicy vegetable-laden broth in this traditional Mexican soup.

Yield:	Prep time:	Initial cook time:	Reheat time:	Serving size:
12 cups	20 minutes	45 minutes	15 minutes	1 cup

½ cup fresh breadcrumbs

1 lb. lean ground beef

3 tsp. minced garlic

1 tsp. salt

1 tsp. black pepper

1 large egg

⅛ cup finely chopped fresh mint or 2 tsp. dried

2 tsp. olive oil

2 medium yellow onions, sliced into ½-in. chunks

2 large celery stalks, or to taste, sliced into ½-in. chunks

2 medium fresh jalapeño peppers

4 medium carrots, peeled and sliced into ½-in. rounds

1 (14-oz.) can crushed tomatoes with green chiles, with juice

8 cups chicken stock

2 tsp. dried oregano

¾ cup loosely packed chopped fresh cilantro leaves

1 TB. cider vinegar

1. In a large bowl, combine breadcrumbs with ground beef, 2 teaspoons minced garlic, salt, pepper, egg, and mint. Using your hands, mix well. Roll into small meatballs using about 1 tablespoon meat mixture per meatball.

2. In a large soup pot over medium heat, heat olive oil. Add onions, celery, jalapeños, and carrots, and cook, stirring frequently, for about 5 to 8 minutes or until softened. Add remaining 1 teaspoon garlic, and cook, stirring for 1 more minute.

3. Add tomatoes and their juice, chicken stock, and oregano, and stir. Bring to a boil, add meatballs, and reduce heat to low. Cover and simmer for 30 minutes.

4. Stir in cilantro and vinegar, and simmer for 10 more minutes. Cool completely, package in zipper-lock plastic freezer bags or rigid freezer containers, label, and freeze.

To reheat after freezing:

1. Heat frozen stew in a saucepan over high heat, stirring frequently, until heated through. Alternatively, microwave stew on high, stopping to stir every minute or so, until heated through.

COOL TIP

To make fresh breadcrumbs, use a food processor to process a few slices of your favorite bread. Any type of nonsweet bread will do. Try white, whole-grain, baguettes, etc. Depending on the bread used, you'll get between ½ and ¾ cup fresh crumbs per slice.

Beef Burgundy Stew

Hearty red wine and bacon give this beef stew a sophisticated, grown-up flavor.

Yield:	Prep time:	Initial cook time:	Reheat time:	Serving size:
16 cups	25 minutes	2 hours	15 minutes	2 cups

3 slices thick-cut bacon, diced

3 lb. stew beef, cut into 2-in. cubes

Salt

Black pepper

2 small onions, minced

1 large celery rib, finely chopped

4 large carrots, peeled and sliced into 1-in. rounds

1 TB. minced garlic

½ cup all-purpose flour

1 (750-ml) bottle red wine, merlot or burgundy

1½ tsp. dried thyme

2 bay leaves

1 (14.5-oz.) can crushed tomatoes, with juice

1 qt. beef stock

1½ cups fresh or frozen pearl onions, peeled if fresh

1 lb. baby potatoes, halved

8 oz. sliced white or cremini mushrooms

1½ cups fresh or frozen green beans, ends removed if fresh

1. Heat a large stockpot over medium heat. Add bacon, and cook, stirring occasionally, for about 5 minutes or until bacon browns.

2. Season beef cubes with salt and pepper. Add to stockpot, and cook, stirring occasionally, for about 10 minutes or until meat is browned on all sides. Remove beef, bacon, and all but about 1 tablespoon fat from the pot, and set aside. Discard excess fat.

3. Add onions, celery, carrots, and garlic to the pot, increase heat to medium-high, and cook, stirring occasionally, for about 5 minutes or until onions are softened and lightly browned. Return meats to the pot.

4. Sprinkle in flour, stir to mix. Pour in wine, and deglaze the pot, scraping up any browned bits on the bottom. Add thyme, bay leaves, tomatoes and their juices, and beef stock, and stir to mix. Bring to a boil, reduce heat to very low, cover, and simmer for about 1½ hours, stirring occasionally, until meat is very tender.

5. Add pearl onions, baby potatoes, and sliced mushrooms, and simmer for 15 minutes.

6. Add green beans, and simmer for about 10 minutes. Season with salt and pepper. Cool completely, remove bay leaf, package in zipper-lock plastic freezer bags or rigid freezer containers, label, and freeze.

To reheat after freezing:

1. Heat frozen stew in a saucepan over high heat, stirring frequently, until simmering. Alternatively, microwave stew on high, stopping to stir every minute or so, until heated through.

COOL TIP

The easiest way to peel fresh pearl onions is to blanch unpeeled onions in boiling water for about 1 minute. Drain and plunge into cold water to stop the cooking process. Cut off the end with a paring knife, and the skins should slip right off.

Posole (Pork and Hominy Stew)

In this classic Mexican soup, savory pork and whole kernel hominy float in a meaty pork and spicy chile broth laden with veggies.

Yield:	Prep time:	Initial cook time:	Reheat time:	Serving size:
16 cups	24 hours	5 hours	15 minutes	1 cup

3 TB. olive oil

6 lb. bone-in pork shoulder

2 large yellow onions, chopped

2 large jalapeño peppers

2 fresh green chiles, such as Anaheim

1 TB. minced garlic

1 gallon water

2 large dried red chiles, such as pasilla, stems and seeds removed and broken into pieces

4 large carrots, peeled and sliced into ½-in. rounds

3 large celery ribs, chopped into ½-in. pieces

2 (29-oz.) cans hominy, rinsed and drained

1 tsp. cumin

1½ tsp. dried oregano

½ cup chopped fresh cilantro

Salt

Black pepper

1. In a large stockpot over medium-high heat, heat 1 tablespoon olive oil. Add pork shoulder, and cook, turning to brown on all sides, for about 3 minutes per side. Remove meat from the pan.

2. Add 1 large chopped onion; 1 cored, seeded, chopped jalapeño; green chiles; and garlic. Sauté for about 3 minutes or until onions start to soften. Return pork to the pot.

3. Add water and dried red chiles, and bring to a boil. Reduce heat to low, cover, and cook for about 4 hours or until meat is falling off the bone and easy to shred.

4. Remove meat from broth. When cool enough to handle, remove and discard fat and bones from meat. Shred meat, and refrigerate.

5. Strain stock and refrigerate overnight. The next day, spoon off the hardened layer of fat from top of stock.

6. In the large stockpot over medium-high heat, heat remaining 2 tablespoons olive oil. Add remaining large chopped onion, remaining chopped jalapeño, carrots, and celery, and sauté for about 5 minutes or until onion softens.

7. Add reserved defatted stock, and bring to a boil. Add hominy, cumin, and oregano. Reduce heat to medium-low, and cook for 20 minutes.

8. Add reserved shredded pork and chopped cilantro, and cook for about 5 minutes or until heated through. Season with salt and pepper. Cool completely, package in zipper-lock plastic freezer bags or rigid freezer containers, label, and freeze.

To reheat after freezing:

1. Heat frozen stew in a saucepan over high heat, stirring frequently, until simmering. Alternatively, microwave stew on high, stopping to stir every minute or so, until heated through.

COOL TIP

This soup isn't difficult to make, but it does take a while. The results are well worth it though! Buy a larger pork roast than what you need for this recipe and save the extra meat for other meals. Pork *carnitas* (what this type of cooked meat would be called on an authentic Mexican restaurant menu) makes great tacos, burritos, taquitos, enchiladas, etc.

Beef and Bean Chili

This family friendly ground beef chili gets its spicy, smoky flavor from *chipotle chiles*.

Yield:	Prep time:	Initial cook time:	Reheat time:	Serving size:
10 cups	10 minutes	45 minutes	20 minutes	1 cup

1 TB. corn, olive, or vegetable oil

2 large yellow onions, diced

2 large green bell peppers, ribs and seeds removed, and diced

2 lb. lean ground beef

1 TB. minced garlic

2 chipotle chiles, or to taste, diced

1 (28-oz.) can crushed tomatoes, with juice

1 (22-oz.) can kidney beans, drained and rinsed

1 (12-oz.) can or bottle beer

4 tsp. chili powder

1½ tsp. cumin

2 TB. unsweetened cocoa powder

1. In a large stockpot over medium-high heat, heat corn oil. Add onions and green bell peppers, and sauté for about 5 minutes or until softened.

2. Add lean ground beef, stirring with a wooden spoon to break up chunks, and cook for 6 to 8 minutes or until beef is browned. Add garlic, and cook, stirring, for 1 more minute.

3. Add chipotle chiles, tomatoes and their juice, kidney beans, beer, chili powder, cumin, and cocoa. Bring to a boil, stirring frequently. Reduce heat to low, and simmer, stirring occasionally, for about 45 minutes.

4. Cool chili completely. Package in rigid freezer containers, label, and freeze; or freeze, flat and labeled, in zipper-lock plastic freezer bags.

To reheat after freezing:

1. Heat frozen chili in a saucepan over high heat, stirring frequently, until heated through. Alternatively, microwave chili on high, stopping to stir every minute or so, until heated through.

TABLE TALK

Chipotle chiles are actually smoked jalapeños. Find them in cans in the Latin section of the supermarket. Chipotles are typically packed in dark red adobo sauce, which is made from chiles, garlic, and vinegar. You'll rarely use an entire can of hot and spicy chipotles in a single recipe, so freeze extras in ice cube trays, 1 chile per cube. When they're frozen, remove them to a zipper-lock plastic freezer bag so you can later use just the amount you need.

What's for Dinner?

When your freezer becomes your personal chef, one of life's biggest domestic challenges becomes a whole lot less challenging. You'll no longer agonize over what to make for dinner or resort to unhealthy take-out foods because you don't have time to shop or cook. Family dinner night actually becomes possible, even for the busiest of families, where even the cook will get to sit down, relax, and enjoy the meal!

Part 4 contains all types of main course recipes you can heat and eat in no time. There are simple family favorite comfort foods, as well as entrées elegant enough for company. You'll also find a variety of side dishes that make it easy to throw together a quick meal with the simple addition of a main dish protein.

Finally, frozen sauces make it easy to add bursts of flavor to all kinds of dishes or perfectly accompany pasta, vegetables, or proteins.

Meaty Mains

In This Chapter

- Successfully storing meat
- Freezing cooked meat
- Beefy main dishes
- Pork and lamb entrées

Buying beef and other red meats can take a major bite out of your average weekly grocery budget, but with your freezer's help, you can take maximum advantage of sales and buying in bulk. If you're lucky enough to live near a sustainable farm or co-op, you might even consider buying a share in a whole cow, pig, or lamb for natural, grass-fed, hormone-free meat.

When freezing raw meats, be sure to wrap them well to ward off freezer burn. Wrap in foil and then paper or plastic to double protect, and finish off by squeezing out as much air as possible from the packing materials.

When freezing cooked meat, always freeze it in its sauce, glaze, or other cooking liquid. Cooked meat frozen without this extra layer of protection tends to turn dry and tough. The one exception is cooked ground meats, which freeze fine, sauce or no sauce.

Spinach-Stuffed Meatloaf

This unique meatloaf holds some healthy secrets, including a savory garlic-spinach filling and sweet roasted red peppers.

Yield:	Prep time:	Initial cook time:	Reheat time:	Serving size:
4 (6½×5-inch) loaves	20 minutes	1 hour	40 minutes	⅓ loaf

2 tsp. olive oil	2 TB. minced fresh Italian parsley
1½ lb. fresh spinach leaves	2 cups dried breadcrumbs
2 tsp. plus 2 TB. minced garlic	2 large eggs
¾ cup grated Parmesan cheese	3 TB. Worcestershire sauce
3 lb. lean ground beef	Salt
3 lb. ground pork	Black pepper
2 large yellow onions, finely diced	⅜ cup ketchup (optional)
1 cup finely diced roasted red peppers	

1. In a large skillet over medium heat, heat olive oil. Wash spinach, but don't dry. Add damp spinach to the skillet, toss with 2 teaspoons garlic, and cook for 1 or 2 minutes or until spinach is wilted. Remove spinach from the skillet and drain well. When cool, take care to squeeze as much water as possible from spinach.

2. Remove spinach to a medium bowl, mix with Parmesan cheese, and set aside.

3. In a large bowl, mix beef, pork, remaining 2 tablespoons minced garlic, onions, roasted peppers, Italian parsley, breadcrumbs, eggs, Worcestershire sauce, salt, and pepper. Using your hands, mix well.

4. Preheat the oven to 350°F. Spray 4 (6½×5-inch) loaf pans with cooking spray.

5. Divide ½ of meat mixture between the prepared pans. Make a small indentation down the center of each meatloaf. Divide spinach mixture evenly between the pans, filling in the indentation and leaving at least a ½-inch border all around. Top spinach mixture with remaining ½ meat mixture, completely encasing spinach filling.

6. Bake for about 1 hour. Spread ketchup (if using) on top during last 15 minutes of baking. Cool meatloaves completely, wrap securely in foil, label, and freeze.

To reheat after freezing:

1. Thaw and eat for cold meatloaf, or reheat in the microwave; timing will depend on portion size. Alternatively, heat frozen meatloaf in 375°F oven for about 40 minutes or until warmed through.

Variation: For a lower-fat meatloaf, substitute all or part of the beef or pork with ground buffalo or ground turkey.

COOL TIP

To make roasted peppers, grill whole sweet or hot peppers over a very hot fire, directly on the grill or over the open flame of a gas stove burner, turning frequently with tongs to blister and blacken the skins. Or roast peppers under a broiler. When the peppers are charred, remove from the fire and place in a plastic bag. Allow some air to remain in the bag, and loosely seal. The steam that forms in the bag will help loosen the skin. Let cool for about 15 minutes or until you can handle the peppers. Remove peppers from the bag and peel off the skins with your fingers. Cut off the stems, and slice the peppers open. Remove the ribs and seeds, and cut into strips.

Beef with Broccoli

This classic beef *stir-fry* in flavorful *oyster sauce* accompanied by crunchy broccoli and rice makes for a quick meal complete from the freezer.

Yield:	Prep time:	Initial cook time:	Reheat time:	Serving size:
5 cups plus rice	10 minutes	10 minutes	4 minutes	1 cup plus rice

2 TB. soy sauce or low-sodium soy sauce

2 TB. cornstarch

2 TB. rice vinegar

2 tsp. sesame oil

1 tsp. sugar

1 lb. flank steak

4 tsp. canola or vegetable oil

3 cups small-cut broccoli florets

¼ cup water

1 large red bell pepper, ribs and seeds removed, and diced

1 medium white or yellow onion, diced

1 tsp. grated peeled fresh ginger

1 tsp. minced garlic

⅓ cup oyster sauce

4 cups cooked white or brown rice

1. In a medium bowl, whisk together soy sauce, cornstarch, rice vinegar, sesame oil, and sugar.

2. Slice flank steak *with the grain* into long 2-inch-wide strips. Slice strips *across the grain* into ¼-inch-thick slices about 2 inches long. Add beef to soy sauce mixture, mix, and set aside.

3. In a wok or a large skillet over high heat, heat 2 teaspoons canola oil until hot but not smoking. A drop of water should sizzle when added to wok. Add broccoli florets, and stir-fry for about 30 seconds. Add water, cover, reduce heat to medium, and cook, stirring once, for about 2 minutes. Remove broccoli from the pan, and set aside.

4. Add remaining 2 teaspoons canola oil to the wok, and set over high heat. Add red bell pepper and onion, and stir-fry for about 3 minutes. Add ginger and garlic, and stir-fry for 1 more minute.

5. Give meat mixture a stir, add to the wok, and stir-fry for about 2 or 3 minutes or until almost done. Add broccoli, and stir. Stir in oyster sauce, and cook until everything is heated through and well coated in sauce. Cool completely. Divide rice among 5 wide microwave-safe rigid freezer containers. Divide beef and broccoli mixture among the 5 containers. Cover, cool completely, label, and freeze.

To reheat after freezing:

1. Microwave frozen on high for about 3 or 4 minutes or until heated through, stopping to stir occasionally.

TABLE TALK

Stir-frying is the method of quickly sautéing small, uniform pieces of food over very high heat. **Oyster sauce,** a thick, dark brown sauce made from ground dried oysters, is a staple of Chinese cuisine. Cuts of meat such as flank steak have distinct visible lines; cut along the lines for slicing **with the grain,** and cut horizontally across these lines for cutting **against the grain.** The latter helps make a usually tough cut less chewy and stringy.

Korean-Style Short Ribs

Bring the sizzling flavors of Korean barbecue—soy, garlic, and tantalizing sesame—
to your home table with this easy grilling recipe.

Yield:	Prep time:	Reheat time:	Serving size:
3 lb.	10 minutes	15 minutes	⅓ lb.

2 TB. sesame seeds

5 green onions, white and green
  parts, minced

3 TB. minced fresh ginger

2 TB. minced garlic

3 TB. sugar

1 tsp. black pepper

1 tsp. crushed red pepper

¼ cup freshly squeezed lemon
  juice

¼ cup soy sauce or low-sodium soy
  sauce

2 TB. sesame oil

3 lb. thinly cut beef short ribs

1. In a medium, dry skillet over medium heat, add sesame seeds. Toast, shaking
   the pan, for about 3 minutes or until seeds begin to brown.

2. In a medium bowl, whisk together toasted sesame seeds, green onions, ginger,
   garlic, sugar, black pepper, crushed red pepper, lemon juice, soy sauce, and
   sesame oil. Or blend in a food processor.

3. Place short ribs in a large zipper-lock plastic freezer bag, pour marinade over
   ribs, close the bag and squeeze out much of the air, and turn the bag to coat ribs
   in marinade. Remove remaining air from the bag, label, and freeze.

To cook after freezing:

1. Thaw ribs in marinade in the refrigerator, the microwave, or via the cold water
   method (see Chapter 1). Grill ribs over a hot fire for about 7 or 8 minutes per
   side or until browned and crisp at edges. Alternatively, grill on an indoor grill or
   roast in a 400°F oven for about 10 to 12 minutes.

COOL TIP

Thinly cut short ribs are easy to find in an Asian market, but not so much in a
general supermarket, although you can commonly find thicker-cut short ribs
there. Ask the butcher to cut some thinly for you. You may have to wait an extra
minute or two, but the price should be the same. In some areas of the country,
thinly cut Asian-style ribs are readily available. Look for "flanken ribs."

Beefy Baked Macaroni

Pasta baked in a meaty tomato sauce and topped with creamy melted mozzarella makes this dish a fabulous family friendly meal.

Yield:	Prep time:	Initial cook time:	Reheat time:	Serving size:
12 cups	10 minutes	30 minutes	50 minutes	1 cup

Salt

1 lb. uncooked elbow macaroni

1 (28-oz.) can crushed or whole tomatoes, with juice

¼ cup tomato paste

2 tsp. olive oil

1½ lb. lean ground beef

1 large yellow onion

½ large red, green, yellow, or orange bell pepper, ribs and seeds removed, and chopped

2 tsp. minced garlic

2 TB. Italian seasoning

2 cups shredded mozzarella cheese

1. Add salt to a large stockpot of water, and bring to a boil over high heat. Add macaroni, and cook until flexible but still very *al dente*. Drain.

2. In a blender or food processor, purée tomatoes with juice and tomato paste.

3. In a large skillet over medium-high heat, heat olive oil. Crumble beef into the skillet, and cook, stirring frequently, for about 6 minutes or until browned. Using a slotted spoon, remove beef and all but about 2 teaspoons fat from the skillet.

4. Add onion and bell pepper, and sauté for about 3 minutes or until softened. Add garlic, and sauté for 1 more minute. Add tomato mixture, and stir to combine. Stir in Italian seasoning, bring to a boil, reduce heat to low, cover, and simmer, stirring occasionally, for 15 minutes. Remove from heat, add cooked pasta, and stir.

5. Spray a 12-cup baking pan with cooking spray. Divide beef mixture among the prepared pans, and sprinkle shredded mozzarella over top. Cool completely, cover with foil, label, and freeze.

To bake after freezing:

1. Bake frozen in a preheated 375°F oven for about 50 minutes or until heated through and cheese on top has melted and started to brown.

TABLE TALK

Al dente is an Italian term meaning "to the tooth," used to describe pasta, risotto, or other foods that are cooked to a consistency that offers a slight resistance when bitten into.

Shepherd's Pie

This one-dish comfort food meal has everything you need on a cold wintry night: ground beef in a savory gravy, carrots, peas, and creamy mashed potatoes.

Yield:	Prep time:	Initial cook time:	Reheat time:	Serving size:
9 cups	10 minutes	20 minutes	55 minutes	1 cup

2 tsp. olive oil

1½ lb. lean ground beef

1 large yellow onion, diced

½ large celery rib, finely diced

2 medium carrots, peeled and finely diced

2 tsp. minced garlic

1 (15-oz.) can crushed tomatoes, with juice

4 TB. tomato paste

2 TB. fresh minced Italian parsley or 1 TB. dried

1 tsp. dried oregano

1 tsp. dried thyme

Salt

Black pepper

1½ cups fresh or frozen green peas

3 cups Real Mashed Potatoes or Roasted Garlic Mashed Potatoes (recipe and variation in Chapter 14)

1. In a large skillet over medium-high heat, heat olive oil. Crumble beef into skillet, and cook, stirring frequently, for about 6 minutes or until browned. Using a slotted spoon, remove beef and all but about 2 teaspoons fat from the skillet.

2. Add onion, celery, and carrots, and sauté for about 3 minutes or until onion has softened. Return beef to the skillet, add garlic, and stir to combine. Reduce heat to medium-low, and continue to cook, stirring occasionally, for 5 minutes.

3. In a blender or food processor, puree tomatoes with juice and tomato paste. Stir into meat mixture, and season with Italian parsley, oregano, thyme, salt, and pepper. Add peas, and stir well. Simmer for 5 more minutes or so or until sauce has slightly thickened.

4. Spray a 9-cup baking or loaf pan with cooking spray. Divide meat mixture among the prepared pans, and cover with a layer of Real Mashed Potatoes. Cool completely, cover with foil, label, and freeze.

To bake after freezing:

1. Thaw in the refrigerator if desired. Bake thawed or frozen in a preheated 375°F oven for about 55 minutes (longer when frozen) or until heated through and tops of potatoes are lightly browned.

COOL TIP

Cut fat and calories in ground beef by cooking and then draining the cooked crumbled meat in a colander to remove as much fat as possible before rinsing in hot tap water to remove even more. This technique can also save you money. The higher the fat content in ground beef, the lower the cost. Use the cook and rinse technique to turn your inexpensive high-fat ground beef into lean ground beef after the fact.

Tamale Pie

Sweet cornbread tops a filling of spicy beef, green chiles, hearty black beans, and sweet corn for a one-dish meal that has it all.

Yield:	Prep time:	Initial cook time:	Reheat time:	Serving size:
4 (5×7-inch) pans	15 minutes	20 minutes	1 hour, 15 minutes	⅓ pan

1 lb. lean ground beef

2 tsp. plus ¼ cup vegetable or canola oil

1 large yellow onion, diced

1 medium green or red bell pepper, ribs and seeds removed, and diced

2 tsp. chili powder

½ tsp. ground cumin

1 (14-oz.) can crushed tomatoes, with juice

1 (15-oz.) can corn, with juice

1 (15-oz.) can black beans, rinsed and drained

1 (4-oz.) can diced green chiles, with juice

½ tsp. salt plus to taste

Black pepper

1½ cups all-purpose flour

1 cup yellow cornmeal

⅓ cup sugar

1 TB. baking powder

1¼ cups milk

2 large eggs, lightly beaten

1½ cups shredded cheddar or Monterrey Jack cheese

1. Spray a large skillet with cooking spray, and set over medium-high heat. Add ground beef, and cook, stirring to break into small crumbles, for about 6 minutes or until browned. Using a slotted spoon, remove beef from the skillet, and drain off excess fat.

2. Return the skillet to heat, and add 2 teaspoons vegetable oil. Add onion and bell pepper, and sauté for about 3 minutes or until softened. Return beef to the skillet, and add chili powder and cumin. Stir in crushed tomatoes with juice, corn, black beans, and green chiles with a wooden spoon. Reduce heat to medium-low, and simmer for 10 minutes. Season with salt and pepper. Cool completely.

3. Meanwhile, in a large bowl, combine all-purpose flour, cornmeal, sugar, baking powder, and ½ teaspoon salt. Add milk, remaining ¼ cup oil, and beaten eggs, and stir until all dry ingredients are moistened. Stir in shredded cheese.

4. Spray 4 (5×7-inch) or 2 (8-inch) square baking pans with cooking spray (recipe will also work in 2 [8-inch] round pans). Divide meat mixture between the prepared pans. Top with cornmeal mixture, and use a rubber spatula to smooth out the top. Cover with foil, label, and freeze.

To bake after freezing:

1. Bake frozen in a 375°F oven for about 1 hour, 15 minutes or until top is puffed and brown and filling is heated through.

COLD FACT

Most baking powder found in grocery stores is "double action," which means it will cause leavening when it first comes into contact with liquid and again in the heat of the oven. Store baking powder in a cool, dry place, and replace it every year or so as it can lose its potency.

Barbecue-Style Pulled Pork

This easy stovetop version of pulled pork satisfies the craving for barbecue without all the work and trouble of smoking the meat.

Yield:	Prep time:	Initial cook time:	Reheat time:	Serving size:
5 lb. pork	10 minutes	2½ hours	15 minutes	¼ lb. pork

5 lb. pork shoulder or Boston butt roast, boneless or bone-in

1 tsp. salt

½ tsp. black pepper

1 TB. olive oil

1 cup ketchup

2 cups water

½ cup cider vinegar

¼ cup Worcestershire sauce

⅓ cup brown sugar, firmly packed

1 TB. dry mustard powder

½ to 1 tsp. crushed red pepper (optional)

1 tsp. *liquid smoke*

1. Cut any large areas of visible fat from pork shoulder. Pat dry with paper towels, and season with salt and pepper.

2. In a large stockpot or Dutch oven with a lid over medium-high heat, heat olive oil. Add pork shoulder and brown, turning, for about 2 minutes per side. Transfer pork to a plate, and set aside.

3. In the same pot, combine ketchup, water, cider vinegar, Worcestershire sauce, brown sugar, dry mustard powder, crushed red pepper (if using), and liquid smoke, and stir well.

4. Return pork shoulder to the pot, and bring liquid to a boil. Reduce heat to low, cover, and simmer for 2½ hours, turning roast every 30 minutes.

5. Remove pork to a plate. Increase heat to high, and boil liquid for 6 or 7 minutes or until slightly thickened.

6. When pork is cool enough to handle, use 2 forks (or your fingers) to shred or "pull" pork. Return pork to sauce. Cool completely, package in zipper-lock plastic freezer bags or rigid freezer containers, label, and freeze.

To reheat after freezing:

1. Thaw in the refrigerator if desired. Place thawed or frozen pork and sauce in a saucepan over medium heat. Heat, stirring frequently, for 15 minutes or until sauce is bubbling and meat is heated through.

> **TABLE TALK**
>
> **Liquid smoke** is a seasoning made from hickory smoke concentrate used to give foods a distinctive smoky flavor. Use sparingly because a little liquid smoke can go a long way. Find it in most grocery stores in the barbecue and steak sauce section.

Crunchy Oven-Baked Pork Chops

The crunchy herbed coating on these tasty pork chops gives them terrific flavor while sealing in moisture.

Yield:	Prep time:	Reheat time:	Serving size:
8 pork chops	15 minutes	40 minutes	1 pork chop

2 TB. Dijon mustard

1 large egg

1¼ cups panko breadcrumbs

1 tsp. onion powder

2 tsp. garlic powder

½ tsp. dried parsley

1 tsp. salt

1 tsp. black pepper

¾ cup all-purpose flour

8 (½-in.-thick) bone-in pork chops

1. In a shallow bowl, beat together Dijon mustard and egg.

2. In a large plastic bag, mix panko breadcrumbs, onion powder, garlic powder, parsley, salt, and pepper.

3. Place all-purpose flour in a third shallow bowl.

4. Dredge each pork chop in flour to lightly coat. Dip in egg mixture. Place in the bag with breadcrumb mixture, and shake to coat.

5. Place coated pork chops on a waxed paper–lined baking sheet, and freeze flat before wrapping tightly in foil or freezer paper and labeling.

To cook after freezing:

1. Preheat the oven to 375°F. Cook frozen pork chops for about 40 minutes or until meat reaches 145°F to 150°F on a meat thermometer. Let rest 5 minutes before serving.

COLD FACT

Today's pork has approximately 16 percent less fat and 27 percent less saturated fat than pork had even 15 years ago—and some pork cuts have a fat content as low as skinless chicken. The change happened when pork producers responded to the public's growing health concerns over saturated fats.

Chinese-Style Pork Tenderloin

Chinese five-spice powder helps infuse this pork loin with an unforgettable flavor. The cooked meat is fabulous as an entrée on its own, or used to make Pork Egg Rolls (variation in Chapter 8), or in a variety of stir-fries.

Yield:	Prep time:	Reheat time:	Serving size:
4½ lb.	5 minutes	20 minutes	¼ lb.

¾ cup *hoisin sauce*

¾ cup rice vinegar

¾ cup low-sodium soy sauce

⅓ cup ketchup

¼ cup brown sugar, firmly packed

2 tsp. grated fresh ginger

2 tsp. minced garlic

¾ tsp. Chinese five-spice powder

3 (1½-lb.) pork tenderloins

1. In a large bowl, combine hoisin sauce, rice vinegar, low-sodium soy sauce, ketchup, brown sugar, grated ginger, garlic, and Chinese five-spice powder.

2. Add pork tenderloins, and toss to completely coat. Place pork and marinade in a zipper-lock plastic freezer bag, or divide among 3 quart-size bags for smaller portions, label, and freeze.

To reheat after freezing:

1. Thaw tenderloins overnight in the refrigerator or using the cold water method (see Chapter 1). Cook in a 375°F oven for about 20 minutes, or sear for about 3 minutes per side on a medium-hot grill before moving to a cooler part of the grill to cook for about 10 more minutes, until pork reaches an inner temperature of 145°F to 150°F. Let rest for 5 minutes before cutting.

TABLE TALK

Chinese five-spice powder is a spice blend of anise and cinnamon plus ginger, cloves, star anise, fennel, licorice, nutmeg, or Szechuan peppercorns. **Hoisin sauce,** a kind of Chinese barbecue sauce, is made from soybeans, sesame seeds, chile peppers, and sugar. You can find it in the Asian foods aisle of the supermarket.

"The Works" Lasagna

Pasta, spicy Italian sausage, meaty mushrooms, tangy tomato sauce, and creamy cheeses come together to make one of the world's ultimate comfort foods.

Yield:	Prep time:	Initial cook time:	Reheat time:	Serving size:
6 (5×7-inch) pans	15 minutes	30 minutes	1 hour	⅓ pan

1 lb. uncooked lasagna noodles

1 TB. olive oil

1 lb. sweet or hot Italian sausage, removed from casings

1 large white or yellow onion, diced

1 large green bell pepper, ribs and seeds removed, and diced

8 oz. sliced white or cremini mushrooms

2 tsp. minced garlic

⅓ cup dry red wine

5 cups Chunky Marinara Sauce (recipe in Chapter 16)

2 tsp. Italian seasoning

Salt

Black pepper

2 large eggs

4 cups whole or part-skim ricotta cheese

¼ cup minced fresh Italian parsley or 3 TB. dried

8 cups grated mozzarella cheese

¾ cup grated Parmesan cheese

1. Bring a large stockpot of salted water to a boil over high heat. Add lasagna noodles, and cook for about 5 minutes. You want noodles to be flexible but not quite cooked. Drain, rinse, and keep noodles moist in a pot of cold water until needed.

2. In a large pot over medium-high heat, heat olive oil. Add sausage, and cook, stirring to break up pieces, for 3 or 4 minutes or until no longer pink. Add onion and bell pepper, and cook, stirring frequently, for 4 or 5 minutes or until onion has softened and is just starting to brown.

3. Add mushrooms, and cook, stirring frequently, for about 4 minutes or until softened. Add garlic, and cook for 2 more minutes. Pour in dry red wine, and deglaze pan, scraping up any brown bits on the bottom.

4. Stir in Chunky Marinara Sauce and Italian seasoning, and season with salt and pepper. Bring to a simmer, reduce heat to low, cover, and simmer for 10 minutes.

5. In a large bowl, beat eggs until frothy. Add ricotta cheese and parsley, and mix well.

6. In a separate bowl, combine grated mozzarella and Parmesan cheese.

7. To begin layering lasagna, spoon a thin layer of sauce on the bottom of 6 (5×7-inch) pans. Arrange a layer of noodles to cover the bottom of the pan, overlapping as necessary to make them fit. Add a layer of ricotta mixture, using about $\frac{1}{2}$ of mixture on this first layer. Add $\frac{1}{3}$ of remaining sauce and $\frac{1}{3}$ of mozzarella-Parmesan mixture. Repeat with another layer of pasta, remaining ricotta mixture, $\frac{1}{2}$ of remaining sauce, and $\frac{1}{2}$ of remaining mozzarella mixture. End with one more layer of pasta and remaining sauce, and top with remaining mozzarella mixture. Cool completely, cover tightly with foil, label, and freeze.

To bake after freezing:

1. Bake uncovered frozen lasagna in a 375°F oven for about 1 hour or until heated through and cheese has melted and browned on top.

COOL TIP

Save time by eliminating step 1 of this recipe and layer uncooked lasagna noodles instead. As long as you take care to ensure the sauce covers everything, there's enough moisture to do the job while the lasagna bakes in the oven. This works with regular pasta; you needn't buy those labeled "no boil," which I find have a different and less-desirable texture.

Herb-Crusted Rack of Lamb

Herbed breadcrumbs and tangy mustard enhance the flavor of the rack of lamb in this elegant entrée.

Yield:	Prep time:	Reheat time:	Serving size:
2 racks of lamb	10 minutes	40 minutes	¼ of 1 rack

1 cup fresh breadcrumbs	1 tsp. black pepper
1 tsp. garlic powder	2 TB. olive oil
1½ tsp. crushed dried rosemary	3 TB. Dijon mustard
½ tsp. dried mint	2 racks of lamb (8 ribs each)
1 tsp. salt	

1. In a small bowl, stir together breadcrumbs, garlic powder, dried rosemary, dried mint, salt, and pepper. Drizzle in olive oil, and stir to mix well. Divide breadcrumbs mixture into 2 halves.

2. Spread Dijon mustard over both sides of racks of lamb. Pat each portion of breadcrumbs onto lamb over mustard, patting with your hands to help coating adhere. Wrap racks of lamb in foil, label, and freeze.

To cook after freezing:

1. Preheat the oven to 400°F. Spray a roasting pan with cooking spray. Roast lamb for about 40 minutes or until a thermometer inserted diagonally into the center (but not touching bone) registers 130°F for medium rare. Let rest for 10 minutes before slicing into chops.

COLD FACT

The meat from a sheep is considered *lamb* if the animal is under 1 year old at the time of slaughter. Meat from animals 12 to 24 months old is referred to as *yearling* (rarely seen in the United States), and after that it becomes *mutton*.

Poultry Pleasers

In This Chapter

- Poultry freezing tips
- Poultry recipes from casual to elegant
- Transforming cooked poultry leftovers

Is there any more versatile ingredient than poultry? Simple chicken and turkey serve as a great culinary blank canvas, just waiting for you to transform them into a seemingly endless variety of interesting and tasty dishes. As a bonus: a lot of those dishes freeze exceptionally well, making it easy to enjoy chicken or turkey for dinner anytime.

Freezing Poultry

You can save money by buying whole chickens, cutting them into pieces, and freezing the meat in the portion sizes best for you or your family. Just be sure to wrap raw poultry well in foil or freezer paper to prevent freezer burn.

Chicken is hearty enough to stand up to being frozen in a marinade, especially one that isn't too acidic. Freeze chicken and marinade together. Thaw using the cold water method (see Chapter 1); discard marinade; and immediately bake, broil, or grill chicken.

You can also freeze cooked poultry, although like cooked meats, cover it in a sauce, broth, or gravy to prevent it from getting tough and dry.

Tandoori-Style Chicken

A marinade of yogurt, lemon, ginger, and curry powder infuses this easy chicken dish with the exotic flavors of India.

Yield:	Prep time:	Reheat time:	Serving size:
6 lb.	10 minutes	30 minutes	2 pieces

2 cups plain yogurt

3 TB. minced garlic

⅓ cup lemon juice

1 tsp. black pepper

2 TB. grated fresh ginger

1 TB. curry powder

1 tsp. turmeric

½ tsp. cayenne or to taste (optional)

6 lb. skin-on, bone-in chicken pieces

1. In a large zipper-lock plastic bag, combine yogurt, garlic, lemon juice, pepper, ginger, curry powder, turmeric, and cayenne (if using). Close bag and squeeze to combine ingredients.

2. Add chicken pieces, and toss to coat. Label, and freeze.

To cook after freezing:

1. Thaw completely in the refrigerator or use the cold water method (see Chapter 1). Heat a grill to medium-high heat, leaving an area unlit for indirect grilling. Lightly spray the grill rack with cooking spray.

2. Remove chicken from marinade, shake off any excess, and discard marinade. Grill chicken, skin side up, for about 8 minutes or until browned. Turn and brown on second side for about 8 minutes. Move chicken from the direct heat and continue to cook via indirect heat for about 10 minutes or until fully cooked and 160°F.

3. Alternatively, bake in a preheated 375°F oven for about 35 minutes or until browned and cooked through.

COLD FACT

Turmeric, a spice that lends its distinctive golden color to many Indian dishes, curries, and mustards, is also prized for its health benefits. Doctors in India have been using it for centuries to treat a host of maladies, including inflammation, liver disorders, arthritis, and pain.

Chicken Cacciatore

In this classic Italian "hunter's stew," chicken is cooked in a tangy, garlic-laden tomato sauce and accented with onions, sweet bell peppers, and meaty mushrooms.

Yield:	Prep time:	Initial cook time:	Reheat time:	Serving size:
3 lb.	15 minutes	40 minutes	1 hour, 15 minutes	¼ lb.

1 cup all-purpose flour

3 lb. bone-in chicken thighs and drumsticks

3 TB. olive oil

1 large yellow onion, diced

1 large red or green bell pepper, ribs and seeds removed, and diced

9 oz. white or cremini mushrooms, sliced

2 TB. minced garlic

½ cup dry red wine

1 (28-oz.) can whole tomatoes, reserve juice

2 TB. tomato paste

1 TB. Italian seasoning

2 bay leaves

¼ cup minced fresh Italian parsley or 1 TB. dried

Salt

Black pepper

1. Place all-purpose flour in a large plastic bag. Add chicken thighs and drumsticks, and shake to lightly coat.

2. In a large skillet (be sure it's large enough to hold chicken in a single layer; if not, use 2 skillets) over medium-high heat, heat olive oil. Add chicken, and cook, turning occasionally, for about 10 minutes or until golden brown on all sides. Remove chicken from the skillet, and set aside.

3. Add onion, bell pepper, and mushrooms to the skillet, and sauté for about 5 minutes or until vegetables are softened. Add garlic, and sauté for 1 more minute. Add red wine, and deglaze the pan, scraping up any browned bits from the bottom.

4. Using your hands, squeeze each tomato into the skillet, breaking it up as you go. Reserve tomato juice in the can. Add tomato paste, and stir well with a wooden spoon.

5. Stir in Italian seasoning, bay leaves, and Italian parsley, and season with salt and pepper. If sauce seems too thick, add some of reserved tomato juice until you achieve a consistency you like. Sauce should be chunky and thick but not dry.

6. Return chicken to the skillet, and coat with sauce. Reduce heat to medium-low, simmer and cook, stirring and turning chicken occasionally, for about 25 minutes or until chicken is just cooked through. Cool completely and remove bay leaf. Package in baking dishes or zipper-lock plastic freezer bags (depending on if you prefer to bake or microwave later), label, and freeze.

To reheat after freezing:

1. Thaw in the refrigerator if desired. Bake thawed or frozen baking pan of chicken and sauce in a preheated 375°F oven for 1 hour, 15 minutes, or until heated through. Alternatively, microwave on high, stopping to stir every minute or so, until heated through.

COOL TIP

Never buy wine labeled "cooking wine." It's an inferior-quality wine and will give your final dish inferior flavor. There's no need to cook with expensive wines, but they should at least be drinkable. Serve the same wine with the meal that you cooked with, and you'll always have a perfect pairing.

Chicken Curry

A ginger and curry–flavored yogurt sauce envelops tender pieces of white meat chicken in this spicy dish.

Yield:	Prep time:	Initial cook time:	Reheat time:	Serving size:
4 cups	10 minutes	25 minutes	15 minutes	1 cup

2 TB. vegetable or olive oil

2 lb. boneless, skinless chicken breasts, cut into 1-in. cubes

1 large yellow onion, cut in ½ and thinly sliced

1 medium fresh jalapeño pepper, ribs and seeds removed, and minced

2 tsp. grated fresh ginger

1 tsp. minced garlic

1 TB. curry powder

½ tsp. turmeric

½ cup plain yogurt

½ cup water

¼ cup minced fresh cilantro

Salt

Black pepper

1 cup cooked rice per serving

1. In a large skillet over medium-high heat, heat vegetable oil. Add chicken, onion, and jalapeño, and cook, stirring frequently with a wooden spoon, for about 5 minutes or until chicken is just beginning to brown and onions are softened.

2. Stir in ginger, garlic, curry powder, and turmeric. Stir in yogurt, and cook, stirring frequently, for about 3 minutes or until thickened.

3. Stir in water and cilantro, and season with salt and pepper. Reduce heat, cover, and simmer, stirring occasionally, for about 15 minutes or until chicken is cooked through. Cool completely, package in zipper-lock plastic freezer bags, and freeze.

4. Alternatively, for a complete frozen meal, top cooled cooked rice with cooled Chicken Curry in a rigid freezer container. Label and freeze.

To reheat after freezing:

1. Thaw in the refrigerator if desired. Heat thawed or frozen in a saucepan over medium heat, stirring frequently, until bubbling and heated through. Serve over rice.

2. Alternatively, microwave thawed or frozen on high (with or without rice), stopping to stir every minute or so, until heated through.

Stuffed Chicken Breasts

Smokey ham and nutty melted Swiss cheese are tucked inside a breaded boneless chicken breast for an elegant and unforgettable entrée.

Yield:	Prep time:	Reheat time:	Serving size:
6 stuffed chicken breasts	20 minutes	50 minutes	1 stuffed breast

6 boneless, skinless chicken breasts

6 thin slices ham or *prosciutto*

6 thin slices Swiss or Gruyère cheese

1 cup all-purpose flour

2 tsp. salt

2 tsp. black pepper

2 large eggs

1 tsp. water

1½ cups panko breadcrumbs

⅛ cup dried parsley

½ cup olive oil

1. Using a sharp knife, butterfly the chicken breasts by slicing each horizontally starting at thinner side and slicing almost all the way through to thicker side of breast. *Do not* slice all the way through. You should have a single piece of meat that opens like a book.

2. Sandwich 1 slice ham and 1 slice Swiss cheese between cut layers of each chicken breast, pushing ham and cheese to fit inside chicken with none hanging over. Fold chicken breast closed over filling, and use your fingers to press closed as much as possible.

3. In a medium bowl, combine all-purpose flour, salt, and pepper.

4. In a shallow bowl, beat eggs with water.

5. In a separate medium bowl, stir together panko breadcrumbs and dried parsley.

6. Ready a piece of plastic wrap big enough to wrap a single breast.

7. Using tongs, and working one at a time, gently coat each stuffed chicken breast in flour. Then dip a floured breast into egg mixture to moisten all surfaces, and coat in panko mixture. Using your fingers, press breadcrumbs onto surface. Place coated breast on plastic wrap, and wrap tightly. Repeat with remaining breasts. Store wrapped breasts together in a large zipper-lock plastic freezer bag, label, and freeze.

To cook after freezing:

1. Preheat the oven to 375°F. In a cast-iron skillet large enough to hold chicken without crowding, heat olive oil. Add frozen stuffed chicken breasts to the pan, and brush top of breasts with remaining ¼ cup olive oil. Bake for 25 minutes. Use a spatula to carefully turn each chicken breast, and bake for 15 to 25 more minutes or until cooked through and juices run clear.

TABLE TALK

Prosciutto (pronounced *pro-SHOOT-oh*) is an aged, dry-cured, intensely flavored Italian ham that comes sliced paper thin and ready to eat. Find prosciutto by the pound in well-stocked delis or packaged in the cold-cut section of the supermarket.

Chicken, Corn, and Black Bean Enchiladas

Enjoy comfort food south-of-the-border style with cheesy chicken, bean, and corn–stuffed enchiladas smothered in a chile-spiced sauce.

Yield:	Prep time:	Reheat time:	Serving size:
16 enchiladas	25 minutes	1 hour	1 enchilada

3 cups cooked diced chicken

1 cup sour cream or low-fat sour cream

1 (15-oz.) can black beans, rinsed and drained

2 (8-oz.) cans diced green chiles, drained

1 (15-oz.) can corn, drained

2½ cups grated Monterrey Jack cheese

1 tsp. ground cumin

½ tsp. dried oregano

½ tsp. garlic powder

2 tsp. chili powder

Salt

Black pepper

16 (8-in.) flour tortillas

1 (28-oz.) can plus 1 (15-oz.) can green enchilada sauce

1. Spray a baking dish or 2 with cooking spray.

2. In a large bowl, combine diced chicken, sour cream, black beans, 1 can green chiles, corn, 2 cups grated Monterrey Jack cheese, ground cumin, dried oregano, garlic powder, and chili powder. Add salt and pepper, and toss to mix well.

3. Place 1 tortilla on a clean surface. Place ½ cup filling mixture down the center, and roll tortilla. Place seam side down in the prepared baking dish. Repeat with remaining tortillas and filling, placing enchiladas with sides touching to completely fill the baking dish(es).

4. In a medium bowl, combine remaining 1 can green chiles with enchilada sauce. Pour sauce over prepared enchiladas. Sprinkle with remaining ½ cup grated Monterrey Jack cheese over top. Tightly cover pans with foil, label, and freeze.

To bake after freezing:

1. Bake uncovered and frozen in a 375°F oven for about 45 minutes for 2 enchiladas, or about 1 hour for 8 enchiladas.

Chicken and Sausage Jambalaya

Made with boneless chicken breasts, this jambalaya is quicker and easier than the usual version but still has all the classic Cajun flavors of sausage, onions, celery, bell peppers, and spice!

Yield:	Prep time:	Initial cook time:	Reheat time:	Serving size:
14 cups	15 minutes	40 minutes	15 minutes	1½ cups

1 TB. olive oil

2 lb. boneless, skinless chicken breasts, cut into 1-in. pieces

2 lb. smoked sausage, sliced into ½-in. pieces

3 large yellow onions, diced

4 large celery stalks, chopped into ½-in. pieces

2 large green bell peppers, ribs and seeds removed, and diced

2 tsp. minced garlic

2½ cups uncooked rice or brown rice

6 cups chicken stock

2 bay leaves

2 tsp. dried thyme

2 tsp. dried oregano

¼ tsp. cayenne, or to taste

1 tsp. hot sauce, or to taste

1. In a large pot over medium heat, heat olive oil. Add chicken, and cook, stirring frequently, for about 5 minutes or until browned on all sides.

2. Add sausage, onions, celery, and green bell peppers, and cook, stirring frequently, for 6 to 8 minutes or until onion begins to brown. Add garlic and rice, and cook, stirring, for 2 more minutes. Add chicken stock, and deglaze pan, scraping up any brown bits on the bottom.

3. Add bay leaves, dried thyme, dried oregano, cayenne, and hot sauce, and stir to blend. Bring to a boil, reduce heat to low, cover, and simmer for 25 to 30 minutes or until liquid is absorbed and rice is tender. Cool completely in the refrigerator, remove bay leaf, package in zipper-lock plastic freezer bags or rigid freezer containers, label, and freeze.

To reheat after freezing:

1. Thaw if desired in the fridge. Heat, thawed or frozen, in a large saucepan sprayed with cooking spray. Heat over medium-low heat, stirring frequently to prevent scorching on the bottom, until heated through. Alternatively, microwave on high, stopping to stir every minute or so, until heated through.

Chicken or Turkey Pot Pies with Puff Pastry Crust

Chicken or turkey, crunchy carrots, celery, and sweet green peas nestle together in a creamy sauce under a flaky puff pastry crust in this classic comfort food.

Yield:	Prep time:	Initial cook time:	Reheat time:	Serving size:
7 cups	15 minutes	12 minutes	45 minutes	1 cup plus crust

2 TB. olive oil

4 medium carrots, peeled and diced small

4 medium celery ribs, diced small

1 large yellow onion, finely diced

1 cup frozen or canned green peas

¼ cup minced fresh Italian parsley

¾ tsp. ground dried sage

½ tsp. dried thyme

4 TB. unsalted butter

½ cup all-purpose flour

1½ cups whole milk

2 cups Poultry Stock (recipe in Chapter 10)

3 cups diced cooked chicken or turkey

Salt

Black pepper

1 (1-lb., 1-oz.) pkg. frozen puff pastry

1. In a large skillet over medium-high heat, heat olive oil. Add carrots, celery, and onion, and cook, stirring frequently, for about 5 minutes or until softened. Stir in peas, Italian parsley, sage, and thyme. Remove from heat.

2. In a large saucepan over medium heat, melt unsalted butter. Whisk in all-purpose flour until smooth. Cook, whisking constantly, for 1 minute.

3. Whisk in whole milk in a steady stream until smooth. Repeat with Poultry Stock. Continue to cook, stirring constantly with a wooden spoon, until mixture comes to a simmer. Cook, stirring, for 2 more minutes or until slightly thickened. Stir in cooked chicken or turkey, cooked vegetables, salt, and pepper.

4. Divide mixture between baking pans or pie pans, filling each about ⅔ full. Cool completely.

5. While chicken mixture is cooling, thaw puff pastry on the countertop until just flexible enough to unfold. Using a sharp knife, cut pastry to the size of the top of the pans, and set on top of chicken mixture. Wrap tightly in foil, label, and freeze.

To bake after freezing:

1. Bake frozen in a 400°F oven until crust is puffed and golden brown and filling is bubbly, about 45 minutes.

COOL TIP

This recipe, along with the Chicken or Turkey and Mushroom–Stuffed Crepes recipe that follows, are great ways to use leftover roast or rotisserie chicken. You may even want to make extra poultry with these recipes in mind. They also make tasty ways to recycle leftover holiday turkey.

Chicken or Turkey and Mushroom–Stuffed Crepes

Savory mushrooms and chicken smothered in a creamy white sauce and spiced with a hint of nutmeg are stuffed into delicate crepes for an impressive entrée.

Yield:	Prep time:	Initial cook time:	Reheat time:	Serving size:
12 stuffed crepes	6 hours	50 minutes	50 minutes	2 crepes

3 large eggs

2½ cups whole or reduced-fat milk

6 TB. unsalted butter, melted

¼ tsp. salt plus to taste

1 cup all-purpose flour

8 oz. sliced white or cremini mushrooms

1 medium yellow onion, diced

½ tsp. minced garlic

2 cups cooked diced chicken or turkey

Black pepper

¼ cup dry sherry or Poultry Stock (recipe in Chapter 10)

¼ tsp. ground nutmeg

1¼ cups shredded Swiss cheese

1. In a medium bowl, and using an electric mixer on high speed or in a blender, combine eggs, 1½ cups milk, 2 tablespoons melted butter, ¼ teaspoon salt, and ¾ cup all-purpose flour. Let batter rest for 5 minutes.

2. Heat an 8-inch nonstick sauté pan over medium heat. Spray lightly with cooking spray, and pour in a scant ¼ cup batter. Immediately tilt the pan in all directions to coat the entire bottom of the pan and slightly up the sides with a paper-thin coating of batter.

3. Cook over medium heat until top of crepe is set and you can easily lift the edge with the corner of a spatula. Watch carefully; with a properly heated skillet the whole process only takes about 30 seconds. As much as possible, avoid browning crepes.

4. Turn cooked crepe onto a plate. (There's no need to flip it and cook the other side if it's properly set.) Repeat with remaining batter, stacking cooked crepes between layers of waxed paper.

5. In a large skillet over medium-high heat, combine 2 tablespoons melted butter, mushrooms, and onion, and sauté for 6 or 7 minutes or until mushrooms have given off most of their liquid and onion has softened. Add garlic and cooked poultry, and sauté 1 more minute. Season with salt and pepper, and stir well.

6. Add dry sherry or Poultry Stock and deglaze pan, scraping up any brown bits on the bottom. Bring to a boil, and cook for 2 or 3 minutes or until most of liquid has evaporated. Place mixture in a large bowl, and cool completely in the refrigerator.

7. Return the skillet to heat, and add remaining 2 tablespoons butter and remaining ¼ cup all-purpose flour, and whisk until smooth. Cook, whisking constantly, for 2 or 3 more minutes or until light tan in color. Whisk in remaining 1 cup milk until smooth.

8. Whisk in nutmeg, and season with additional salt and pepper, if necessary. Bring mixture to a boil, stirring frequently with a wooden spoon. Reduce heat to low, and simmer, stirring often, for 7 or 8 minutes or until thickened. Remove from heat and whisk in shredded Swiss cheese until smooth. Transfer to a bowl, cover, and cool completely in the refrigerator.

9. To assemble, spray a 10×7 baking dish with cooking spray. Remove about 2 cups sauce, and spread a thin layer over the bottom of the dish. Place 1 crepe on a clean work surface and run a line of filling, about ⅓ cup, down center of crepe. Tightly roll crepe around filling, and place seam down in the prepared dish. Repeat with remaining crepes, packing stuffed crepes side by side in a line, until dish is full. Spread remaining sauce over top, cover tightly with foil, label, and freeze.

To bake after freezing:

1. Bake frozen in a 375°F oven for about 50 minutes (for a pan of 4 stuffed crepes) or until lightly browned on top and filling is bubbly.

COOL TIP

It's easiest to make the filling, crepes, and sauce for this recipe ahead of time and assemble and freeze later or even the following day. Stack crepes with a layer of waxed paper between each pancake, wrap tightly in foil, place in a zipper-lock plastic freezer bag, and freeze. Thaw in the refrigerator and use as directed. Oh, and as a beginner, you'll probably waste a few crepes as you learn to make them, but nearly everyone does that. You'll be a pro in no time, and the ones you mess up make great snacks.

Rolled Stuffed Turkey Breast

When cooking a whole turkey is just too much, this roasted stuffed turkey breast delivers all the flavors of a traditional turkey dinner in a smaller package.

Yield:	Prep time:	Reheat time:	Serving size:
1 large roll	20 minutes	1 hour, 10 minutes	1 slice

1 TB. butter or margarine	1 tsp. dried thyme
2 tsp. olive oil	½ tsp. dried sage
½ medium yellow onion, minced	¾ cup fresh breadcrumbs
½ small celery rib, minced	Salt
½ tsp. minced garlic	Black pepper
3 TB. minced fresh Italian parsley	1 (2-lb.) boneless turkey breast half

1. In a medium skillet over medium heat, heat butter and olive oil. Add onion and celery, and cook, stirring frequently, for about 4 minutes or until softened.

2. Stir in garlic, and sauté for another 30 seconds. Remove from heat, and stir in Italian parsley, dried thyme, dried sage, and breadcrumbs. Season with salt and pepper, and stir until well combined.

3. Carefully remove skin from turkey breast and set aside. Place breast on a cutting board. Using a chef's knife, and starting at the rounded side, butterfly the breast by carefully making a horizontal cut about halfway down. Cut to within 1 inch of the other side to open the breast as you would a book.

4. Spread stuffing mixture over surface of turkey. Roll lengthwise into a cylinder, and secure in 2 or 3 spots with kitchen twine. Cover rolled turkey with skin, season with salt and pepper, and wrap tightly in plastic wrap. (If you prefer smaller portions, cut the stuffed roll in ½ and wrap separately.) Label and freeze.

To roast after freezing:

1. Spray a baking dish with nonstick cooking spray. Bake frozen in the prepared dish in a 350°F oven for about 1 hour, 10 minutes or until browned and cooked to an internal temperature of 165°F. Remove from the oven, and let rest for 10 minutes before slicing. Serve with Poultry Gravy (recipe in Chapter 16).

COOL TIP

When cooking foods from a frozen state, it can be difficult to determine when they're actually cooked all the way through. With meats, it's important for safety reasons to check. An inexpensive probe-type kitchen thermometer solves the problem by instantly accessing the food's inner temperature.

Sensational Seafood

In This Chapter

- Fish and the freezer
- Ensuring success with seafood
- Sumptuous seafood dishes

You might be surprised to find a seafood chapter in this book, having heard that fish and seafood don't stand up well to freezing and thawing. Although that can be true, with a little care, you can enjoy some seafood dishes from your freezer—without sacrificing taste or texture.

For best results, wrap fresh fish very well in freezer paper or foil in the appropriate portion sizes. Then double-wrap them in a zipper-lock plastic freezer bag to help prevent freezer burn.

You'll notice this seafood chapter doesn't contain as many recipes as some of the other chapters. There's a reason for that. Just because you *can* freeze something, doesn't mean you *should*. Most fish filet dishes cook quickly, so you don't really need to make them ahead of time and risk sacrificing the seafood's delicate texture. More elaborate seafood dishes like those in sauces—like the Shrimp Creole and Elegant Seafood Crepes—make more sense for the freezer. Just cook the seafood until no longer translucent, add it to the sauced dish at the last minute, and enjoy!

Old-Fashioned Tuna Noodle Casserole

This cheesy, creamy family favorite comfort-food casserole topped with crunchy breadcrumbs is just the thing to bring both kids and adults to the table.

Yield:	Prep time:	Initial cook time:	Reheat time:	Serving size:
8 cups	5 minutes	20 minutes	50 minutes	1 cup

12 oz. uncooked wide egg noodles

6 TB. unsalted butter

4 TB. all-purpose flour

2 cups milk

2 cups shredded cheddar cheese

2 (6-oz.) cans oil- or water-packed tuna, drained well

1½ cups frozen green peas

Salt

Black pepper

½ tsp. minced garlic

1½ cups *panko breadcrumbs*

1. In a large saucepan over high heat, cook egg noodles according package directions until flexible but still very *al dente*. Drain and set aside.

2. In a large saucepan over medium heat, melt 4 tablespoons unsalted butter. Whisk in all-purpose flour until a smooth *roux* forms. Whisk in milk until smooth. Bring mixture to a boil, stirring frequently, and cook for about 3 minutes or until slightly thickened. Remove from heat, and stir in cheddar cheese until melted and smooth. Stir in tuna and peas, and season with salt and pepper.

3. Spray baking pans that meet your portion needs with cooking spray. Fill the prepared pans ¾ full with tuna mixture.

4. In a medium skillet over medium-high heat, melt remaining 2 tablespoons butter. Add garlic, and stir for 30 seconds. Add panko breadcrumbs, and stir until well combined. Sprinkle garlic crumbs over tops of filled baking dishes. Cool completely, cover with foil, label, and freeze.

To bake after freezing:

1. Bake frozen in a 375°F oven for about 50 minutes (for a 4-cup portion) or until heated through, bubbly, and lightly browned on top.

Variation: You can add all kinds of vegetables to this casserole. Try blanched baby carrots, green beans, broccoli, or sliced and sautéed mushrooms.

TABLE TALK

Panko breadcrumbs are coarse Japanese-style breadcrumbs that create a wonderful crunchy coating for fried foods. Find them in Asian markets and in the Asian section of well-stocked supermarkets. A **roux** is a mixture of butter or another fat and flour. It's used to thicken sauces and soups.

Shrimp Creole

Sweet shrimp swim in a spicy, Cajun-style tomato sauce in this classic Southern dish. Serve it over rice.

Yield:	Prep time:	Initial cook time:	Reheat time:	Serving size:
8 cups	10 minutes	35 minutes	10 minutes	1 cup

2 TB. unsalted butter

2 TB. olive oil

3 TB. all-purpose flour

1 small onion, diced

1 small green bell pepper, ribs and seeds removed, and diced

3 medium celery ribs, finely diced

2 tsp. minced garlic

1 (15-oz.) can crushed tomatoes, with juice

2 cups Poultry Stock or Vegetable Stock (recipes in Chapter 10)

2 bay leaves

¼ tsp. cayenne, or to taste

3 TB. chopped fresh Italian parsley or 1 TB. dried

Salt

1½ lb. medium shrimp, peeled

1 cup cooked white or brown rice per serving at serving time

1. In a large skillet over medium heat, melt unsalted butter and olive oil. Whisk in all-purpose flour, and cook, whisking constantly, for 3 or 4 minutes or until a golden brown roux forms.

2. Add onion, green bell pepper, and celery, and stir with a wooden spoon to combine well. Cook, stirring constantly, for about 4 minutes or until vegetables are softened. Stir in garlic, and cook for 1 more minute.

3. Stir in tomatoes with juice, Poultry Stock, bay leaves, cayenne, Italian parsley, and salt. Increase heat to high, and bring mixture to a boil. Reduce heat to low, and simmer for about 25 minutes.

4. Add shrimp, stir to combine, and cook for 4 or 5 minutes or until shrimp are no longer translucent. Remove from heat. Cool completely and remove bay leaf. Package in zipper-lock plastic freezer bags, and freeze. Alternatively, for a complete frozen meal, top cooled cooked rice with cooled Shrimp Creole in a rigid freezer container, label, and freeze.

To reheat after freezing:

1. Thaw in the refrigerator if desired. Heat thawed or frozen (without rice) in a saucepan over medium heat, stirring frequently, until bubbling and heated through. Alternatively, microwave thawed or frozen on high (with or without rice), stopping to stir every minute or so, until heated through. Serve over rice.

FREEZER BURN

One of the first and most important lessons instilled in any Cajun cook is to never leave a roux while it's on the stove. The cooking combination of flour and fat can turn into a burned mess in a matter of seconds. Don't even think about leaving the stove, and stir constantly—and I do mean *constantly*—until other liquid ingredients are incorporated.

Elegant Seafood Crepes

Sweet lobster, crab, or shrimp is encased in a creamy sherry-flavored Newburg sauce and wrapped in delicate crepes for a rich, special occasion entrée.

Yield:	Prep time:	Initial cook time:	Reheat time:	Serving size:
12 stuffed crepes	6 hours	40 minutes	50 minutes	2 crepes

3 large eggs

1½ cups whole or reduced-fat milk

5 TB. unsalted butter, melted

¼ tsp. salt plus to taste

1 cup all-purpose flour

½ tsp. dried dill (optional)

1 medium shallot, peeled and minced

1¼ cups half-and-half

Black pepper

½ tsp. paprika (preferably smoked paprika)

1 large egg yolk

3 TB. dry sherry or white wine

2½ cups cooked chopped lobster, crabmeat, or shrimp

1. In a medium bowl, and using an electric mixer on high speed or in a blender, combine eggs, whole milk, 2 tablespoons melted butter, ¼ teaspoon salt, ¾ cup all-purpose flour, and dried dill (if using). Let batter rest for 5 minutes.

2. Heat an 8-inch nonstick sauté pan over medium heat. Spray lightly with cooking spray, and pour in a scant ¼ cup batter. Immediately tilt the pan in all directions to coat the entire bottom of the pan and slightly up the sides with a paper-thin coating of batter.

3. Cook over medium heat until top of crepe is set and you can easily lift the edge with the corner of a spatula. Watch carefully; with a properly heated skillet the whole process only takes about 30 seconds. As much as possible, avoid browning crepes.

4. Turn cooked crepe onto a plate. (There's no need to flip it and cook the other side if it's properly set.) Repeat with remaining batter, stacking cooked crepes between layers of waxed paper.

5. In a medium saucepan over medium heat, add remaining 3 tablespoons butter and shallot, and cook, stirring, for about 2 minutes or until softened. Whisk to combine. Whisk in half-and-half slowly, stirring constantly, until smooth, and stir in remaining salt, pepper, and paprika.

6. In a small bowl, whisk together egg yolk and dry sherry. Whisk a small amount of hot sauce into egg mixture, add it back into the saucepan, and bring to a simmer, stirring constantly. Remove from heat, remove about ¾ cup sauce, and stir cooked lobster into remaining sauce. Cool mixture and extra sauce completely.

7. To assemble, spray a 10×7 baking dish with cooking spray. Spread ¾ cup of sauce in a thin layer over the bottom of the dish. Place 1 crepe on a clean work surface and run a line of filling, about ¼ cup, down center of crepe. Tightly roll crepe around filling, and place seam down in the prepared dish. Repeat with remaining crepes, taking care to use most if not all of pieces of seafood inside crepes. Pack stuffed crepes side by side in a line, until dish is full. Spread remaining sauce over top, cover tightly with foil, label, and freeze.

To bake after freezing:

1. Bake frozen in a 375°F oven for about 50 minutes (for a pan of 4 stuffed crepes) or until lightly browned on top and filling is bubbly.

COOL TIP

Both rock lobsters, which have meaty tails, and Maine lobsters, which contain substantial meat in both the claws and tail, work well for this recipe. Most seafood markets offer lobster already cooked. If you want to cook your own lobster, plunge a live lobster into heavily salted, rapidly boiling water. Do not overcook. Figure between 10 to no more than 15 minutes, depending on the size of your lobster.

Shrimp Egg Rolls

Sweet shrimp and gingery seasoned vegetables are encased in a crispy fried wrapper for a fabulous starter for an Asian-inspired meal.

Yield:	Prep time:	Initial cook time:	Reheat time:	Serving size:
18 egg rolls	1 hour	3 minutes	5 minutes	1 egg roll

1 cup finely chopped carrots (about 2 large)

2 celery ribs, finely chopped

3 whole green onions, minced

6 cups packed shredded napa cabbage

1 cup bean sprouts

2 cups chopped cooked shrimp

2 cloves garlic, minced

2 tsp. minced fresh ginger

18 egg roll wrappers

Vegetable oil for frying

1. Bring a large pot of water to boil over high heat.

2. Add carrots, celery, onions, napa cabbage, and bean sprouts, and blanch for 1 minute. Drain, rinse with cold water, and let drain well.

3. Mix cooled drained vegetables with chopped shrimp, garlic, and ginger, and stir until well combined.

4. Place 1 egg roll wrapper on a clean surface, and use a pastry brush to wet all 4 edges. Place ¼ cup filling near bottom edge about 1 inch from border, and spread to within ¾ inch of the left and right edges. Fold in left and right edges over filling and then fold up the bottom edge over filling and sides of wrapper. Begin rolling, tucking in the sides to encase any escaping filling as necessary, until you have a tight cylinder. Seal seam with a little water.

5. Freeze in a single layer on a waxed paper–lined baking sheet. Once frozen, remove to a rigid freezer container or a zipper-lock plastic freezer bag, label, and freeze.

To cook after freezing:

1. Heat enough vegetable oil to cover egg rolls to 375°F in a deep fat fryer, or in a wok or a deep skillet over medium-high heat. Carefully add frozen rolls to hot oil—use caution because oil may spit and splatter, so stand back. Fry for about 5 minutes or until egg rolls are golden brown. Serve with Pineapple Sweet and Sour Dipping Sauce (recipe in Chapter 16) or hot Chinese mustard.

Variations: Eliminate shrimp from the filling mixture for **Vegetarian Egg Rolls** (you'll need 8 less wrappers as the yield decreases to 18), or substitute 2 cups cooked finely diced Chinese-Style Pork Tenderloin (recipe in Chapter 11) for the shrimp to make **Pork Egg Rolls.**

COOL TIP

The secret to success with frozen egg rolls is to get the filling ingredients as dry as possible before filling and freezing. Use clean hands to squeeze out excess water, and blot with paper towels to get as much moisture out as possible. Take this extra step, and the finished egg rolls will be every bit as good as those freshly made.

Eat Your Vegetables!

In This Chapter

- Versatile veggie main dishes
- Spectacular side dishes
- Bountiful beans
- Perfect potato recipes

You've probably been told to "Eat your vegetables!" countless times over your life, and with the delicious veggie main and side dishes in this chapter, along with help from your freezer, you'll soon look forward to eating your greens, oranges, and yellows—even if you're not a vegetarian!

By keeping a variety of vegetable-based main dishes such as Vegetable Lasagna, Spinach-Stuffed Shells, or Curried Veggies with Lentils in the freezer, you're free to make a whole meal of vegetables. Or you can mix and match sides like Maple-Glazed Carrots, Boston Baked Beans, Southern Succotash, or Candied Sweet Potatoes with Crumb Topping to create an endless variety of meals just by adding a piece of meat and a salad.

You already know from Chapter 1 that you should blanch vegetables destined for the freezer. Think twice about freezing or preparing recipes made with delicate veggies. Since they rarely need anything more than a quick steam, there's little time advantage.

Vegetable Lasagna

Meaty eggplant and mushrooms provide substance in this vegetarian version of the classic pasta dish. Sliced zucchini, creamy ricotta, tangy tomato sauce, and melted mozzarella round out the flavors.

Yield:	Prep time:	Reheat time:	Serving size:
2 (8-inch-square) pans	1 hour, 15 minutes	40 minutes	⅓ pan

1 lb. lasagna noodles

2 medium eggplants

2 TB. salt

¼ cup plus 2 TB. olive oil

2 tsp. plus 1 TB. minced garlic

6 medium zucchini, ends trimmed and sliced into ¼-in.-thick planks

Black pepper

8 oz. sliced white or cremini mushrooms

1 large yellow onion, diced

2 medium red, green, orange, or yellow bell peppers, ribs and seeds removed, and diced

1 (28-oz.) can plus 1 (15-oz.) can crushed tomatoes, with juice

1 (6-oz.) can tomato paste

2 TB. balsamic vinegar

1 bay leaf

2 TB. Italian seasoning

½ tsp. crushed red pepper, or to taste (optional)

2 large eggs

1 (32-oz.) pkg. whole or part-skim ricotta cheese

1 cup grated Parmesan cheese

¼ cup minced fresh Italian parsley, or 3 TB. dried

1½ cups grated mozzarella cheese

1. Bring a large stockpot of salted water to a boil over high heat. Add lasagna noodles, and cook for about 5 minutes. You want noodles to be flexible but not quite cooked. Drain, rinse, and keep moist in a pot of cold water until needed.

2. Preheat the oven to 375°F. Spray 2 large baking sheets with cooking spray.

3. Cut ends off eggplants, and slice eggplants into ½-inch slices. Coat eggplants liberally with salt, and set aside.

4. In a small bowl, combine ¼ cup olive oil with 2 teaspoons minced garlic.

5. Rinse salt off eggplant, and pat dry with paper towels. Liberally brush eggplant and zucchini slices with garlic oil, and season with salt and pepper. Arrange vegetables in a single layer on the prepared baking sheets (you may need to do this in batches), and roast for about 20 minutes. Turn with a metal spatula, and continue to roast for another 20 minutes or until browned. Remove from the oven and cool.

6. In a large Dutch oven over medium-high heat, heat remaining 2 tablespoons olive oil. Add sliced mushrooms and diced onion, and sauté for about 5 minutes. Reduce heat to medium, add diced bell pepper and 1 remaining tablespoon garlic, and sauté for 5 more minutes. Add tomatoes with juice, and stir with a wooden spoon to combine.

7. Add tomato paste, balsamic vinegar, bay leaf, Italian seasoning, and crushed red pepper (if using), and stir to fully incorporate tomato paste into sauce. Increase heat to medium-high, and bring to a boil. Reduce heat to low, cover, and simmer, stirring often, for 20 minutes. Remove from heat, and remove bay leaf.

8. In a large bowl, beat eggs until frothy. Add ricotta cheese, Parmesan cheese, and Italian parsley, and mix well.

9. To begin layering lasagna, spoon a thin layer of tomato sauce on the bottom of 2 (8-inch-square) baking pans. Arrange a layer of noodles to cover the bottom of the pan, overlapping as necessary to make them fit. Add a layer of roasted eggplant slices, followed by a layer of zucchini. Add a layer of egg-ricotta mixture followed by a thin sprinkling of mozzarella. Cover with tomato sauce. Repeat with a pasta layer, vegetables, ricotta, mozzarella, and sauce. End with a layer of pasta, cover with sauce, and sprinkle remaining mozzarella on top. Cool completely, cover tightly with foil, label, and freeze.

To bake after freezing:

1. Thaw in the refrigerator. Bake uncovered in a 375°F oven for about 40 minutes or until heated through, cheese has melted and browned on top, and sauce is bubbling. Alternatively, bake frozen in a 375°F oven for about 3 hours or until heated through, cheese has melted and browned on top, and sauce is bubbling.

COOL TIP

Taking the time to salt the eggplant helps take away any bitterness it may have. It also shrinks the pores, making the vegetable less absorbent. Without this extra step, the eggplant can end up soaking up most of the sauce's moisture and you're left with a dry finished product.

Spinach-Stuffed Shells

Spinach combines with creamy ricotta and mozzarella in these savory stuffed pasta shells covered with tangy marinara sauce.

Yield:	Prep time:	Initial cook time:	Reheat time:	Serving size:
30 stuffed shells	10 minutes	20 minutes	60 minutes	2 stuffed shells

1 TB. salt plus to taste

1 (12-oz.) box jumbo pasta shells

1 TB. olive oil

2 medium yellow onions, finely chopped

2 tsp. minced garlic

1 (10-oz.) box frozen spinach, thawed and squeezed dry

2 cups whole milk or part-skim ricotta cheese

2 large eggs

1 cup grated Parmesan cheese

2 cups grated mozzarella cheese

1 TB. dried parsley

1½ tsp. dried basil

1½ tsp. dried oregano

½ tsp. black pepper

3½ cups Chunky Marinara Sauce (recipe in Chapter 16)

1. Add about 1 tablespoon salt to a large pot of water over high heat. Bring to a boil, add jumbo pasta shells, and cook for about 5 or 6 minutes or until just barely *al dente*. Drain.

2. In a medium skillet over medium heat, heat olive oil. Add onions, and cook, stirring occasionally, for about 5 minutes or until starting to brown. Add garlic and spinach, and cook, stirring frequently, for 5 minutes. Remove from heat, drain excess water, and cool.

3. In a large bowl, combine ricotta cheese, eggs, Parmesan cheese, mozzarella cheese, dried parsley, dried basil, dried oregano, and salt and pepper to taste, using a wooden spoon to stir well. Stir in cooled spinach mixture.

4. Spray baking dishes to hold the desired number of shells to meet your portion needs with cooking spray. Fill each pasta shell with about ¼ cup filling mixture. Place shells, barely touching and not overcrowded, in the baking dishes. Spoon about 2 tablespoons cooled Chunky Marinara Sauce on each shell. Cover baking dishes tightly with foil, label, and freeze.

To bake after freezing:

1. Bake frozen in a 375°F oven for about 1 hour or until heated through.

COOL TIP

When testing this recipe the first time, I happened upon a happy accident when I grabbed a bag of shredded white cheddar cheese instead of the similar-in-appearance mozzarella I thought I was adding to the dish. The result was a stuffed shell filling with a stronger, more robust flavor. Not traditional, but an improvement in the opinion of all my recipe tasters.

Curried Veggies with Lentils

A hearty vegetable medley and good-for-you lentils swim in a spicy curry sauce in this satisfying Indian-inspired vegan entrée. Serve over rice.

Yield:	Prep time:	Initial cook time:	Reheat time:	Serving size:
7 cups	20 minutes	25 minutes	15 minutes	1 cup

½ tsp. ground cumin

½ tsp. ground turmeric

1 tsp. ground dried ginger

½ tsp. ground cinnamon

1 tsp. curry powder

2 TB. vegetable or canola oil

1 medium yellow onion, diced into ¼-in. pieces

1 medium potato, peeled and diced into ¼-in. pieces

1 medium carrot, peeled and sliced into ⅜-in. rounds

1 medium parsnip, peeled and sliced into ⅜-in. chunks

1 small eggplant, ends trimmed, cut into ¾-in. chunks

1½ cups chopped cauliflower florets

½ cup red lentils or split yellow peas

3½ cups boiling Vegetable Stock (recipe in Chapter 10) or water

¼ cup tomato paste

7 cups cooked white or brown rice

1. In a small bowl, mix together ground cumin, ground turmeric, ground ginger, ground cinnamon, and curry powder.

2. In a large skillet over medium heat, heat vegetable oil. Add spices, and stir for about 10 seconds. Add onion, and cook, stirring constantly, for about 3 or 4 minutes or until just softened. Add potato, carrot, parsnip, eggplant, and cauliflower, and stir to combine.

3. Stir in red lentils and boiling Vegetable Stock. Stir in tomato paste until dissolved and all ingredients are well combined. Increase heat to high and bring to a boil.

4. Reduce heat to medium-low, cover, and simmer for 10 minutes. Remove from heat, and cool completely. Package in zipper-lock plastic freezer bags or rigid freezer containers, and freeze. Alternatively, for a complete frozen meal, top cooled cooked rice with cooled Curried Veggies with Lentils in a rigid freezer container, label, and freeze.

To reheat after freezing:

1. Thaw in the refrigerator if desired. Heat thawed or frozen (with or without rice) in a large saucepan on the stovetop over medium heat, stirring frequently, until bubbling and heated through. Alternatively, microwave thawed or frozen (with or without rice), stopping to stir every minute or so, until heated through. Serve over rice.

COLD FACT

Anytime you see the word *dal* on an Indian menu, legumes are involved. Most often it's lentils, but *dal* can also refer to dried peas (which you can substitute in this recipe) or beans.

Charro Beans

Smokey bacon and spicy jalapeño chiles flavor these cowboy beans.

Yield:	Prep time:	Initial cook time:	Reheat time:	Serving size:
8 cups	10 minutes	2 hours, 15 minutes	15 minutes	1 cup

1 lb. dried pinto beans, rinsed and *picked over*

½ lb. bacon, diced

1 large yellow onion, diced

1 TB. minced garlic

2 jalapeño peppers, ribs and seeds removed, and minced

1 (12-oz.) can or bottle beer

1 (15-oz.) can crushed tomatoes, with juice

1 cup tomato juice

2 cups Poultry Stock or Meat Stock (recipes in Chapter 10)

Salt

Black pepper

1. Place pinto beans in a large stockpot over high heat, and cover with cold water. Bring to a boil, and boil for 1 minute. Remove from heat, cover, and let sit for at least 1 hour. Drain.

2. In a large stockpot over medium-high heat, add bacon. Cook, stirring occasionally, for about 4 minutes or until beginning to brown. Add onion and cook, stirring frequently with a wooden spoon, for about 5 minutes or until lightly browned.

3. Add garlic and jalapeños, stir to combine, and cook, stirring constantly, for 1 more minute. Add beer and deglaze pot, scraping up any brown bits on the bottom of the pan. Bring to a simmer, stir in tomatoes with juice, tomato juice, Poultry Stock, and pinto beans.

4. Return to a boil, reduce heat to low, cover, and simmer for about 2 hours or until beans are almost tender. Much of sauce will have been absorbed, but you should still have an inch or so of liquid. Season with salt and pepper. Cool completely, package in zipper-lock plastic freezer bags or rigid freezer containers, label, and freeze.

To reheat after freezing:

1. Thaw in the refrigerator if desired. Heat frozen or thawed in saucepan over medium heat and cook, stirring frequently to prevent scorching on the bottom, until heated through. Alternatively, microwave on high, stirring every minute or two, until heated through.

TABLE TALK

You'll notice that dried bean recipes always advise you to wash and **pick over** the beans. This means to spread them out and look through them to remove any dried, withered beans or small stones that might have accidentally gotten into the mix.

Boston Baked Beans

Sweet, smoky, and slightly spiced, these baked beans never fail to please.

Yield:	Prep time:	Initial cook time:	Reheat time:	Serving size:
6 cups	1 hour	4 hours, 20 minutes	14 minutes	½ cup

2 cups dried navy or white beans, rinsed and picked over

½ lb. bacon, diced

1 large yellow onion, diced

1 TB. prepared mustard

¼ cup molasses

¼ cup maple syrup

¼ cup brown sugar, firmly packed

2 bay leaves

⅛ cup cider vinegar

1 tsp. salt

1 tsp. black pepper

9 cups boiling water

1. Place navy beans in a large stockpot over high heat, and cover with cold water. Bring to a boil, and boil for 1 minute. Remove from heat, cover, and let sit for 1 hour. Drain.

2. Preheat the oven to 350°F.

3. In a stockpot over medium heat, add bacon. Cook, stirring occasionally, for about 10 minutes or until crisp. Add onion and cook, stirring, for about 10 minutes or until onion begins to brown. Add navy beans, prepared mustard, molasses, maple syrup, brown sugar, bay leaves, cider vinegar, salt, pepper, and boiling water. Bring to a boil.

4. Cover and transfer pot to the oven, and bake, stirring occasionally, for about 4 hours or until liquid thickens and beans are tender. Remove bay leaves. Cool completely, package in zipper-lock plastic freezer bags or rigid freezer containers, label, and freeze.

To reheat after freezing:

1. Heat frozen or thawed in a saucepan over medium heat, and cook, stirring frequently to prevent scorching on the bottom, until heated through. Alternatively, microwave frozen or thawed on high, stirring every minute or two, until heated through.

Green Bean Casserole

Crunchy green beans and hearty mushrooms blend in a creamy sauce and are topped with caramelized onions in this classic American side dish casserole.

Yield:	Prep time:	Initial cook time:	Reheat time:	Serving size:
4 cups	10 minutes	30 minutes	1 hour	½ cup

1 lb. fresh green beans, ends trimmed and cut in ½

1 TB. olive oil

2 medium yellow onions, cut into very thin slices

½ cup panko breadcrumbs

2 TB. unsalted butter

1 oz. sliced white or cremini mushrooms

½ tsp. minced garlic

½ tsp. black pepper

¼ tsp. ground nutmeg

3 TB. all-purpose flour

1 cup Poultry Stock (recipe in Chapter 10)

1 cup half-and-half

1. Bring a large pot of water to a boil over high heat. Add green beans, and blanch for 2 minutes. Drain. Rinse with cold water to stop cooking process, and drain again.

2. In a large, preferably cast-iron, skillet over medium heat, heat olive oil. Add onions, and cook, stirring and turning occasionally with a spatula, for about 20 minutes or until deep brown and caramelized. Remove caramelized onions to a medium bowl, add panko breadcrumbs, and toss to coat. Set aside.

3. In the same skillet over medium heat, heat unsalted butter. Add mushrooms, and cook, stirring occasionally, for about 4 minutes or until mushrooms have released their water. Add minced garlic, pepper, and ground nutmeg, and cook, stirring, for 1 more minute.

4. Sprinkle in all-purpose flour, and cook, stirring, for 2 more minutes. Stir in Poultry Stock slowly while whisking, and bring to a simmer. Stir in half-and-half, and cook, stirring often, for about 6 minutes or until mixture thickens.

5. Meanwhile, spray a 1½-quart baking dish with cooking spray.

6. Remove the skillet from heat, and stir in ¼ of onion-panko mixture along with blanched green beans. Fill the prepared dish ¾ full with bean mixture. Spread remaining onion-panko mixture over the top of the pan. Cool completely, cover with foil, label, and freeze.

To bake after freezing:

1. Bake frozen uncovered in a 375°F oven for about 1 hour or until bubbly and top is browned.

COLD FACT

Green beans are also known as "string beans" because of the fibrous string that runs along their seam. You can pull the string out when snapping off the ends (although many of today's varieties no longer have this problem). The snapping sound and motion is the reason why fresh green beans are also sometimes labeled "snap beans."

Corn Pudding

Sweet corn and sweet red bell peppers pair well in this indulgent cheesy, eggy side dish.

Yield:	Prep time:	Initial cook time:	Reheat time:	Serving size:
6 cups	10 minutes	8 minutes	1½ hours	½ cup

2 TB. butter or margarine	4 cups fresh, frozen, or canned corn kernels
1 large yellow onion, diced	
1 large red bell pepper, ribs and seeds removed, and diced	8 large eggs
	2 cups shredded cheddar or Monterrey Jack cheese
½ tsp. minced garlic	

1. Butter 2 (1½-quart) baking dishes.

2. In a large skillet over medium heat, heat butter. Add diced onion and red bell pepper, and sauté for about 5 minutes or until softened but not yet beginning to brown. Add garlic and corn kernels, and sauté for another 3 minutes. Remove from heat and allow to cool.

3. In a large bowl, whisk eggs until frothy and well combined. Add cheddar cheese, and stir well with a wooden spoon.

4. Stir in cooled corn mixture and divide between the prepared baking dishes. Cool completely, cover with foil, label, and freeze.

To bake after freezing:

1. Bake frozen in a 375°F oven for about 1½ hours or until pudding is set and puffed and top is nicely browned.

Variation: You can bake this before freezing. Bake in a 375°F oven for about 30 minutes for 1½-quart dish or about 20 minutes for individual ramekins. Cool completely, cover with foil, and freeze. Reheat in the microwave.

COOL TIP

Instead of one big dish, try baking Corn Pudding in small ramekins or individual portions for each person at the table. You'll cut baking time down to about 35 to 40 minutes when starting from an unbaked, frozen state.

Southern Succotash

This vegetable medley marries sweet corn and red bell peppers with crunchy zucchini and lima beans. Tarragon adds a touch of sophisticated flavor.

Yield:	Prep time:	Initial cook time:	Reheat time:	Serving size:
4 cups	10 minutes	8 minutes	5 minutes	½ cup

1 TB. olive oil

2 cups fresh or frozen corn kernels

1 large zucchini, ends trimmed and diced small

1 large red bell pepper, ribs and seeds removed, and finely diced

½ cup finely diced whole green onions

1 cup fresh or frozen lima beans, shelled if fresh

½ cup Vegetable Stock (recipe in Chapter 10) or water

1 TB. minced fresh Italian parsley or 1 tsp. dried

¼ tsp. dried tarragon

Salt

Black pepper

1. In a large skillet over medium heat, heat olive oil. Add corn, zucchini, red bell pepper, green onions, and lima beans, and cook, stirring often, for 5 minutes. Add Vegetable Stock, cover, and cook for another 3 minutes or until vegetables are tender.

2. Remove from heat and stir in Italian parsley, dried tarragon, salt, and pepper. Cool completely, package in zipper-lock plastic freezer bags or rigid freezer containers, label, and freeze.

To reheat after freezing:

1. Thaw if desired. Microwave (thawed or frozen) on high until heated through. Alternatively, heat (thawed or frozen) in a saucepan over medium heat. Add a few tablespoons water, and cook, stirring frequently, until heated through.

COLD FACT

Lima beans, named after Lima, Peru, where they originated, are also known as butter beans—thanks to their smooth, buttery flavor—or fordhook beans. Also commonly available are baby lima beans, which tend to be more tender and can be used interchangeably in most recipes.

Cauliflower Gratin

Similar to mac and cheese, but without the mac, this rich and creamy side dish is perfect for special occasion dinners.

Yield:	Prep time:	Initial cook time:	Reheat time:	Serving size:
6 cups	10 minutes	10 minutes	1 hour	½ cup

1 small head cauliflower, cut into small florets	1¼ cups whole milk or half-and-half
4 whole green onions, finely chopped	1¼ cups grated cheddar cheese
3 TB. unsalted butter or margarine	Salt
3 TB. all-purpose flour	Black pepper
	½ cup panko breadcrumbs

1. Bring a large pot of water to a boil over high heat. Add cauliflower florets and green onions and blanch for 3 minutes. Drain, rinse in cold water to stop the cooking process, and drain again.

2. In a medium saucepan over medium-high heat, melt unsalted butter. Whisk in all-purpose flour to make a roux, and cook, whisking constantly, for about 2 minutes or until mixture turns light tan in color.

3. Whisk in whole milk slowly until smooth. Continue to cook, stirring frequently, for about 7 minutes or until mixture has thickened and begins to boil. Remove from heat.

4. Stir in cheddar cheese until cheese has melted and mixture is smooth. Add blanched cauliflower and green onions, and stir to coat. Season with salt and pepper.

5. Spray baking pans that meet your portion size needs with cooking spray.

6. Fill the prepared pans ¾ full with cauliflower mixture, and sprinkle panko breadcrumbs over top. Cool completely, cover with foil, label, and freeze.

To bake after freezing:

1. Bake frozen in a 375°F oven for about 1 hour or until bubbly and top has browned.

COLD FACT

If you ever thought that cauliflower physically resembled cheese, you're not alone. The white, edible portion of cauliflower is called the curd.

Maple-Glazed Carrots

The glaze on these carrots is subtle, with delicate undertones of maple and just a hint of heat from the cayenne.

Yield:	Prep time:	Initial cook time:	Reheat time:	Serving size:
6 cups	10 minutes	15 minutes	10 minutes	½ cup

⅓ cup maple syrup

⅓ cup water

1 TB. unsalted butter

⅛ to ¼ tsp. cayenne

¼ tsp. salt

Black pepper

10 medium carrots, peeled and sliced on the diagonal into ½-in. pieces

1. In a large saucepan over medium-high heat, combine maple syrup, water, unsalted butter, cayenne, salt, and pepper. Bring to a boil, stirring frequently.

2. Add carrots, and stir to coat. Lower heat to a high simmer, partially cover, and cook, stirring occasionally, for about 13 to 15 minutes or until carrots are *crisp-tender* and sauce has reduced to glaze. Remove from heat. Cool completely, package carrots and glaze in zipper-lock plastic freezer bags or rigid containers, label, and freeze.

To reheat after freezing:

1. Thaw in the refrigerator, if desired. Microwave (frozen or thawed), covered with a damp paper towel, until heated through. Alternatively, heat (thawed or frozen) in a saucepan over medium heat. Stir frequently to prevent scorching, and add a small amount of water if carrots seem dry.

TABLE TALK

Similar to *al dente*, vegetables cooked until they are **crisp-tender** are just beginning to cook and still retain some of their crunch in the center.

Roasted Root Vegetables

Healthful root vegetables are roasted in an apple juice reduction that infuses them with a sweet yet sophisticated flavor.

Yield:	Prep time:	Initial cook time:	Reheat time:	Serving size:
5 cups	15 minutes	20 minutes	50 minutes	½ cup

3 cups apple juice

1 TB. lemon juice

3 TB. unsalted butter

1 tsp. dried crumbled rosemary

Salt

Black pepper

3 medium carrots, peeled and sliced into ⅜-in. pieces

1 large *parsnip*, peeled and sliced into ⅜-in. pieces

1 small sweet potato or yam, peeled, quartered, and sliced into ⅜-in. slices

1 small white *turnip*, peeled and diced into ½-in. chunks

1. In a small saucepan over high heat, combine apple juice and lemon juice. Bring to a boil, reduce heat to medium, and boil for about 12 to 15 more minutes or until mixture is reduced to about ¼ cup.

2. Whisk in unsalted butter and dried rosemary, and season with salt and pepper.

3. Bring a large pot of water to a boil over high heat. Add carrots, parsnip, sweet potato, and turnip, and blanch for 4 minutes. Drain. Rinse with cold water to stop cooking process, and drain again.

4. Add blanched veggies to reduced sauce, and toss to coat. Cool completely, package veggies and sauce in baking pans sprayed with cooking spray and filled ¼ full, cover with foil, label, and freeze.

To roast after freezing:

1. Roast, uncovered and frozen in a 375°F oven for about 50 minutes or until vegetables are tender. Remove vegetables from sauce with a slotted spoon, and serve.

TABLE TALK

Similar in appearance to a white carrot, **parsnips** are a cream-colored root vegetable with a pleasantly sweet flavor. Look for firm parsnips without signs of shriveling. **Turnips,** shaped somewhat like a top, have tinges of deep purple on their white skin. Look for turnips that are heavy for their size. These are younger and will have a subtle sweet flavor and delicate texture. Older turnips can turn coarse and woody. Peel both parsnips and turnips with a vegetable peeler before use.

Candied Sweet Potatoes with Crumb Topping

Sweet potatoes become even sweeter with the addition of brown sugar, maple syrup, and toasted pecans. The dish gets topped with a crunchy brown sugar crumb topping.

Yield:	Prep time:	Initial cook time:	Reheat time:	Serving size:
8 cups	15 minutes	5 minutes	45 minutes	½ cup

1½ cups brown sugar, firmly packed

½ cup all-purpose flour

3 TB. plus ½ cup unsalted butter

4 lb. sweet potatoes or yams, peeled and cut into ⅜-in. slices

1 TB. grated orange zest

⅓ cup fresh orange juice (juice of 1 orange)

2 tsp. ground cinnamon

1 cup chopped toasted pecans (optional)

1. In a food processor, combine ½ cup brown sugar and flour, and pulse until well mixed. Add 3 tablespoons unsalted butter, cut in small pieces, and pulse until butter is well incorporated into flour and sugar. Set aside.

2. Bring a large pot of water to a boil over high heat. Add sweet potatoes, and blanch for 5 minutes. Drain, rinse in cold water to stop the cooking process, and drain again.

3. In a small saucepan over medium heat, melt remaining ½ cup unsalted butter. Using a wooden spoon, stir in remaining 1 cup brown sugar, orange zest, orange juice, ground cinnamon, and pecans (if using). Cook, stirring, for 1 or 2 minutes or until sugar has dissolved.

4. Coat baking pans that meet your portion needs with cooking spray.

5. Place drained sweet potatoes in a large bowl. Pour brown sugar mixture over sweet potatoes, and toss to coat. Divide potatoes between the prepared baking pans, filling each about ⅔ full. Spread brown sugar–flour mixture on top. Cool completely, cover with foil, label, and freeze.

To bake after freezing:

1. Bake frozen sweet potatoes in a 375°F oven for 45 minutes or until potatoes are cooked through and topping is beginning to brown.

TABLE TALK

The outermost part of a citrus fruit, **zest** adds an intense flavor to recipes. When zesting a fruit, be careful to get only the thin, colorful, outermost layer and none of the bitter white pith underneath. A *citrus zester* makes quick work of this, or you can use a vegetable peeler to zest strips you'll then need to mince. A Microplane creates a fine, recipe-ready zest. An inexpensive rasp that you can pick up at any hardware store works just as well.

French-Style Roast Potatoes

The unique combination of nutmeg and lemon zest gives these potatoes their unique aroma and amazing flavor.

Yield:	Prep time:	Initial cook time:	Reheat time:	Serving size:
8 cups	25 minutes	40 minutes	45 minutes	¾ cup

3 TB. plus 1 tsp. salt	2 TB. chopped fresh Italian parsley
3 lb. yellow or russet potatoes, peeled and sliced into ½-in. rounds	½ tsp. ground nutmeg
	1 tsp. black pepper
1 large yellow onion, diced	1 tsp. lemon zest
3 TB. all-purpose flour	Juice of ½ fresh lemon (optional at serving time)
⅓ cup olive oil	

1. Bring a large pot of water with 3 tablespoons salt to a boil. Add potatoes, and cook for 5 minutes. Add onion during last 2 minutes of cooking. Drain.

2. Butter 3 (7-inch-square) baking dishes, or equivalent size(s) to meet your serving needs.

3. In a large mixing bowl, combine flour, olive oil, Italian parsley, nutmeg, remaining salt, pepper, and lemon zest.

4. Add blanched potatoes and onion, and toss to coat. Divide potatoes among prepared dishes, no more than 4 thin layers of potato rounds deep. Cool completely, cover with foil, label, and freeze.

To bake after freezing:

1. Bake frozen in a 400°F oven for 45 minutes or until potatoes are cooked through and just beginning to brown on top. Place under the broiler for about 5 minutes to finish browning and crisp the top layer. Sprinkle with fresh lemon juice (if desired) just before serving.

COOL TIP

While ground spices will lose their potency over time, you can buy whole nutmeg, which keeps indefinitely, and easily grind your own with a Microplane or fine grater whenever you need some. Just pass the surface of the whole nutmeg over the rasp until you have the right amount.

Real Mashed Potatoes

Creamy potatoes, with just the right amount of lumps to let you know they're real and not instant, are the ultimate comfort food side dish.

Yield:	Prep time:	Initial cook time:	Reheat time:	Serving size:
8 cups	15 minutes	15 minutes	45 minutes	1 cup

5 lb. russet or Yukon Gold potatoes, peeled and cut into 2-in. chunks	1 large egg
5 TB. unsalted butter	Salt
4 oz. cream cheese	Black pepper

1. Bring a large pot of salted water to a boil over high heat. Add russet potatoes, reduce heat to medium, and boil for about 15 minutes or until potatoes are soft. Drain potatoes in a colander.

2. Add potatoes to a large bowl along with unsalted butter, cream cheese, and egg. Using an electric mixer on medium speed, whip until all ingredients are well combined and little or no lumps remain, according to your preference. Do not whip more than necessary, as you run the risk of turning the texture gummy.

3. Season with salt and pepper, and cool completely. Depending on if you plan on baking or microwaving potatoes later, package in baking dishes that have been sprayed with cooking spray, in rigid freezer containers, or in zipper-lock plastic freezer bags; label; and freeze.

To reheat after freezing:

1. Bake thawed in a 375°F oven for 35 to 40 minutes or frozen for 1 to 1½ hours or until heated through and top has browned. Alternatively, microwave thawed or frozen, stopping to stir every minute or two, until heated through.

Variation: The addition of roasted garlic makes wonderful **Roasted Garlic Mashed Potatoes.** To roast garlic, peel away the loose outer white skin from 2 heads of garlic. Place in the center of a small square of aluminum foil, drizzle with a few drops of olive oil, and sprinkle with salt and pepper. Gather up the sides of the foil and twist at the top. Bake packet in a 375°F oven for about 45 minutes or until garlic pulp is tender. Cool until you can handle garlic, and squeeze the pulp from the remaining peels. Add to potatoes with other ingredients and mash. Roasting mellows and sweetens garlic's normally hot and pungent flavor.

COOL TIP

Whenever you're making mashed potatoes, it's a good time to think about making Shepherd's Pie (recipe in Chapter 11), too. The savory one-dish meal is topped with mashed potatoes, so why not make a little extra now for use later?

Breads and Grains

In This Chapter

- Freezing baked goods
- Fresh-from-the-freezer pizzas
- Perfect pastas
- Rice and grain dishes

Breads and grains are the glue that holds many a meal together. When you use your freezer, fresh-baked dinner rolls, pizza doughs, savory dressings, creamy risotto, and other usually time-consuming starch staples are just a few minutes away.

As I discussed in Chapter 1, most yeasted baked goods freeze well, whether in their raw or baked form. Surprisingly, you can also freeze quick-bread batters, like this chapter's Popovers, to thaw and bake fresh later.

Cooked rice and grains do well from the freezer. Undercook them slightly before freezing, and package them with as little air surrounding the food as possible to prevent freezer burn.

Likewise, when cooking pasta, cook for less time than you would normally to help preserve the texture. You want it just flexible enough to have some give but still have a firm core.

Popovers

Light, eggy, and puffed oh-so-high, these popovers will delight both the young and the old.

Yield:	Prep time:	Reheat time:	Serving size:
12 popovers	5 minutes	20 minutes	1 popover

2 large eggs	1 cup all-purpose flour
1 cup milk	¼ tsp. salt
1 TB. melted vegetable shortening	

1. In a medium bowl, whisk eggs until frothy. Whisk in milk, melted shortening, all-purpose flour, and salt.

2. Package batter in a lidded plastic bottle, zipper-lock plastic freezer bag, or rigid freezer container. Label and freeze.

To bake after freezing:

1. Thaw batter in the refrigerator or using the cold water method (see Chapter 1). Preheat the oven to 425°F. Spray cups in a 12-cup muffin tin or cast-iron muffin pan with cooking spray. Fill each muffin cup ½ full with batter. Bake for about 20 to 25 minutes or until puffed and golden brown.

COOL TIP

Serve these popovers immediately after baking. Set out with butter or one of the compound butter recipes in Chapter 16. Include jam or preserves if you're serving at breakfast.

Dinner Rolls

Everyone loves fresh-baked, soft, yeasty dinner rolls. Now you can serve this restaurant staple anytime.

Yield:	Prep time:	Reheat time:	Serving size:
16 rolls	2 hours	40 minutes	1 roll

¾ cup milk

2 TB. unsalted butter

2¼ tsp. dry yeast (1 packet)

¼ cup sugar

3 cups all-purpose flour

1 tsp. salt

¼ cup nonfat powdered milk

1 large egg

1 TB. olive or vegetable oil

1. In a microwave-safe bowl, microwave milk and butter in a small bowl for about 1 minute or until very hot and butter is melted. Remove from heat and set aside until warm to the touch, about 120°F.

2. In a food processor fitted with the dough blade (or the regular blade if you don't have one), combine milk mixture, dry yeast, and sugar, and pulse to mix. Let rest for 5 minutes or until small bubbles start to form in liquid.

3. In a small bowl, combine all-purpose flour, salt, and powdered milk. Add to the food processor along with egg, and process for about 1 minute or until a ball of dough forms. Process 2 more minutes to knead dough, stopping occasionally to push down dough as needed. Alternatively, use an electric stand mixer fitted with the dough hook.

4. Pour olive oil into the bottom of a large bowl, and put a little on your hands. Remove dough from the food processor, and form it into a ball. Place dough in the bowl, and turn once to coat lightly with oil. Cover with a clean kitchen towel, and place in a warm, draft-free place. Let rise for about 1 hour or until doubled in size.

5. Punch down dough, and knead it a few times on a lightly floured surface. Reshape dough into a ball, return it to the bowl, turn dough to coat in oil again, and cover with the kitchen towel. Let rise for about 45 more minutes or until doubled in size.

6. Spray baking dishes to hold the number of rolls you will want to freeze together with cooking spray.

7. Punch down dough, and divide into 16 equal pieces. Using your hands, roll each piece into a round ball. Place rolls in the prepared baking dish. Cover with foil, label, and freeze.

To bake after freezing:

1. Bake frozen in a 375°F oven for 10 minutes. Brush tops of rolls with melted butter, and bake for about 30 more minutes or until cooked through and lightly browned on top. Serve with butter or, better yet, one of the compound butters in Chapter 16.

FREEZER BURN

Watch the milk and butter carefully as you cook it. All microwaves are different, and the mixture could easily boil over if it's left to cook too long.

Pizzeria-Style Pizza Dough

This recipe makes a perfect pizza crust with a chewy and crunchy texture—just like you'd get at a pizzeria. Nobody will guess the dough only takes 5 minutes in a food processor to make!

Yield:	Prep time:	Initial cook time:	Reheat time:	Serving size:
3 (12-inch) pizzas	1 hour	5 minutes	18 minutes	½ pizza

1½ cups very warm water (120°F)

2 tsp. yeast

2 tsp. sugar

2¾ cups bread flour

½ cup *semolina* flour

1¼ tsp. salt

1 TB. olive oil

1 cup Chunky Marinara Sauce (recipe in Chapter 16), or your favorite pizza sauce

3 cups shredded mozzarella cheese

Your favorite pizza toppings: pepperoni, cooked crumbled sausage, sliced onions, bell peppers, mushrooms, etc. (optional)

1. In a food processor, combine warm water, yeast, and sugar, and pulse once or twice to mix. Let rest for 2 or 3 minutes or until small bubbles start to form in liquid.

2. Add bread flour, semolina flour, and salt, and turn on the food processor. After about 1 minute, dough should form into a ball going around in your food processor. If dough is too wet, add a bit of bread flour, but know that too wet is better than too dry and the dough will lose some of its stickiness as it rises. Let the processor run for about 2 minutes. Alternatively, use an electric stand mixer fitted with the dough hook.

3. Pour olive oil into the bottom of a large bowl, and put a little on your hands. Remove dough from the food processor, and form it into a ball. Place dough in the bowl, and turn once to coat lightly with oil. Cover with a clean kitchen towel, and place in a warm, draft-free place. Let rise for about 1 hour or until doubled in size.

4. At this point, you either can freeze dough or roll it out to make pizza crusts and freeze those. If you opt to freeze dough now, when you're ready to make pizza, let dough ball thaw in the refrigerator and bring to room temperature before continuing with these instructions.

5. To make crusts, preheat the oven to 475°F. Place a baking stone in the oven. If you don't have a baking stone, oil a pizza pan.

6. Divide dough ball into 3 pieces. On a lightly floured surface and using your hands and a rolling pin, roll out each piece into a 12-inch circle. Lightly sprinkle baking stone and pizza peel (if using a stone) with cornmeal. Place dough on peel and slide onto stone—the cornmeal act like little ball bearings. Bake for 5 minutes.

7. Remove crust from oven, push down any bubbles that formed during baking, and let cool.

8. In a blender or food processor, purée Chunky Marinara Sauce. Spread each crust with about ⅓ cup puréed sauce. Sprinkle 1 cup shredded mozzarella over top, and add your favorite pizza toppings. (Don't forget to blanch fresh vegetables first!) Wrap in foil, label, and freeze.

To bake after freezing:

1. Bake unwrapped frozen on a baking stone or an oiled pizza pan in a 450°F oven for about 18 minutes or until cheese is melted and bubbly, crust is beginning to brown, and pizza is heated through.

Variation: To make a **California-Style Thai Chicken Pizza,** substitute Thai-Style Peanut Sauce (recipe in Chapter 16) for the Chunky Marinara Sauce. Top each pizza with cheese and sprinkle with ⅓ cup diced cooked chicken, ¼ cup blanched shredded carrots, ¼ cup finely chopped blanched green onions, ¼ cup blanched bean sprouts, and 3 tablespoons minced fresh cilantro.

TABLE TALK

Semolina is a coarse low-starch durum wheat flour that's an essential component of good pasta and is what gives this recipe its unique texture. Look for it in the flour aisle of well-stocked supermarkets, health food stores, and Italian markets. If you can't find it, substitute bread flour.

Whole-Wheat Pizza Dough

This partly whole-grain recipe makes a thicker crust pizza with a distinctive nutty flavor.

Yield:	Prep time:	Initial cook time:	Reheat time:	Serving size:
3 (12-inch) pizzas	1 hour	5 minutes	18 minutes	½ of 1 pizza

1¼ cups very warm water (120°F)	1 cup whole-wheat flour
1 TB. yeast	2 cups bread flour
2 TB. honey	1 tsp. salt
¼ cup plus 1 TB. olive oil	

1. In a food processor, combine warm water, yeast, honey, and ¼ cup olive oil, and pulse once or twice to mix. Let rest for 2 or 3 minutes or until small bubbles start to form in liquid.

2. Add whole-wheat flour, bread flour, and salt, and turn on the food processor. After about 1 minute, dough should form into a ball going around in your food processor. If dough is too wet, add a bit of flour, but know that too wet is better than too dry and the dough will lose some of its stickiness as it rises. Let the food processor run for about 2 minutes. Alternatively, use an electric stand mixer fitted with the dough hook.

3. Pour remaining 1 tablespoon olive oil into the bottom of a large bowl, and put a little on your hands. Remove dough from the food processor, and form it into a ball. Place dough in the bowl, and turn once to coat lightly with oil. Cover with a clean kitchen towel, and place in a warm, draft-free place. Let rise for about 1 hour or until doubled in size.

4. At this point, you either can freeze dough or roll it out to make pizza crusts and freeze those. If you opt to freeze dough now, when you're ready to make pizza, let dough ball thaw in the refrigerator and bring to room temperature before continuing with these instructions.

5. To make crusts, preheat the oven to 475°F. Place a baking stone in the oven. If you don't have a baking stone, oil a pizza pan.

6. Divide dough ball into 3 pieces. On a lightly floured surface and using your hands and a rolling pin, roll out each piece into a 12-inch circle. Place on the baking stone, and bake for 5 minutes.

7. Remove crust from oven, push down any bubbles that formed during baking, and let cool.

8. In a blender or food processor, purée Chunky Marinara Sauce. Spread each crust with about ⅓ cup puréed sauce. Sprinkle 1 cup shredded mozzarella over top, and add your favorite pizza toppings. (Don't forget to blanch fresh vegetables first!) Wrap in foil, label, and freeze.

To bake after freezing:

1. Bake unwrapped frozen on a baking stone or an oiled pizza pan in a 450°F oven for about 18 minutes or until cheese is melted and bubbly, crust is beginning to brown, and pizza is heated through.

COOL TIP

While most recipes will tell you to only heat the liquid for yeast doughs to lukewarm, I find it better to heat until very warm to the touch, as it will cool by the time it hits the surface of your bowl or food processor's surface. Those small bubbles you see forming in the liquid-yeast mixture mean the yeast is working or feeding on carbohydrates and creating carbon dioxide as a by-product.

Herbed Sausage Dressing

Sausage and sweet apples pair beautifully in a dressing equally at home as a side dish for poultry or pork.

Yield:	Prep time:	Reheat time:	Serving size:
6 cups	15 minutes	1 hour	¾ cup

6 cups dried bread cubes

1 lb. lite bulk sausage

1 tsp. minced garlic

1 large celery stalk, finely diced

1 large yellow onion, diced

1 large Granny Smith apple,
  peeled, cored, and diced

⅛ cup minced fresh Italian parsley,
  or 1 TB. dried

2 large eggs

¼ cup melted butter

1½ cups Poultry Stock (recipe in
  Chapter 10)

1 tsp. dried thyme

Salt

Black pepper

1. In a large bowl, combine dried bread cubes, sausage, garlic, celery, onion, Granny Smith apple, Italian parsley, eggs, melted butter, Poultry Stock, thyme, salt, and pepper. Using your hands, mix well.

2. Spray baking pans that meet your portion needs with cooking spray.

3. Divide dressing among prepared baking dishes, filling each about ¾ full. Cover with foil, label, and freeze.

To bake after freezing:

1. Bake frozen in a 375°F oven for about 1 hour or until heated through.

COOL TIP

If you're in a hurry, you can buy boxes of dried bread cubes at the supermarket. Look for stuffing or dressing mix. It's also easy to make your own. Slice day-old or stale bread (any kind that isn't sweet) into small cubes, place on a dry baking sheet, and bake in a 350°F oven for about 10 to 12 minutes or until dried. A regular slice of white or wheat bread yields about ½ cup cubes.

Baked Macaroni and Cheese

This creamy, cheesy, satisfying comfort food topped with crunchy breadcrumbs goes from freezer to oven for a quick dinner.

Yield:	Prep time:	Initial cook time:	Reheat time:	Serving size:
9 cups	20 minutes	20 minutes	1 hour	1 cup

3 TB. salt

16 oz. uncooked elbow macaroni

6 TB. unsalted butter

4 TB. all-purpose flour

1 TB. dry mustard powder

4 cups whole or reduced-fat milk

1 medium yellow onion, minced

1 bay leaf

½ tsp. paprika

4 oz. cream cheese

5 cups shredded extra-sharp cheddar cheese

Salt

Black pepper

1 cup panko breadcrumbs

1. Add salt to a large stockpot of water, and bring to a boil over high heat. Add macaroni, and cook for about 4 minutes or until flexible but still very *al dente*. Drain.

2. In a large saucepan over medium heat, melt 4 tablespoons butter. Whisk in all-purpose flour and mustard powder, and cook, whisking constantly, for 2 minutes. Gradually whisk in milk.

3. Stir in onion, bay leaf, and paprika. Increase heat to medium-high and bring to a boil. Reduce heat to low, and simmer for 15 minutes. Remove from heat, and remove bay leaf.

4. Stir in cream cheese and ½ of shredded cheddar cheese, and stir until cheese is melted. Season with salt and pepper, and stir in cooked macaroni.

5. Spray baking dishes that meet your portion needs with cooking spray. Divide ½ of macaroni mixture between prepared baking dishes. Sprinkle with ½ of remaining cheddar cheese. Top with remaining pasta followed by a sprinkling of remaining cheese. Each dish should be about ¾ full.

6. In a small skillet over medium heat, melt remaining 2 tablespoons butter. Add panko breadcrumbs, and stir to coat. Sprinkle buttered breadcrumbs over tops of the baking dishes. Cool completely, cover tightly with foil, label, and freeze.

To reheat after freezing:

1. Bake frozen in a 375°F oven for about 1 hour or until filling is bubbly, top is lightly browned, and dish is heated through.

COLD FACT

Ever wonder why Yankee Doodle called the feather in his cap "Macaroni"? Because back in the eighteenth century, when British soldiers wrote the song to ridicule the "county bumpkin" colonials, the word *macaroni* was slang for excellence; perfection; or, in the case of the Yankee's hat, the pinnacle of style.

Mushroom Risotto

Creamy rice flavored with earthy mushrooms and sharp Parmesan cheese makes an impressive side dish or even light entrée.

Yield:	Prep time:	Initial cook time:	Reheat time:	Serving size:
7 cups	15 minutes	25 minutes	5 minutes	½ cup

5 cups chicken stock

1 TB. olive oil

2 medium stalks celery, minced

2 medium yellow onions, minced

8 oz. sliced white or cremini mushrooms

1 tsp. minced garlic

2 cups *arborio rice*

½ cup dry vermouth or dry white wine

¾ tsp. dried thyme

⅛ cup minced fresh Italian parsley or 1 TB. dried

Salt

Black pepper

3 TB. unsalted butter

1½ cups grated Parmesan cheese

1. In a medium pot over high, bring chicken stock to a simmer. Reduce heat to low and keep warm.

2. In a large skillet over medium-high heat, heat olive oil. Add celery, onions, and mushrooms, and sauté for about 4 minutes or until softened. Add garlic, and sauté for 1 more minute.

3. Increase heat to high, and add arborio rice. Cook, stirring constantly, for about 4 minutes or until rice begins to look translucent. Add dry vermouth, and keep stirring.

4. When vermouth has cooked away, stir in about 1½ cups hot chicken stock along with thyme, Italian parsley, salt, and pepper. Reduce heat to medium-low, and cook, stirring frequently, until almost all chicken stock has been absorbed. Repeat with another ladle of chicken stock, and continue cooking, stirring and adding stock, until it's all been added to rice and has been mostly absorbed. Rice should be very moist but not swimming in stock at this point.

5. Season with salt and pepper, remove from heat, and stir in butter and Parmesan until everything is well combined. Cool completely, package in rigid freezer containers or zipper-lock plastic freezer bags, label, and freeze.

To reheat after freezing:

1. Microwave frozen on high, stopping to stir every minute or so, until heated through.

TABLE TALK

Arborio rice is a short-grain Italian rice. Its high starch content helps create risotto's distinctive creamy texture. Find arborio rice in the Italian section of the supermarket.

Vegetable Fried Rice

Studded with colorful veggies and eggs, this flavorful rice is anything but ordinary.

Yield:	Prep time:	Initial cook time:	Reheat time:	Serving size:
8 cups	20 minutes	10 minutes	5 minutes	1 cup

2 tsp. vegetable or canola oil

4 whole green onions, finely chopped

1½ tsp. fresh grated ginger

½ tsp. minced garlic

1 medium carrot, peeled and diced

½ cup fresh or frozen green peas

6 cups steamed short-grain rice, preferably cold

2 large eggs, beaten

¼ cup soy sauce or reduced-sodium soy sauce

1 tsp. sesame oil

1. In a wok or large skillet over high heat, heat vegetable oil. Add green onions, ginger, and garlic, and stir-fry for about 10 seconds. Add carrots and green peas, and stir-fry for another 20 seconds. Add steamed rice, and stir-fry for about 5 more minutes or until rice is heated.

2. Make a well in middle of rice. Add beaten eggs, and let sit for about 30 seconds or until eggs are just beginning to set. Stir to scramble, breaking eggs into chunks as you go, until eggs and rice are well combined.

3. In a small bowl, whisk together soy sauce and sesame oil. Pour soy sauce mixture over rice, and continue to stir-fry for 2 minutes or until everything is well mixed. Cool completely, package in zipper-lock plastic freezer bags or rigid freezer containers, label, and freeze.

To reheat after freezing:

1. Microwave frozen on high, stopping to stir every minute or so, until heated through.

2. Alternatively, thaw rice in the refrigerator. Place a small amount of oil in a wok or skillet over high heat, add thawed rice, and stir-fry until heated through.

Variation: Add 1 cup cooked shrimp, scallops, diced chicken, or diced Chinese-Style Pork Tenderloin (recipe in Chapter 11) after adding vegetables.

Grilled Vegetable Couscous

Fire-grilled veggies bring a smoky flavor and delicate crunch to whole-grain couscous in this side dish that can double as a lunchtime salad.

Yield:	Prep time:	Initial cook time:	Reheat time:	Serving size:
6 cups	15 minutes	25 to 30 minutes	5 minutes	1 cup

1 tsp. minced garlic	1 large yellow onion, diced
¼ cup olive oil	8 oz. white or cremini mushrooms
1 large zucchini, ends trimmed and cut into 1-in. rounds	1¾ cups water
	1½ cups couscous
1 large green, red, yellow, or orange bell pepper, ribs and seeds removed, and cut into 2-in. chunks	Salt
	Black pepper

1. Preheat the grill to medium-hot.

2. In a small bowl, combine garlic and olive oil.

3. Thread zucchini, bell pepper, onion, and mushrooms onto wooden skewers. Brush with garlic oil.

4. Grill vegetables, turning to grill on all sides, for about 20 to 25 minutes. Remove skewers from heat, take vegetables off skewers, cool slightly, and chop into ½-inch chunks.

5. In a medium saucepan over high heat, bring water to a boil. Add couscous and chopped grilled vegetables, and stir. Cover, turn off heat, and let sit for 10 minutes. Fluff with a fork to remove any lumps and season with salt and pepper. Cool completely, package in zipper-lock plastic freezer bags or rigid freezer containers, label, and freeze.

To eat after freezing:

1. Microwave frozen on high until heated through.

Variation: For lunchbox-ready **Grilled Vegetable Couscous Salad,** toss in ¼ cup of your favorite vinegar and oil–based Italian dressing with cold, thawed Grilled Vegetable Couscous, and serve cold.

COOL TIP

Threading different vegetables and meats onto a kebab skewer looks pretty, but the food cooks more evenly if you thread all the same type of food cut to a similar size on a single skewer. In recipes like this, where you won't be serving the skewers, it's the only way to go.

Sauces and Accompaniments

In This Chapter

- Great gravy!
- Creative cooking with sauces
- Delicious dipping sauces
- Compound butters and chutneys

Perhaps sauces aren't the first thing you think of when contemplating cooking for the freezer, but perhaps they should be. The splashes of flavor sauces add to dishes can turn a humdrum dish into something special.

When you have a variety of sauce selections in the freezer, you can quickly throw together a tasty meal anytime. A piece of chicken or fish, or a plate of steamed veggies, transforms into something exotic and glamorous with just a touch of pesto or chutney or Thai peanut sauce.

The sauces in this chapter, and the suggestions for using them, are mere jumping-off points. You're sure to come up with new uses as well as new freezer-friendly sauce recipes your family will love. Many of your favorite sauces are already freezer-friendly, so why not stock up?

Especially friendly to the freezing process are any vegetable concoctions, with or without meat. Avoid egg or cream emulsions as these tend to separate and turn watery after freezing. Otherwise, fill your freezer with pasta sauces, dipping sauces, and any other sauces you can think of, and you'll be ready to whip up tasty impromptu recipes at a moment's notice.

Meat or Poultry Gravy

Here's a handy gravy to pull out of the freezer anytime you need gravy but don't have pan drippings. Use over roasted meats or poultry or mashed potatoes.

Yield:	Prep time:	Initial cook time:	Reheat time:	Serving size:
1 cup	3 minutes	10 minutes	5 minutes	¼ cup

2 TB. unsalted butter

2 TB. all-purpose flour

1 cup cold beef or chicken stock

2 tsp. powdered beef or chicken bouillon

¼ tsp. black pepper

1. In a small saucepan over medium heat, melt unsalted butter. Whisk in all-purpose flour until smooth, and cook for about 3 minutes, whisking constantly, or until mixture is a light blonde color.

2. Whisk in cold beef stock and powdered beef bouillon. Cook, stirring constantly, for about 5 minutes or until mixture thickens slightly. Stir in pepper. Cool completely, package in a lidded freezer container or zipper-lock plastic freezer bag, label, and freeze.

To heat after freezing:

1. Thaw in the refrigerator if desired. Heat thawed or frozen gravy in the microwave, stopping to stir every minute or so, until heated through. Timing will depend on portion size.

2. Place thawed or frozen gravy in a saucepan, heat over medium heat, stirring frequently to prevent scorching on the bottom, until heated through.

COOL TIP

When you reheat the gravy, add a little of whatever seasonings you used in the main course for extra flavor.

Chunky Marinara Sauce

This tangy, flavorful tomato sauce is chunky, perfect for dipping foods like bread-sticks or Mozzarella Sticks (recipe in Chapter 8). It also serves as the base for Pizza Bites (recipe in Chapter 8). For a quick spaghetti dinner, serve hot marinara sauce over cooked pasta.

Yield:	Prep time:	Initial cook time:	Reheat time:	Serving size:
8 cups	15 minutes	4 to 8 hours	10 minutes	1/3 cup

4 tsp. olive oil

2 large yellow onions, finely chopped

2 large green bell peppers, ribs and seeds removed, and finely chopped

3 medium celery stalks, finely chopped

1 TB. minced garlic

2 (28-oz.) cans crushed tomatoes, with juice

2 (6-oz.) cans tomato paste

1/8 cup balsamic vinegar

1/8 cup water

2 tsp. sugar

1 TB. Italian seasoning

1 tsp. dried oregano

2 bay leaves

1 tsp. salt, or to taste

3/4 tsp. black pepper, or to taste

1. In a large skillet over medium-high heat, heat 2 teaspoons olive oil. Add onions, and sauté, stirring occasionally, for about 5 minutes or until onions are softened and translucent. Transfer onions to a 3½- to 4-quart slow cooker.

2. In the skillet over medium-high heat, heat remaining 2 teaspoons oil. Add green bell peppers and celery, and sauté, stirring occasionally, for 3 minutes. Stir in garlic, and sauté for 2 more minutes. Add remaining vegetables to slow cooker.

3. Add crushed tomatoes, tomato paste, balsamic vinegar, water, sugar, Italian sea-soning, oregano, bay leaves, salt, and pepper to the slow cooker, and stir well. Cook on low for 6 to 8 hours or on high for 4 or 5 hours. Cool completely, remove bay leaves, and package in lidded freezer containers or small zipper-lock plastic freezer bags, label, and freeze.

To heat after freezing:

1. Microwave frozen or thawed sauce on high, stirring frequently, until heated through. Alternatively, heat sauce in a saucepan over low heat, stirring frequently, until heated through.

Variations: You also can cook on the stovetop by substituting a stockpot for the skillet in step 1. Simmer over low for about 1½ hours, watching carefully and stirring frequently to prevent scorching on the bottom. Or for sophisticated **Vodka Cream Pasta Sauce,** thaw 4 cups Chunky Marinara Sauce, and purée in a blender or food processor until smooth. Heat puréed sauce along with ⅔ cup vodka in a medium saucepan over low heat. Simmer for 20 minutes, stirring frequently. Stir in ½ cup heavy cream, and cook, stirring, just until heated through. Remove from heat and stir in ½ cup grated Parmesan cheese. Season with salt and pepper. Makes 6 cups, or enough to cover about 1 pound cooked pasta such as penne.

COLD FACT

Conventional wisdom holds that raw foods generally have higher nutrient levels than cooked, but tomatoes are the exception. Cooked tomatoes actually display higher levels of lycopene, an important antioxidant, than their fresh counterparts.

Pineapple Sweet-and-Sour Dipping Sauce

Sweet pineapple juice gets a sour tang thanks to rice vinegar in this tantalizing sauce. To turn up the heat, *sriracha* hot sauce will do the trick. Serve with Wonton Shrimp or Shrimp and Pork Pot Stickers (recipes in Chapter 7) or Shrimp Egg Rolls (recipe in Chapter 13).

Yield:	Prep time:	Initial cook time:	Serving size:
2½ cups	3 minutes	4 minutes	2 tablespoons

1 cup unsweetened pineapple juice	½ tsp. sesame oil
½ cup rice vinegar	½ tsp. salt
¼ cup brown sugar, firmly packed	2 tsp. cornstarch
3 TB. ketchup	1 tsp. sriracha hot sauce, or to taste (optional)

1. In a small saucepan, and using a large spoon, stir together pineapple juice, rice vinegar, brown sugar, ketchup, sesame oil, and salt.

2. Whisk in cornstarch, and set over medium heat. Cook, whisking constantly, for about 4 minutes or until just beginning to boil.

3. Remove from heat, and stir in sriracha (if using). Cool completely, package in small containers, label, and freeze.

To use after freezing:

1. Thaw in the refrigerator and use.

TABLE TALK

Sriracha is a Thai hot sauce made from a paste of chiles, garlic, sugar, and salt. It's used to season recipes and can be a dipping sauce in its own right. Huy Fong, with its familiar rooster on the bottle, is the most commonly found brand. Find it in the Asian foods section of most supermarkets.

Pesto

With strong flavors like fresh basil, garlic, olive oil, and Parmesan cheese, a little dab of Pesto can add an intense flavor blast to any dish.

Yield:	Prep time:	Serving size:
1 cup	5 minutes	1 tablespoon

1 cup loosely packed fresh basil

¾ tsp. minced garlic

½ cup freshly grated Parmesan cheese

¼ cup toasted pine nuts or walnuts

½ cup olive oil

Salt

1 tsp. black pepper, or to taste

1. In a food processor or blender, combine basil, garlic, Parmesan cheese, and pine nuts, and process to mix.

2. With the machine running, slowly drizzle in olive oil, and season with salt and pepper. Package in a lidded freezer container, label, and freeze.

To use after freezing:

1. Spoon out the amount of pesto you need and use directly from the freezer. For larger amounts, thaw in the fridge or on the countertop and use.

COOL TIP

Pesto is potent, and a little can go a long way. Freeze pesto in ice cube trays and store pesto cubes in a zipper-lock plastic freezer bag. You'll have just enough to flavor a small piece of chicken or fish, drizzle over 1 or 2 cups steamed veggies, or top a small portion of pasta.

Thai-Style Peanut Sauce

Peanut butter flavors this versatile Thai-style sauce. Use it on grilled vegetables, chicken, or beef; serve over pasta with tofu or veggies; or make a California-Style Thai Chicken Pizza (variation in Chapter 15).

Yield:	Prep time:	Serving size:
1 cup	5 minutes	2 tablespoons

¼ cup chopped yellow or sweet onion

¼ cup chopped celery

¼ cup grated carrot

½ tsp. minced garlic

2 tsp. grated ginger

¼ cup minced fresh cilantro

1 tsp. lime zest

¼ cup freshly squeezed lime juice

½ cup smooth or chunky peanut butter

1. In a food processor or in a blender, combine onion, celery, carrot, garlic, peeled ginger, cilantro, lime zest, lime juice, and peanut butter.

2. Process or blend on high until smooth and ingredients are well combined. Package in a rigid freezer container, label, and freeze.

To use after freezing:

1. Thaw sauce in the refrigerator and use, or add frozen sauce to recipes that will be heated.

COLD FACT

In the last year, more than 75 percent of all American families purchased peanut butter. Americans eat more peanut butter per capita than any other country—about 3 pounds of peanut butter per person per year.

Garlic-Herb Compound Butter

You can use this *compound butter*, vibrant with fresh garlic and herbs, in so many ways, you'll wonder how you ever lived without it! Use it to flavor just about any type of plain baked, grilled, or steamed fish, poultry, or meat. Or add a dab to melt on a baked potato or steamed veggies.

Yield:	Prep time:	Serving size:
1 cup	5 minutes	1 or 2 teaspoons

1 cup unsalted butter, softened	1 tsp. finely chopped fresh rosemary leaves
1 TB. minced fresh chives	½ tsp. minced garlic
1 TB. minced fresh basil	¼ tsp. salt
1 tsp. minced fresh oregano	

1. In a medium bowl, and using an electric mixer on high speed, or in a food processor, whip unsalted butter until light and fluffy.

2. Add minced chives, basil, oregano, rosemary, garlic, and salt, and beat until well combined. Package in ice cube trays and freeze before removing to a zipper-top plastic bag, labeling, and freezing.

To use after freezing:

1. For melted butter, use straight from the freezer and melt as necessary. For spreading butter, allow to come to room temperature.

TABLE TALK

Compound butter, a favorite pantry staple of savvy chefs, is butter creamed with other ingredients. The two recipes in this chapter offer both a sweet and a savory compound butter. Use your imagination and come up with your own blends. Compound butters generally freeze well and can add a lot of instant flavor to your cooking or be used as flavorful toppings for breads, vegetables, and grilled proteins.

Orange-Honey Compound Butter

A splash of this sweet compound butter, accented by zesty orange, can turn ordinary morning toast or biscuits into something extraordinary. Add a dab to grilled chicken or fish and sprinkle with salt and cayenne for a quick yet sophisticated entrée.

Yield:	Prep time:	Serving size:
½ cup	5 minutes	1 to 2 teaspoons

½ cup unsalted butter, softened

1 TB. grated orange zest

3 TB. honey

1. In a medium bowl, and using an electric mixer on high speed, or in a food processor, whip butter until light and fluffy.

2. Add orange zest and honey, and beat until well combined. Package in ice cube trays, and freeze before removing to a zipper-top plastic bag, labeling, and freezing.

To use after freezing:

1. For spreading butter, allow to come to room temperature. For use in cooking, add frozen or melted butter (depending on intended use) to your recipe.

COOL TIP

Honey comes in many different flavors, depending on the type of plants the bees that made it were pollinating. Orange blossom is nice when keeping with the citrus theme. Lavender honey will make a more exotic version. Any kind will work with this recipe, but experiment for different, subtle results and to find your favorites.

Mango Chutney

Sweet gets an unexpected kick of heat in this fruity chutney. It's not for the meek, although you can leave out the serrano chile and crushed red pepper for a less-hot version. Serve with Mini Samosas or Wonton Shrimp (recipes in Chapter 7) or Tandoori-Style Chicken (recipe in Chapter 12).

Yield:	Prep time:	Initial cook time:	Serving size:
5 cups	10 minutes	35 minutes	¼ cup

2 tsp. vegetable or canola oil	1 TB. grated fresh ginger
1 large red onion, finely diced	1 cup cider vinegar
½ large red bell pepper, ribs and seeds removed, and finely diced	½ cup brown sugar, firmly packed
	1 tsp. crushed red pepper
1 serrano chile, or to taste, finely minced	1½ tsp. curry powder
	½ tsp. salt or to taste
4 large mangoes, peeled, pitted, and finely diced	½ tsp. black pepper or to taste

1. In a medium saucepan over medium-high heat, heat oil. Add red onion, red bell pepper, and serrano chile, and cook for 2 or 3 minutes or until soft.

2. Add mangoes, ginger, cider vinegar, brown sugar, crushed red pepper, curry powder, salt, and pepper, and stir well to combine. Bring to a boil, reduce heat to low, and simmer for about 30 minutes, stirring occasionally. Cool completely, package in small lidded containers, label, and freeze.

To use after freezing:

1. Thaw in the refrigerator or bring to room temperature and use.

COOL TIP

Peeling mangoes intimidates some people, but it need not be so. Simply use a vegetable peeler to peel the mango and cut the fruit away from the pit, a flat oval that runs down the center of the fruit. Cut the fruit on all 4 sides, getting as close to the pit as possible.

Sweet Endings

Part 5 explores the sweeter side of freezer cooking. You'll find casual sweet-tooth treats perfect for packing in a lunchbox or for coffee breaks. There are also plenty of recipes for when you want to impress—or desserts elegant enough to serve at holiday meals and for special occasions.

Maybe you don't want to eat dessert every day (or you want to but don't *allow* yourself to). Your freezer can provide the perfect compromise by letting you have sweet indulgences on hand, but not too closely on hand. Package and thaw treats individually, and enjoy a sensible portion of dessert while taking away the ability to immediately overindulge.

Cakes, Cobblers, and Pies

In This Chapter

- Cake: the cure for sweet cravings
- Desserts from elegant to comfort food
- Baked-fresh fruity desserts

"Life is uncertain, eat dessert first."

—Ernestine Ulmer, writer

When your freezer is stocked with sweet treats, there's nothing uncertain about it. You know a fabulous dessert is always close at hand, whenever the mood strikes.

One of the best parts of freezer desserts is that although they're accessible, they're not *too* close. You do have to heat, bake, or at minimum thaw before eating, making it harder to overindulge. Packaging desserts in individual portions also helps keep temptation at bay.

Of course, there are exceptions to the rule. Recipes like the Old-Fashioned Whoopee Pies taste darn good right from the freezer. You've been warned!

Celebration Chocolate Layer Cake

This rich, moist chocolate cake, encased in an even richer fudge frosting, makes the perfect celebration dessert.

Yield:	Prep time:	Initial cook time:	Serving size:
1 (9-inch) frosted double layer cake	70 minutes	30 minutes	1/10 of cake

1 cup cocoa powder

2 cups boiling water

2¾ cups all-purpose flour

½ tsp. baking powder

2 tsp. baking soda

½ tsp. salt

1¾ cups unsalted butter, at room temperature

2½ cups sugar

4 large eggs

1 TB. vanilla extract

4 oz. unsweetened baking chocolate

⅓ cup heavy whipping cream

3 cups confectioners' sugar

1. Preheat the oven to 350°F. Grease 2 (9-inch) cake pans with vegetable shortening, and lightly dust with flour.

2. In a small bowl, and using a wooden spoon, combine cocoa and boiling water until smooth. Set aside to cool.

3. In a medium bowl, stir together flour, baking powder, baking soda, and salt.

4. In a large bowl, and using an electric mixer on high speed, beat 1 cup unsalted butter and sugar for 4 or 5 minutes or until fluffy. Beat in the eggs, 1 at a time, and vanilla extract. Alternately add the flour mixture and cooled cocoa mixture in 3 additions, and continue beating until everything is well combined and no lumps remain.

5. Divide batter between the prepared pans, and bake for about 30 minutes or until a toothpick inserted into center of cake comes out clean. Cool for 5 minutes, invert pans onto a wire rack, and allow cakes to cool completely.

6. Meanwhile, in a double boiler set over low heat, melt remaining ¾ cup butter and unsweetened baking chocolate. Remove from heat as soon as chocolate has melted, and whisk in heavy whipping cream. Allow mixture to cool to the point where it's just starting to thicken.

7. Using an electric mixer on high speed, beat cooled chocolate mixture with confectioners' sugar. Refrigerate for at least 1 hour before frosting cake.

8. To frost cake, place 1 cake on a cake plate. Using an offset or rubber spatula, coat top of cake with a thin coating of frosting. Place second cake on top, and frost top and sides, completely covering cake in icing. Refrigerate for at least 30 minutes, carefully cover with plastic wrap or foil, label, and freeze.

To enjoy after freezing:

1. Allow cake to thaw at room temperature, and enjoy.

FREEZER BURN

This recipe has one potential trouble spot: if you fail to let the butter–unsweetened chocolate mixture part of the frosting cool sufficiently, the butter will separate and you'll be left with a stiff, grainy, lumpy mess. Be sure to cool until it is starting to thicken before continuing.

Diner-Style Coconut Layer Cake

This moist cake, covered in a sweet and tangy cream cheese frosting and topped with sweet nutty coconut, makes an unforgettable meal finale.

Yield:	Prep time:	Initial cook time:	Serving size:
1 (9-inch) frosted double layer cake	30 minutes	30 minutes	¹⁄₁₀ of cake

2¾ cups all-purpose flour

1 tsp. baking powder

½ tsp. baking soda

½ tsp. salt

1¾ cups unsalted butter, at room temperature

1¾ cups sugar

4 large eggs, separated

1 cup *cream of coconut*

1 tsp. vanilla extract

1½ tsp. coconut extract

1 cup buttermilk

1 (8-oz.) pkg. plus 1 (3-oz.) pkg. cream cheese

3 cups sweetened shredded coconut

1. Preheat the oven to 350°F. Grease 2 (9-inch) cake pans with vegetable shortening, and lightly dust with flour.

2. In a small bowl, combine all-purpose flour, baking powder, baking soda, and salt.

3. In a large bowl, and using an electric mixer on high speed, beat together 1 cup unsalted butter and sugar for 4 or 5 minutes or until light and fluffy. Beat in egg yolks one at a time, stopping once or twice to scrape down the sides of the bowl.

4. Beat in cream of coconut, vanilla extract, 1 teaspoon coconut extract, and buttermilk until well combined. Reduce speed to low, and beat until dry ingredients are just blended in.

5. In a clean medium-size glass or stainless-steel bowl, and using an electric mixer with clean beaters on high speed, beat egg whites until stiff but not dry. (Take care that there isn't even a tiny speck of egg yolk or grease in the bowl or on the beaters or egg whites won't whip.)

6. Gently fold egg whites into batter. Continue folding batter over on itself using a rubber spatula until just combined. Divide batter between the prepared cake pans, and bake for about 40 minutes or until golden brown on top and a toothpick inserted into center of cake comes out clean. Cool in pans for 5 minutes before inverting the pans on a wire rack to remove cake. Allow cakes to cool completely.

7. Meanwhile, in a large bowl, and using an electric mixer on high speed, beat cream cheese and remaining ¾ cup unsalted butter until light and fluffy. Beat in remaining ½ teaspoon coconut extract, reduce speed to medium, and slowly beat in confectioners' sugar, stopping occasionally to scrape down the bowl. Chill icing for at least 15 minutes.

8. To frost cake, place 1 cake layer on a cake plate. Using an offset or rubber spatula, coat top of cake with a thin coating of frosting. Lightly sprinkle about ½ cup coconut over cake. Place second cake on top, and frost top and sides, completely covering cake in icing. Cover top and sides of cake with shredded coconut, using your hands to gently press coconut into sides of cake. Refrigerate for at least 30 minutes, carefully cover with plastic wrap or foil, label, and freeze.

To enjoy after freezing:

1. Allow cake to thaw at room temperature, and enjoy.

> **TABLE TALK**
>
> **Cream of coconut** (or coconut cream) is a sweet, syrupy coconut flavored mixture primarily used for making piña coladas, but it can also be a delicious baking ingredient, as in this recipe. Coco López is the most commonly found brand. Do not confuse cream of coconut with unsweetened coconut milk or cream. They're not the same.

Raspberry Swirl Cheesecake

The ultimate rich and creamy moist cheesecake is made even better by a swirl of tart raspberry sauce.

Yield:	Prep time:	Initial cook time:	Serving size:
1 (10-inch) cake	35 minutes	2 hours	1/12 of cake

1 (14.4-oz.) pkg. graham crackers	1½ cups sugar
½ cup melted unsalted butter	4 (8-oz.) pkg. cream cheese
1 cup fresh raspberries	2½ tsp. vanilla extract
⅓ cup water	4 large eggs
1 TB. freshly squeezed lemon juice	1 pt. sour cream

1. Preheat the oven to 350°F.

2. Use a food processor to pulverize graham crackers to crumbs, and use the pulse feature to mix in melted butter. Press mixture into the bottom and up the sides of a 10-inch *springform pan*. Bake for about 8 minutes or until set. Remove crust from oven and set aside.

3. Reduce oven temperature to 300°F.

4. In a medium saucepan over medium-high heat, combine raspberries, water, lemon juice, and ¼ cup sugar. Bring to a boil, reduce heat to low, and cook for 10 minutes. Remove from heat and pour mixture through a cheesecloth-lined sieve to strain out seeds. (If you don't mind raspberry seeds, you can forego the straining.) Set aside.

5. In a large bowl, and using an electric mixer on high speed, beat cream cheese, remaining 1¼ cups sugar, and vanilla until smooth, light, fluffy, and lump-free. Beat in eggs, one at a time, until blended. Quickly beat in sour cream just until blended.

6. Spoon ⅓ of cheese mixture into the baked crust. Drop 6 or so tablespoons raspberry sauce randomly over batter. Spoon ⅓ more batter in, followed by another round of raspberry sauce spoonfuls, topped with remaining cheesecake batter. Try to space out raspberry sauce so one layer isn't directly on top of another. Using a blunt knife, swirl raspberry sauce through batter to distribute, taking care not to go so deep you disturb crust on bottom.

7. Bake in the lower part of the oven for 1 hour. After 1 hour, turn off oven but do not open the door. Let cake sit in oven for 1 more hour.

8. Transfer cake to a wire rack to cool before covering and chilling in the refrigerator for at least 6 hours. If you want to freeze cake whole, run a knife around the edges, slightly loosen the pan's ring, and tighten it again before labeling and freezing cake, covered with foil, in the pan. Otherwise, remove cake from the pan and freeze portions in labeled, rigid freezer containers.

To enjoy after freezing:

1. Allow cake to thaw in the refrigerator, and enjoy.

Variation: Substitute blackberries, strawberries, or blueberries for the raspberries. Or if you're a cheesecake purist, you may leave out the fruit swirls entirely.

TABLE TALK

A **springform pan** is characterized by a removable bottom and hinged sides. The sides make it easy to remove the cake from the pan, as they loosen their grasp when the hinge is opened. This is especially useful with delicate crumb crusts like this one.

Blueberry Peach Cobbler

Summer-sweet peaches and blueberries come together in this old-fashioned rustic dessert finished with a delicately sweet biscuit topping.

Yield:	Prep time:	Initial cook time:	Reheat time:	Serving size:
2 (8-inch square) pans	25 minutes	25 minutes	45 minutes	$\frac{1}{9}$ of 1 pan

1 cup plus 2 TB. sugar

3 TB. cornstarch

4 cups fresh, frozen, or canned sliced peaches

4 cups fresh or frozen blueberries

3 TB. lemon juice

¼ cup cold water

¼ tsp. ground cardamom (optional)

3 cups all-purpose flour

1 TB. baking powder

1 tsp. baking soda

½ tsp. salt

½ cup unsalted butter

1½ cups plus 2 TB. heavy whipping cream

1. Preheat the oven to 400°F. Grease 2 (8-inch) glass or ceramic baking dishes.

2. In a large saucepan over medium-high heat, combine ½ cup sugar and cornstarch. Add sliced peaches, blueberries, lemon juice, cold water, and cardamom (if using), and stir to combine. Bring to a boil, stirring constantly. Reduce heat to low, and simmer for 5 minutes, stirring frequently. Remove from heat, and divide between the prepared pans.

3. In a food processor, combine all-purpose flour, ½ cup sugar, baking powder, baking soda, and salt, and pulse to combine. Add unsalted butter, and pulse until butter is well combined and mixture resembles coarse crumbs. Alternatively, use a pastry blender or 2 knives to cut butter into dry ingredients.

4. Add 1½ cups heavy whipping cream, and pulse until just combined and a soft dough forms.

5. Turn out dough onto a lightly floured surface, and knead a few times. Roll out to about ½-inch thickness. Using a 3-inch cookie cutter (or the top of a drinking glass approximately that size), cut dough into 18 biscuits. Gather scraps and reroll as necessary.

6. Brush biscuits with remaining 2 tablespoons heavy whipping cream and sprinkle with remaining 2 tablespoons sugar. Place biscuits on top of fruit filling, touching but not crowded (3 rows of 3 if using 8-inch square baking dishes). Bake for about 25 minutes or until tops of biscuits are lightly browned. Cool completely, cover tightly with foil, label, and freeze.

To reheat after freezing:

1. Bake frozen in a 375°F oven for about 40 to 45 minutes or until fruits are bubbling. Alternatively, thaw in the refrigerator and bake at 375°F for about 20 minutes or until bubbling.

2. Or freeze cobbler unbaked. Let filling cool completely before placing cut biscuits on top. Cover in foil, label, and freeze. Bake, frozen, at 400°F for about 50 minutes or until biscuits are puffed and brown, and filling is bubbling.

Variation: This recipe works with most any type of fresh or frozen fruit, so it's adaptable year round. Try mixing and matching apples, pears, plums, nectarines, rhubarb, strawberries, raspberries, blackberries, cherries, and fresh cranberries.

COLD FACT

The type of creams are determined by their milk fat content. Lightest is half-and-half—half milk, half cream and weighing in at 10 to 12 percent milk fat. Light cream contains about 20 percent (but by law can be labeled light if it contains between 18 to 30 percent). Half-and-half and light cream cannot be whipped. Light whipping cream comes in at between 30 to 36 percent. Heavy cream, also known as heavy whipping cream, contains between 36 to 40 percent milk fat.

Apple Crumb Pie

A flaky piecrust holds sweet, cinnamon-spiced apples steeped in tangy orange juice and topped with a sweet buttery crumb topping in this unforgettable twist on an American classic.

Yield:	Prep time:	Initial cook time:	Reheat time:	Serving size:
2 (10-inch) deep-dish pies	1 hour	10 minutes	55 minutes	⅛ of 1 pie

3½ cups all-purpose flour

½ tsp. salt

1½ cups sugar

½ cup plus 6 TB. unsalted butter, cut into small chunks and chilled

½ cup vegetable shortening, chilled

8 TB. ice water

10 lb. (about 30 medium) Granny Smith or your favorite baking apples, peeled, cored, quartered, and sliced in ⅓s

2 tsp. ground cinnamon

½ tsp. ground nutmeg

4 TB. cornstarch

⅓ cup frozen undiluted orange juice concentrate, thawed

1 cup brown sugar, firmly packed

1. In a food processor, combine 2½ cups flour, salt, and ¼ cup sugar, and pulse until combined. Add ½ cup chilled butter and shortening, and pulse about 20 times or just until butter is well incorporated and mixture is crumbly. Add ice water, and pulse about 10 times or until just combined.

2. Remove dough from the food processor, divide into 2 equal pieces, and flatten each piece into a disc. Wrap discs in plastic, and freeze for about 10 minutes.

3. Cut 2 pieces of waxed paper about a third larger than the size of the finished crust, and very lightly sprinkle with flour.

4. Place dough between sheets of floured waxed paper, and roll to about 12 inches, or 2 inches larger than the circumference of the pie plate. (No worries if a little crust hangs out of the waxed paper. Just keep it sprinkled lightly with flour.)

5. Remove one layer of waxed paper, and center an upside-down pie plate on rolled dough. Pick up bottom layer of waxed paper (as well as dough and pie plate), and flip the entire thing over. Press dough into place in the pie plate, and peel off waxed paper. Straighten out the edges. Using a thumb and forefinger of one hand, pinch dough around the forefinger of your other hand to make a scalloped edge all around the rim. Freeze crust. Repeat with remaining dough. Cover with plastic wrap or foil after crust is frozen.

6. In a large bowl, toss sliced apples with cinnamon, nutmeg, and cornstarch.

7. In a large stockpot over medium heat, combine orange juice concentrate and remaining 1¼ cups sugar, and cook, stirring, until well combined and sugar has melted. Bring to a boil, add apples, and toss to coat in orange syrup. Cook, stirring frequently, for about 7 minutes or until apples are not quite tender. Remove from heat and cool completely. Package cooled pie filling in zipper-lock plastic freezer bags, label, and freeze.

8. In a food processor, combine brown sugar and remaining 1 cup flour, and pulse until well mixed. Add remaining 6 tablespoons butter, and pulse until butter is well incorporated. Package crumb topping in a zipper-lock plastic freezer bag or rigid freezer container, label, and freeze.

To prepare pie after freezing:

1. Thaw pie filling in the refrigerator or using the cold water method (see Chapter 1). If you'll be baking the pie right away, you can even thaw the sealed bag of filling in hot water. Pour ½ thawed apple filling into each frozen prepared piecrust. Top each with ½ crumb mixture, cover loosely with foil, and bake in a 375°F oven for 25 minutes. Remove foil and bake for another 30 minutes or until top is golden brown. Cool on a wire rack for at least 15 minutes before serving.

COLD FACT

If, like me, you think the bottom crust comes out a bit soggy when you bake filled and frozen fruit pies, freeze the pie deconstructed, as in this recipe. It takes only minutes to toss thawed fruit pie filling into a prepared frozen piecrust, and the final result is well worth the extra effort. Need a top crust instead of crumb topping for a fruit pie? Freeze the top crust dough in a plastic-wrapped disc. Let it sit at room temperature for about 15 minutes, and it'll be pliable enough to roll and top your fruit pie. The dough portion of this recipe also makes a great all-purpose crust for most dessert pies and tarts.

Old-Fashioned Whoopee Pies

Two soft devil's food cookies sandwich fluffy marshmallow filling in this old-fashioned lunchbox favorite.

Yield:	Prep time:	Initial cook time:	Serving size:
17 filled pies	30 minutes	15 minutes	1 pie

12 TB. unsalted butter

2 cups all-purpose flour

1 cup sugar

¾ cup unsweetened cocoa powder

1 tsp. baking soda

¼ tsp. salt

1 cup milk

1 large egg

1 cup confectioners' sugar

1 (7-oz.) jar marshmallow crème

1½ tsp. vanilla extract

1. Preheat the oven to 350°F. Grease 2 large cookie sheets with vegetable shortening or spray with cooking spray.

2. In a small bowl in the microwave or a small saucepan on the stovetop, melt 6 tablespoons unsalted butter.

3. In a large bowl, combine all-purpose flour, sugar, cocoa, baking soda, and salt. Add melted unsalted butter, milk, 1 teaspoon vanilla extract, and egg, and stir with a wooden spoon until everything is well mixed.

4. Drop batter by heaping tablespoons onto the prepared baking sheet about 2 inches apart. You should have 34 cookies. Bake cookies for about 12 minutes or until a toothpick inserted into the center comes out clean. Using a spatula, transfer cookies to a wire rack to cool completely before filling.

5. In a large bowl, and using an electric mixer on high speed, beat remaining 6 tablespoons unsalted butter for about 3 minutes or until fluffy. Reduce speed to medium, and gradually beat in confectioners' sugar. Beat in marshmallow crème and remaining ½ teaspoon vanilla extract until well combined and filling is light and fluffy.

6. Spread about 1 tablespoon filling on the flat side of 17 cookies. Top with remaining 17 cookies. Wrap individually in plastic wrap, store in zipper-lock plastic freezer bags, label, and freeze.

To enjoy after freezing:

1. Let thaw at room temperature, and enjoy.

 COOL TIP

If you're in a hurry, these whoopee pies are good directly from the freezer.

More Delicious Desserts

In This Chapter

- Sweet-tooth-satisfying cookies and brownies
- Decadent soufflés
- Frozen delights
- Complementary sauces and toppings

Dessert from the freezer is more than just cakes and pies. This chapter explores additional ways your freezer can be sweet to you. You'll find eclectic dessert recipes along with some sweet sauces you can use to throw together a quick meal finale with the addition of fresh fruit, ice cream, or a simple piece of cake.

I offer a versatile and customizable cookie recipe here, but you should note that most cookie doughs freeze well. Try freezing your favorites. You can take out a small amount and bake up a few fresh hot cookies anytime you want. Unbaked frozen cookie dough, packaged with baking instructions, also makes a thoughtful homemade gift.

Cookies Your Way

This basic recipe makes a crunchy, buttery, texture-packed base for a cookie you can then customize with your favorite add-ins. Freeze the dough, slice it, and bake for hot cookies anytime.

Yield:	Prep time:	Reheat time:	Serving size:
about 90 cookies	10 minutes	12 minutes	2 cookies

2¼ cups all-purpose flour

1 tsp. baking powder

1 tsp. baking soda

¼ tsp. salt

1 cup sugar

1 cup brown sugar, firmly packed

1 cup old-fashioned oats

1 cup crushed corn flake cereal

½ cup toffee chips

2 eggs, beaten

2 tsp. vanilla extract

1 cup unsalted butter, melted

2¼ cups chocolate chips, peanut butter chips, raisins, nuts, shredded coconut, and/or M&M's

1. In a medium bowl, combine flour, baking powder, baking soda, and salt.

2. In a large bowl, combine sugar, brown sugar, old-fashioned oats, crushed corn flake cereal, and toffee chips. Add beaten eggs, vanilla extract, and melted butter, and stir until well combined and butter is completely incorporated. Stir in flour mixture.

3. Add desired mix-ins, and stir well. Divide dough into 3 pieces, and roll each portion into a log about 2½ inches in diameter. Wrap logs tightly in plastic wrap and then freezer paper or foil, label, and freeze.

To bake after freezing:

1. Spray a baking sheet with cooking spray. Slice dough into ½-inch slices (if dough crumbles, gather up and press together). Place on cookies about 2 inches apart on the prepared baking sheet, and bake in a 375°F oven for about 12 minutes or until tops are browned and cookies are set.

COOL TIP

Forgo rolling the dough into a log and instead package in a small tub. When it comes time to bake, use a small scoop to spoon out the number of cookies you want to bake.

Best-Ever Brownies

If you're a fan of decadent, dense, fudgy brownies, you'll love these. They live up to their name!

Yield:	Prep time:	Initial cook time:	Serving size:
32 small brownies	10 minutes	30 minutes	1 brownie

1 cup (2 sticks) butter

5 (1 oz.) squares unsweetened baking chocolate

1 cup semisweet chocolate chips

2¼ cups sugar

2 tsp. vanilla extract

5 large eggs

½ tsp. salt

1½ cups all-purpose flour

1. Preheat the oven to 350°F. Butter 2 (8½-inch) square baking pans.

2. In the top of a double boiler (or in a large metal bowl placed over a saucepan of simmering water), melt butter, unsweetened baking chocolate, and chocolate chips, stirring frequently. Remove from heat and use a wooden spoon to stir in sugar and vanilla extract. Beat in eggs, one at a time. Stir in salt and flour until just combined.

3. Divide batter between the prepared pans, and bake for about 30 minutes or until a toothpick inserted about 2 inches from the edge comes out clean. Cool completely in the pan. Slice into small squares, wrap, label, and freeze.

To eat after freezing:

1. Thaw and enjoy.

COOL TIP

If you're in a hurry and have no time to wait for them to thaw, these brownies are also terrific frozen.

Chocolate Soufflés

Light and airy yet rich and chocolaty, this classic French dessert never fails to impress.

Yield:	Prep time:	Reheat time:	Serving size:
12 (3.5 oz.) soufflés	15 minutes	25 minutes	1 soufflé

8 oz. bittersweet chocolate

4 TB. unsalted butter

⅓ cup plus ¼ cup sugar plus extra for ramekins

3 TB. water

5 large egg yolks

⅛ tsp. salt

½ tsp. vanilla extract

8 large egg whites

¼ tsp. cream of tartar

3 TB. whipped cream per soufflé at serving time

1. Prepare 12 (3.5-ounce) ramekins by coating lightly with butter (you may have some butter left over). Fill one of the butter-coated ramekins with sugar and hold in one hand. Hold a second ramekin underneath the first and tilt the top one and spin, allowing excess sugar to fall into the ramekin below. Repeat with remaining ramekins until all have a light coating of sugar covering their buttered inner surface. Return excess sugar to the sugar bowl.

2. Set a medium glass or stainless-steel bowl over a saucepan of simmering water. Add chocolate to the bowl, and stir occasionally until melted, about 8 minutes.

3. Meanwhile, in a small saucepan over medium heat, combine ⅓ cup sugar with 3 tablespoons water, and cook for about 30 seconds or until sugar dissolves. Remove from heat.

4. In a medium bowl, and using an electric mixer on high speed, beat egg yolks until thick. Slowly beat in syrup. With the mixer on low, mix salt, vanilla extract, and melted chocolate into egg yolk mixture. Set aside.

5. In a clean glass or stainless-steel bowl, and using a mixer on high speed with clean beaters, beat egg whites with cream of tartar until foamy. Gradually beat in remaining ¼ cup sugar, and beat until stiff peaks form.

6. Stir ¼ of egg whites into chocolate mixture to lighten it, stirring until well combined. Using a rubber spatula, gently fold remaining egg whites into chocolate mixture until just combined. Divide batter among the prepared ramekins, filling each just to the top. Cover with plastic wrap, label, and immediately freeze.

To bake after freezing:

1. Bake frozen in a 375°F oven for 25 minutes. Remove from the oven, place hot ramekins on small plates, and serve immediately with whipped cream on the side.

COOL TIP

Eggs are easier to separate when cold, but egg whites will whip faster at room temperature.

Nut-Covered Chocolate-Dipped Bananas

Rich, dark chocolate enrobes sweet creamy frozen bananas. Toasted nuts top off this treat for an unforgettable guilt-free indulgence.

Yield:	Prep time:	Initial cook time:	Serving size:
8 frozen bananas	5 minutes	10 minutes	1 frozen banana

2½ cups finely chopped toasted peanuts, pecans, walnuts, almonds, or hazelnuts

8 medium bananas

1 lb. dark chocolate

1 TB. unsalted butter

1. Place toasted nuts on a large, flat plate or a small baking sheet, and set aside.

2. Line 2 more baking sheets with waxed paper.

3. Peel bananas, cut 1 inch off one end, and insert a wooden craft (Popsicle) stick into the cut end, leaving about a 2-inch portion of the stick outside the banana for a handle. Place bananas on one of the prepared baking sheets and place in the freezer while you prepare the chocolate.

4. In a metal bowl placed over a pan of simmering water, melt dark chocolate and unsalted butter together, stirring frequently.

5. When chocolate mixture is smooth and completely melted, remove from heat and remove 1 banana from the freezer. Dip chilled banana into melted chocolate, and using a large spoon, scoop additional chocolate over banana until it's completely encased. Lift to let excess chocolate drip back into bowl, and immediately roll banana in toasted nuts. Place on the prepared baking sheet, and repeat with remaining bananas. Immediately place in the freezer.

To use after freezing:

1. Let sit at room temperature for 5 to 10 minutes, and enjoy.

Variation: Instead of rolling dipped bananas in nuts, try mixing and matching toasted coconut, toffee chips, jimmies, granola, crushed cookies, or graham crackers.

COLD FACT

The average American eats 27 pounds of bananas per year!

Neapolltan Ice Cream Cake

All the flavors of a childhood birthday party—vanilla cake, chocolate ice cream, and strawberry ice cream—are contained within this impressive yet easy-to-make dessert.

Yield:	Prep time:	Serving size:
1 (8-inch) cake	4 hours	⅛ cake

1 (8-in.) angel food cake

2 cups chocolate ice cream, softened

2 cups strawberry ice cream, softened

1 cup Hot Fudge Sauce (recipe later in this chapter), at room temperature

1½ cups heavy whipping cream

⅓ cup confectioners' sugar

1 tsp. vanilla extract

1. Using a large serrated knife, slice cake horizontally into 3 equal layers.

2. Place each flavor ice cream in a large bowl. Using a large spoon or rubber spatula, mash chocolate ice cream and then strawberry ice cream until almost the consistency of soft-serve ice cream.

3. Using a knife or small spatula, spread ½ of Hot Fudge Sauce over top of first cake layer. Top fudge sauce with chocolate ice cream, using a rubber spatula to spread ice cream into an even layer covering surface of cake. Top with next cake layer, followed by another layer of fudge sauce, followed by strawberry ice cream. Top with remaining cake layer. Place in freezer.

4. In a large bowl, and using an electric mixer on high speed, beat heavy whipping cream, confectioner's sugar, and vanilla extract for about 10 minutes or until stiff peaks form.

5. Remove cake from the freezer, and using a rubber spatula, frost top and sides of cake. Return cake to the freezer for at least 4 hours before serving, or wrap in plastic wrap for longer storage. Alternatively, after freezing, slice and wrap individual portions.

To serve after freezing:

1. Allow cake to sit out at room temperature for 10 minutes, slice, and enjoy.

Cream Cheese Frosting

This frosting makes the Cinnamon Rolls in Chapter 6 out of this world, but you can also use this versatile icing on all kinds of muffins, cakes, and cupcakes or even on graham crackers for a sweet snack.

Yield:	Prep time:	Serving size:
4 cups	5 minutes	1 tablespoon

1 (8-oz.) pkg. cream cheese	3½ cups *confectioners' sugar*
½ cup unsalted butter, softened	1 tsp. vanilla extract

1. In a large bowl, and using an electric mixer on high speed, beat cream cheese with softened unsalted butter for about 3 minutes or until light and fluffy.

2. Gradually beat in confectioners' sugar, followed by vanilla extract. Package frosting in small containers, label, and freeze.

To use after freezing:

1. You can defrost in the refrigerator if you want, but it's not necessary because this icing stays soft enough to spread right from the freezer.

> **TABLE TALK**
>
> Also known as powdered sugar, **confectioners' sugar** is nothing more than granulated sugar ground to a fine powder and mixed with a little cornstarch to prevent clumping. While it may seem like you could make it yourself, home food processors don't get the sugar fine enough for the job. You can, however, use them to make superfine sugar (also known as castor or caster sugar), which is handy for making cocktails and meringues, as it dissolves faster than regular granulated sugar.

Hot Fudge Sauce

Rich and chocolaty, this versatile sauce can dress up all kinds of desserts like ice cream, pound cake, or even fresh fruits.

Yield:	Prep time:	Initial cook time:	Reheat time:	Serving size:
4 cups	5 minutes	10 minutes	30 seconds to 1 minute	¼ cup

5 (1-oz.) squares unsweetened chocolate

½ cup (1 stick) unsalted butter

2¾ cups sugar

½ tsp. salt

1 (12 oz.) can evaporated milk

2 tsp. vanilla extract

1. In the top of a double boiler (or in a large metal bowl placed over a saucepan of simmering water), melt chocolate and unsalted butter, stirring to combine.

2. Stir in sugar in 3 additions, stirring to combine and incorporate before adding more. Stir in salt.

3. Slowly stir in evaporated milk, a little at a time, until everything is completely mixed. Continue to cook, stirring, for about 3 minutes or until sugar has completely melted and sauce is smooth. Stir in vanilla extract. Cool completely, package in appropriately sized rigid freezer containers, label, and freeze.

To reheat after freezing:

1. Microwave for 30 seconds to 1 minute, depending on amount being heated. Take care and err on the side of under thawing because even a second too long in the microwave will result in sauce boiling over.

COLD FACT

Want to try the world's most indulgent sundae? New York City's Serendipity 3 restaurant, with 48 hours' advance notice and $1,000, offers their "Golden Opulence Sundae." It consists of 5 scoops of Tahitian vanilla bean ice cream covered in 23K edible gold leaf; drizzled with the world's most expensive chocolate, Amedei Porceleana; and covered with chunks of rare Chuao chocolate, exotic Parisian candied fruits, gold dragets, truffles, and Marzipan cherries. Instead of a cherry on top, you'll find a tiny glass bowl of Grand Passion Caviar, an exclusive dessert caviar. The whole thing is served in a baccarat crystal goblet with an 18K gold spoon and topped with a huge gilded sugar flower.

Blueberry Compote

Blueberry Compote makes a perfect sweet-tart counterpart to the creaminess of the Cheese Blintzes recipe in Chapter 6, but you can also use this versatile fruit sauce to top pancakes, waffles, and French toast, or stir into plain yogurt for a lower-sugar alternative to commercial fruit-flavored yogurts. It even makes a great dessert topping over ice cream or pound cake.

Yield:	Prep time:	Initial cook time:	Reheat time:	Serving size:
3 cups	3 minutes	6 minutes	1 to 2 minutes	¼ cup

3½ cups or 2 (12-oz.) bags frozen blueberries

2 TB. freshly squeezed lemon juice

½ cup sugar

1 TB. cornstarch

1 TB. cold water

1. In a medium saucepan over medium-high heat, combine blueberries, lemon juice, and sugar.

2. In a small bowl, stir together cornstarch and cold water. Drizzle cornstarch mixture into blueberry mixture, and bring to a boil. Reduce heat to medium-low, and simmer for about 5 minutes or until thickened.

3. Cool completely, package in small containers (or even ice cube trays), and freeze. Pop frozen compote out of the freezer containers and into a zipper-lock plastic freezer bag for long-term storage, label, and freeze.

To reheat after freezing:

1. Defrost in the microwave for a minute or 2, and enjoy hot compote.

Variation: Substitute frozen raspberries, blackberries, or chopped apples or peaches for the blueberries in this recipe.

COLD FACT

Blueberries are one of only three fruits native to North America. (Concord grapes and cranberries are the others.) A single blueberry bush can produce as many as 6,000 berries in a single year.

accoutrement   An accompaniment, trapping, or garnish.

al dente   Italian for "against the teeth." Refers to pasta or rice that's neither soft nor hard, but just slightly firm against the teeth.

all-purpose flour   Flour that contains only the endosperm, or inner part of the wheat grain, unlike whole wheat, which adds the bran and germ. It is made from wheat with an equal amount of starch and protein, making it suitable for all purposes, from cakes to gravies.

allspice   Named for its flavor echoes of several spices (cinnamon, cloves, nutmeg), allspice is used in many desserts and in rich marinades and stews.

almonds   Mild, sweet, and crunchy nuts that combine nicely with creamy and sweet food items.

arborio rice   A plump, short-grained Italian rice used, among other purposes, for risotto.

artichoke heart   The center part of the artichoke flower, often found canned in grocery stores.

au gratin   The quick broiling of a dish before serving to brown the top ingredients. When used in a recipe name, the term often implies cheese and a creamy sauce.

au jus   French for "with juice," an expression that refers to a dish served with juices that result from cooking (as in roast beef).

bake   To cook in a dry oven. Dry-heat cooking often results in a crisping of the exterior of the food being cooked. Moist-heat cooking, through methods such as steaming, poaching, etc., brings a much different, moist quality to the food.

baking stone   Unglazed stone used for baking breads and pizzas. Placed in the oven (and kept there when not in use) a baking stone retains heat and makes an ideal surface for baking yeast doughs.

balsamic vinegar   Vinegar produced primarily in Italy from a specific type of grape and aged in wood barrels. It is heavier, darker, and sweeter than most vinegars.

bamboo shoots   Crunchy, tasty white parts of the growing bamboo plant, often purchased canned.

barbecue   To quick-cook over high heat, or to cook something long and slow in a rich liquid (barbecue sauce).

basil   A flavorful, almost sweet, herb delicious with tomatoes and used in all kinds of Italian- and Mediterranean-style dishes.

baste   To keep foods moist during cooking by spooning, brushing, or drizzling with a liquid.

beat   To quickly mix substances.

black pepper   A biting and pungent seasoning, freshly ground pepper is a must for many dishes and adds an extra level of flavor and taste.

blanch   To place a food in boiling water for about 1 minute (or less) to partially cook the exterior and then submerge in or rinse with cool water to halt the cooking.

blend   To completely mix something, usually with a blender or food processor, more slowly than beating.

blue cheese   A blue-veined cheese that crumbles easily and has a somewhat soft texture, usually sold in a block. The color is from a flavorful, edible mold that's often added or injected into the cheese.

boil   To heat a liquid to a point at which water is forced to turn into steam, causing the liquid to bubble (212°F at sea level). To boil something is to insert it into boiling water. A rapid boil is when a lot of bubbles form on the surface of the liquid.

bouillon (dried)   Dried essence of stock from chicken, beef, vegetable, or other ingredients. This is a popular starting ingredient for soups because it adds flavor (and often a lot of salt). Bouillon comes in cubes or granules.

braise   To cook with the introduction of some liquid, usually over an extended period of time.

bread flour   Wheat flour with a high gluten content and a large part of its starch removed.

breadcrumbs   Tiny pieces of crumbled dry bread, often used for topping or coating.

Brie   A creamy cow's milk cheese from France with a soft, edible rind and a mild flavor.

broil To cook in a dry oven under the overhead high-heat element.

broth *See* stock.

brown To cook in a skillet, turning, until the food's surface is seared and brown in color.

brown rice Whole-grain rice including the germ with a characteristic pale brown or tan color; more nutritious and flavorful than white rice.

Cajun cooking A style of cooking that combines French and Southern characteristics and includes many highly seasoned stews and meats.

Cajun seasoning A boldly flavored seasoning blend typically consisting of garlic, onion, cayenne and black peppers, chilies, mustard, celery, and other seasonings.

Canadian bacon Lean smoked pork from the eye of loin, closer in taste and texture to ham than traditional bacon.

caramelize To cook sugar over low heat until it develops a sweet caramel flavor. The term is increasingly gaining use to describe cooking vegetables (especially onions) or meat in butter or oil over low heat until they soften, sweeten, and develop a caramel color.

carbohydrate A nutritional component found in starches, sugars, fruits, and vegetables that causes a rise in blood glucose levels. Carbohydrates supply energy and many important nutrients, including vitamins, minerals, and antioxidants.

cardamom An intense, sweet-smelling spice, common to Indian cooking, used in baking and coffee.

cayenne A fiery spice made from (hot) chile peppers, especially the cayenne chile, a slender, red, and very hot pepper.

cheddar The ubiquitous hard cow's milk cheese with a rich, buttery flavor that ranges from mellow to sharp. Originally produced in England, cheddar is now produced worldwide.

chile (or **chili**) Any one of many different "hot" peppers, ranging in intensity from the relatively mild ancho pepper to the blisteringly hot habañero.

chili powder A seasoning blend that includes chile pepper, cumin, garlic, and oregano created for the Texan stew. Proportions vary among different versions, but they all offer a warm, rich flavor.

Chinese five-spice powder A seasoning blend of cinnamon, anise, ginger, fennel, and pepper.

chipotle chile   A dried, smoked jalapeño pepper that has a wrinkled brown skin and a smoky flavor. It's most commonly found canned in adobo sauce.

chives   A member of the onion family, chives grow in bunches of long leaves that resemble tall grass or the green tops of onions and offer a light onion flavor.

chop   To cut into pieces, usually qualified by an adverb such as "coarsely chopped," or by a size measurement such as "chopped into ½-inch pieces." "Finely chopped" is much closer to mince.

chutney   A thick condiment often served with Indian curries made with fruits and/ or vegetables with vinegar, sugar, and spices.

cider vinegar   Vinegar produced from apple cider, popular in North America.

cilantro   A member of the parsley family used in Mexican cooking (especially salsa) and some Asian dishes. Use in moderation, as the flavor can overwhelm. The seed of the cilantro plant is the spice coriander. Also called fresh coriander or Chinese parsley.

cinnamon   A rich, aromatic spice commonly used in baking or desserts. Cinnamon can also be used for delicious and interesting entrées.

cocoa   An unsweetened dry powder made by separating most of the cocoa butter out of the cocoa bean.

compound butter   Butter creamed with other ingredients such as garlic, herbs, and/ or spices.

confectioners' sugar   Granulated sugar that's been ground to a fine powder and mixed with a tiny amount of cornstarch to prevent clumping. Also known as powdered sugar.

coriander   A rich, warm, spicy seed used in all types of recipes, from African to South American, from entrées to desserts. Coriander comes in whole round seeds or ground into a powder.

cornmeal   Dried corn kernels that have been ground to a coarse, medium, or fine consistency, used for cooking, baking, and breading.

cornstarch   A white powder made from the endosperm portion of a corn kernel commonly used as a thickening agent in food.

count   In terms of seafood or other foods that come in small sizes, the number of that item that compose 1 pound. For example, 31 to 40 count shrimp are large appetizer shrimp often served with cocktail sauce; 51 to 60 are much smaller.

couscous Granular semolina (durum wheat) that's cooked and used in many Mediterranean and North African dishes.

cream of coconut A sweet coconut-flavored syrup used to make cocktails or in cooking.

cream of tartar A white acidic powder derived from a crystalline acid deposit found on the inside of wine barrels, used for stabilizing beaten egg whites and activating baking soda. Find it in the spice aisle of the market.

cremini mushrooms A relative of the white button mushroom but brown in color and with a richer flavor. The larger, fully grown version is the portobello.

croutons Chunks of bread, usually between ¼ and ½ inch in size, sometimes seasoned and baked, broiled, or fried to a crisp texture and used in soups and salads.

crudités Fresh vegetables served as an appetizer, often all together on one tray.

crushed red pepper Hot and spicy flakes of dried red chile peppers.

cumin A fiery, smoky-tasting spice popular in Middle Eastern and Indian dishes. Cumin is a seed; ground cumin seed is the most common form used in cooking.

curry Rich, spicy, Indian-style sauces and the dishes prepared with them. A curry uses curry powder as its base seasoning.

curry powder A ground blend of rich and flavorful spices used as a basis for curry and many other Indian-influenced dishes. Common ingredients include hot pepper, nutmeg, cumin, cinnamon, pepper, and turmeric. Some curry can also be found in paste form.

custard A cooked mixture of eggs and milk popular as a base for desserts.

dash A few drops, usually of a liquid, released by a quick shake of, for example, a bottle of hot sauce.

deglaze To scrape up the bits of meat and seasoning left in a pan or skillet after cooking by adding a liquid such as wine or broth and creating a flavorful stock that can be used to create sauces.

dice To cut into small cubes about ¼-inch square.

Dijon mustard Hearty, spicy mustard made with white wine in the style of the Dijon region of France.

dill A herb perfect for eggs, salmon, cheese dishes, and, of course, vegetables (pickles!).

dollop   A spoonful of something creamy and thick, like sour cream or whipped cream.

double boiler   A set of two pots designed to nest together, one inside the other, and provide consistent, moist heat for foods that need delicate treatment. The bottom pot holds water (not quite touching the bottom of the top pot); the top pot holds the ingredient you want to heat.

dredge   To cover a piece of food with a dry substance such as flour or cornmeal.

drizzle   To lightly sprinkle drops of a liquid over food, often as the finishing touch to a dish.

dry   In the context of wine, a wine that contains little or no residual sugar, so it's not very sweet.

emulsion   A combination of liquid ingredients that do not normally mix well, beaten together to create a thick liquid, such as a fat or oil with water. Creation of an emulsion must be done carefully and rapidly to ensure that particles of one ingredient are suspended in the other.

entrée   The main dish in a meal. In France, however, the entrée is considered the first course.

evaporated milk   Concentrated, unsweetened milk made by evaporating some of the liquid in whole milk.

extra-virgin olive oil   *See* olive oil.

fillet   A piece of meat or seafood with the bones removed.

floret   The flower or bud end of broccoli or cauliflower.

flour   Grains ground into a meal. Wheat is the most common flour. Flour is also made from oats, rye, buckwheat, soybeans, etc. *See also* all-purpose flour; whole-wheat flour.

fold   To combine a dense and light mixture with a circular action from the middle of the bowl.

freezer paper   Heavy paper with a grease and waterproof wax coating on one side, ideal for wrapping meats before freezing.

fry   To cook food in fat.

garlic A member of the onion family, a pungent and flavorful element in many savory dishes. A garlic bulb contains multiple cloves. Each clove, when chopped, provides about 1 teaspoon garlic. Most recipes call for cloves or chopped garlic by the teaspoon.

garnish An embellishment not vital to the dish but added to enhance visual appeal.

ginger The root (or rhizome) of a tropical flowering plant, available fresh, ground, pickled, or candied. Ginger adds a pungent, sweet, and spicy quality to a dish.

grate To shave into tiny pieces using a sharp rasp or grater.

grind To reduce a large, hard substance, often a seasoning such as peppercorns, to the consistency of sand.

grits Coarsely ground hominy corn, served in the southern United States as a porridge.

Gruyère A rich, sharp, cow's milk cheese made in Switzerland that has a nutty flavor.

hazelnuts (also **filberts**) A sweet nut popular in desserts and, to a lesser degree, in savory dishes.

hoisin sauce A sweet Asian condiment similar to ketchup made with soybeans, sesame, chili peppers, and sugar.

hominy Dried yellow or white corn with its hull and germ removed by soaking in lye or slaked lime. Find hominy dried (in which case it will need to be reconstituted before use) or canned (more common).

hors d'oeuvre French for "outside of work" (the "work" being the main meal), an hors d'oeuvre can be any dish served as a starter before the meal.

horseradish A sharp, spicy root in the radish family that forms the flavor base in many condiments from cocktail sauce to sharp mustards. Prepared horseradish contains vinegar and oil, among other ingredients. Use pure horseradish much more sparingly than the prepared version, or try cutting it with sour cream.

infusion A liquid in which flavorful ingredients such as herbs have been soaked or steeped to extract that flavor into the liquid.

Irish oatmeal Unrolled oat groats that result in a chewier, hardier textured dish with higher fiber and nutritional content than typical rolled oats. Also known as steel-cut oats or Scotch oats.

Italian seasoning   A blend of dried herbs, including basil, oregano, rosemary, and thyme.

jalapeño pepper   A small green chile pepper that turns bright red when ripe and ranges from hot to very hot.

kalamata olives   Traditionally from Greece, these medium-small long black olives have a salty, rich flavor.

kidney beans   Firm, medium-size beans with a dark red skin and white flesh available dried or canned.

knead   To work dough to make it pliable and activate elastic gluten proteins so it holds carbon dioxide gas bubbles as it bakes. Kneading is fundamental in the process of making yeast breads.

kosher salt   A coarse-grained salt made without any additives or iodine.

lentils   Tiny lens-shape pulses used in European, Middle Eastern, and Indian cuisines.

liquid smoke   A liquid seasoning made from hickory smoke concentrate that imparts a distinctive smoky flavor to foods. Find it in most grocery stores in the barbecue and steak sauce section.

malted milk powder   A mixture of malted barley and wheat mixed with whole milk and evaporated until it forms a powder. Some brands also add sugar.

marinate   To soak meat, seafood, or other food in a seasoned sauce, called a marinade, that's high in acid content. The acids break down the muscle of the meat, making it tender and adding flavor.

marjoram   A sweet herb, a cousin of and similar to oregano, popular in Greek, Spanish, and Italian dishes.

marshmallow crème   A thick, spreadable version of marshmallow candy, made primarily from egg whites, corn syrup, and gelatin.

meld   To allow flavors to blend and spread over time. Melding is often why recipes call for overnight refrigeration and is also why some dishes taste better as leftovers.

Microplane or micro-grater   A kitchen gadget consisting of a long, sharp rasp with an attached handle, used to grate citrus zest, ginger, nutmeg, and hard cheeses.

mince   To cut into very small pieces smaller than diced pieces, about $\frac{1}{8}$ inch or smaller.

mortadella   An Italian smoked beef and pork sausage, similar to bologna, with added garlic flavoring and cubes of pork fat.

nutmeg   A sweet, fragrant, musky spice used primarily in baking.

Old Bay seasoning   A seasoning blend consisting of bay leaves, celery seeds, and other spices used primarily in seafood dishes. Look for the McCormick brand.

olive oil   A fragrant liquid produced by crushing or pressing olives. Extra-virgin olive oil—the most flavorful and highest quality—is produced from the first pressing of a batch of olives; oil is also produced from later pressings.

olives   The fruit of the olive tree commonly grown on all sides of the Mediterranean. Black olives are also called ripe olives. Green olives are immature, although they're also widely eaten. *See also* kalamata olives.

oregano   A fragrant, slightly astringent herb used in Greek, Spanish, and Italian dishes.

oyster sauce   A thick, dark brown sauce, a staple of Chinese cuisine, made from ground dried oysters. Find it at Asian markets or well-stocked grocery stores. It will keep indefinitely in the refrigerator.

panko   Coarse, Japanese-style breadcrumbs that create a wonderful crunchy coating for fried foods. Find them in Asian markets and in the Asian food sections of well-stocked supermarkets.

paprika   A rich, red, warm, earthy spice that also lends a rich red color to many dishes.

parboil   To partially cook in boiling water or broth, similar to blanching (although blanched foods are quickly cooled with cold water).

Parmesan   A hard, dry, flavorful cheese primarily used grated or shredded as a seasoning for Italian-style dishes.

parsley   A fresh-tasting green leafy herb, often used as a garnish.

parsnip   A cream-colored root vegetable that resembles white carrots with a pleasantly sweet flavor.

pastry blender   A small wire kitchen gadget used for cutting fats into flour when making pastry crusts. You can get similar results (although with more work) by using two knives, by pressing with a fork, or by pulsing ingredients in a food processor.

pearl onions   Small, marble-size, mild-flavored onions available fresh, frozen, or pickled.

pecans   Rich, buttery nuts, native to North America, that have a high unsaturated fat content.

peppercorns   Large, round, dried berries ground to produce pepper.

pesto   A thick spread or sauce made with fresh basil leaves, garlic, olive oil, pine nuts, and Parmesan cheese. Some newer versions are made with other herbs.

phyllo dough   A pastry dough characterized by wafer-thin layers that are stacked with melted butter or oil between to give the final product a flaky consistency. It's possible to make your own phyllo (pronounced *FEE-low*) dough, but it's tricky and time-consuming. It's far easier to buy frozen phyllo dough at the grocery store.

pilaf   A rice dish in which the rice is browned in butter or oil and then cooked in a flavorful liquid such as a broth, often with the addition of meats or vegetables. The rice absorbs the broth, resulting in a savory dish.

pine nuts (also **pignoli** or **piñon**)   Nuts grown on pine trees, that are rich (read: high fat), flavorful, and a bit piney. Pine nuts are a traditional component of pesto and add a wonderful hearty crunch to many other recipes.

pizza peel   A wide, wooden paddlelike spatula used for moving pizzas on and off an oven's baking stone.

pizza stone   Preheated with the oven, a pizza stone cooks a crust to a delicious, crispy, pizza-parlor texture. It also holds heat well, so pizza or other food removed from the oven on the stone stay hot for as long as 30 minutes at the table.

poach   To cook a food in simmering liquid, such as water, wine, or broth.

preheat   To turn on an oven, broiler, or other cooking appliance in advance of cooking so the temperature will be at the desired level when the assembled dish is ready for cooking.

prosciutto   Dry, salt-cured ham that originated in Italy.

purée   To reduce a food to a thick, creamy texture, usually using a blender or food processor.

raw sugar or **sugar-in-the-raw**   The purified residue left after sugar cane has been processed to remove the molasses and refine the sugar crystals, resulting in a coarse crystal brown-tinged sugar.

reduce To boil or simmer a broth or sauce to remove some of the water content, resulting in more concentrated flavor and color.

render To cook a meat to the point where its fat melts and can be removed.

reserve To hold a specified ingredient for another use later in the recipe.

rice vinegar Vinegar produced from fermented rice or rice wine, popular in Asian-style dishes. This isn't the same as rice wine vinegar.

ricotta A fresh Italian cheese smoother than cottage cheese with a slightly sweet flavor.

risotto A popular Italian rice dish made by browning arborio rice in butter or oil and then slowly adding liquid to cook the rice, resulting in a creamy texture.

roast To cook something uncovered in an oven, usually without additional liquid.

Roma tomatoes Small, oblong-shape tomatoes especially suited for cooking. Also known as plum tomatoes.

rosemary A pungent, sweet herb used with chicken, pork, fish, and especially lamb. A little of it goes a long way.

roux A mixture of butter or another fat and flour, used to thicken sauces and soups.

saffron A spice made from the stamens of crocus flowers, saffron lends a dramatic yellow color and distinctive flavor to a dish. Use only tiny amounts of this expensive herb.

sage An herb with a musty yet fruity, lemon-rind scent and "sunny" flavor.

salami A general term for a family of boldly spiced cured, ready-to-eat sausages.

sauté To pan-cook in oil over high heat while keeping food in constant motion.

savory A popular herb with a fresh, woody taste. The term also refers to the flavor of foods that are not sweet.

sear To quickly brown the exterior of a food, especially meat, over high heat to give foods an appetizing color and carbonized flavor.

semolina flour A coarse durum wheat flour that's an essential component of good pasta and pizza. Find semolina flour in Italian markets, health food stores, and in the flour and grain section of most well-stocked supermarkets.

serrano chile   A small, green, very hot chile pepper that can be used raw or cooked. As they mature, the serrano chile's smooth bright green skin will turn red and then yellow.

sesame oil   An oil, made from pressing sesame seeds, that's tasteless if clear and aromatic and flavorful if brown.

shallot   A member of the onion family that grows in a bulb somewhat like garlic and has a milder onion flavor. When a recipe calls for shallot, use the entire bulb.

short-grain rice   A starchy rice popular for Asian-style dishes because it readily clumps (perfect for eating with chopsticks).

shred   To cut into many long, thin slices.

sieve   A fine-mesh strainer.

simmer   To cook liquid gently, just under the boil, so the liquid barely bubbles.

skewers   Thin wooden or metal sticks, usually about 8 inches long, used for assembling kebabs, dipping food pieces into hot sauces, or serving single-bite food items with a bit of panache.

skillet (also **frying pan**)   A generally heavy, flat-bottomed cast-iron pan with a handle designed to cook food over heat on a stovetop or campfire.

skim   To remove fat or other material from the top of liquid.

slice   To cut into thin pieces.

springform pan   A baking pan characterized by a removable bottom and hinged sides that make it easy to remove the cake from the pan because they loosen their grasp when the hinge is opened.

sriracha sauce   A Thai hot sauce made from a paste of chiles, garlic, sugar, and salt.

steam   To suspend a food over boiling water and allow the heat of the steam (water vapor) to cook the food. A quick-cooking method, steaming preserves the flavor and texture of a food.

steel-cut oats   *See* Irish oatmeal.

steep   To let sit in hot water, as in steeping tea in hot water, for 10 minutes.

stew   To slowly cook pieces of food submerged in a liquid. Also, a dish that's been prepared by this method.

sticky rice (or **glutinous rice**)   *See* short-grain rice.

stir-fry   To cook small pieces of food in a wok or skillet over high heat, moving and turning the food quickly to cook all sides.

stock   A flavorful broth made by cooking meats and/or vegetables with seasonings until the liquid absorbs these flavors. This liquid is then strained and the solids discarded. Stock can be eaten alone or used as a base for soups, stews, etc.

strata   A savory bread pudding usually made with eggs and cheese layered with other ingredients.

succotash   A cooked vegetable dish made of corn and lima beans.

tapenade   A thick, chunky spread made from olives, lemon juice, and anchovies.

tarragon   A sweet, rich-smelling herb perfect with seafood, vegetables (especially asparagus), chicken, and pork.

teriyaki sauce   A Japanese-style sauce composed of soy sauce, rice wine, ginger, and sugar that works well with seafood as well as most meats.

thyme   A minty, zesty herb.

toast   To heat something, usually bread, so it's browned and crisp.

toffee chips   Small bits of English toffee candy used in baking. Find them in your grocery store next to the chocolate chips.

tomato paste   A concentrated paste made from tomatoes available in cans or in tubes.

turmeric   A spicy, pungent yellow root used in many dishes, especially Indian cuisine, for color and flavor. Turmeric is the source of the yellow color in many prepared mustards.

turnip   A top-shape root vegetable with a delicate sweet flavor.

vegetable shortening   A solid, virtually tasteless fat made from hydrogenated vegetable oils typically used to make piecrusts flaky and for frying.

vegetable steamer   An insert for a large saucepan or a special pot with tiny holes in the bottom designed to fit on another pot to hold food to be steamed above boiling water. *See also* steam.

vinegar   An acidic liquid widely used as dressing and seasoning, often made from fermented grapes, apples, or rice. *See also* balsamic vinegar; cider vinegar; rice vinegar; white vinegar; wine vinegar.

walnuts   A rich, slightly woody-flavored nut.

water chestnuts   A tuber, popular in many types of Asian-style cooking. The flesh is white, crunchy, and juicy, and the vegetable holds its texture whether cool or hot.

whisk   To rapidly mix, introducing air to the mixture. Also the wire kitchen tool that accomplishes this task.

white mushrooms   Button mushrooms. When fresh, they have an earthy smell and an appealing "soft crunch."

white vinegar   The most common type of vinegar, produced from grain.

whole-wheat flour   Wheat flour that contains the bran and germ of the grain.

wine vinegar   Vinegar produced from red or white wine.

wok   A round-bottom cooking vessel used for stir-frying, braising, stewing, and deep-frying.

wonton wrappers   Paper-thin squares (usually) or circles of dough typically used for making stuffed dumplings.

Worcestershire sauce   Originally developed in India and containing tamarind, this spicy sauce is used as a seasoning for many meats and other dishes.

yeast   Tiny fungi that, when mixed with water, sugar, flour, and heat, release carbon dioxide bubbles, which in turn cause bread to rise.

zest   Small slivers of peel, usually from a citrus fruit such as lemon, lime, or orange.

zester   A kitchen tool used to scrape zest off a fruit into thin, stringy slivers. A small grater also works well.

Resources for Freezer Cooks

Don't let your freezer cooking adventures start and end with this book. In this appendix, you'll find more terrific books, blogs, and websites to help you expand your recipe repertoire and keep your freezer filled with tasty fare. The Internet can also be a great place to shop for frequently used pantry staples, unusual or hard-to-find ingredients, and supplies to package your freezer food creations.

Books

Brown, Ellen. *The Complete Idiot's Guide to Slow Cooker Cooking, Second Edition.* Indianapolis, IN: Alpha Books, 2007.
Although this isn't specifically a freezer cookbook, I bet you'll still find this nice collection of recipes handy, because most slow cooker recipes do well in the freezer.

Clegg, Holly. *Holly Clegg's Trim and Terrific Freezer Friendly Meals.* Philadelphia, PA: Running Press, 2006.
This cookbook from the queen of cooking light offers a huge collection of quick-and-easy freezer-friendly recipes for all occasions.

Slagle, Nanci, and Carol Santee. *30-Day Gourmet's Big Book of Freezer Cooking.* Brownsburg, IN: 30-Day Gourmet Press, 2010.
The recipes here are a long way from the promise of "gourmet," but this is a great guide for serious cooks who plan to cook only once a month.

Websites

Cheri On Ice
www.cherionice.com
The author's blog on freezer and make-ahead cooking for foodies, Cheri On Ice focuses on the sophisticated side of make-ahead cooking.

ENERGY STAR

www.energystar.gov

This joint program of the U.S. Environmental Protection Agency and the U.S. Department of Energy helps us all save money and protect the environment through energy-efficient appliances, products, and practices.

Favorite Freezer Foods

www.favoritefreezerfoods.com/index.html

Log on here for a blog, e-zine, and cooking community, all dedicated to freezer cooking.

Once a Month Mom

www.onceamonthmom.com

This site offers freezer cooking recipes and menus for family friendly, once-a-month cooking. It even includes homemade baby foods!

USDA's Freezing and Food Safety

www.fsis.usda.gov/factsheets/focus_on_freezing/index.asp

Here you'll find essential freezing facts and information from the U.S. Department of Agriculture.

Tools, Supplies, and Ingredients

Amazon.com

www.amazon.com

Most people don't realize Amazon.com sells groceries. True, you have to buy in quantity, but with good prices and free shipping on orders over $25, it's a great place to buy frequently used pantry staples as well as food-packaging supplies.

DealTime

www.dealtime.com

With the click of a button, this site searches the net to find the best deals on all sorts of merchandise, especially helpful when shopping for big-ticket items like refrigerators and freezers.

King Arthur Flour

www.kingarthurflour.com

If your supermarket doesn't stock them, you can find the bread flour and semolina needed to make perfect pizzeria-style pizza here.

The Well-Stocked Kitchen

Having a well-stocked pantry and refrigerator can save you lots of time and money because you can avoid having to run to the store for forgotten ingredients. Before going shopping, check your supplies and stock up!

Pantry Checklist

Herbs and spices:

- ❑ Allspice
- ❑ Basil
- ❑ Bay leaves
- ❑ Cajun seasoning
- ❑ Cardamom
- ❑ Cayenne
- ❑ Cinnamon
- ❑ Coriander
- ❑ Crushed red pepper
- ❑ Cumin
- ❑ Curry powder
- ❑ Garlic powder
- ❑ Ginger
- ❑ Italian seasoning
- ❑ Marjoram

- ❑ Mustard powder
- ❑ Nutmeg
- ❑ Old Bay seasoning
- ❑ Onion powder
- ❑ Oregano
- ❑ Paprika
- ❑ Parsley
- ❑ Pepper (black and white)
- ❑ Rosemary
- ❑ Sage
- ❑ Salt
- ❑ Tarragon
- ❑ Thyme
- ❑ Turmeric

Oils:

- ❏ Canola
- ❏ Grapeseed
- ❏ Olive
- ❏ Peanut
- ❏ Sesame
- ❏ Vegetable
- ❏ Additional nut and/or flavored oils you like

Vinegars:

- ❏ Balsamic
- ❏ Cider
- ❏ Rice
- ❏ White and red wine
- ❏ Additional flavored and specialized vinegars you like

Condiments:

- ❏ Hot sauce
- ❏ Jams
- ❏ Jellies
- ❏ Ketchup
- ❏ Mayonnaise
- ❏ Mustard
- ❏ Soy sauce
- ❏ Worcestershire sauce

Extracts:

- ❏ Almond
- ❏ Butter
- ❏ Coconut
- ❏ Lemon
- ❏ Maple
- ❏ Peppermint
- ❏ Vanilla—a must!

Dry ingredients:

- ❏ Baking powder
- ❏ Baking soda
- ❏ Brown sugar
- ❏ Cornstarch
- ❏ Cream of tartar
- ❏ Flour
- ❏ Sugar
- ❏ Yeast

Canned goods:

- ❏ Beans
- ❏ Soup stocks
- ❏ Tuna
- ❏ Additional fruits and vegetables you like

Dry foods:

- ❏ Beans
- ❏ Chiles
- ❏ Couscous
- ❏ Mushrooms
- ❏ Nuts
- ❏ Pasta
- ❏ Rice
- ❏ Sun-dried tomatoes

Produce:

- ❏ Garlic
- ❏ Onions
- ❏ Potatoes
- ❏ Shallots
- ❏ Sweet potatoes
- ❏ Tomatoes

Syrups:

- ❏ Corn
- ❏ Honey
- ❏ Maple
- ❏ Molasses

Refrigerator Checklist

Dairy:

- ❏ Butter or margarine
- ❏ Cream or half-and-half (if you use them)
- ❏ Eggs
- ❏ Milk
- ❏ Parmesan and other cheeses you like
- ❏ Plain yogurt or sour cream

Produce:

- ❏ Bell peppers
- ❏ Carrots
- ❏ Celery
- ❏ Cilantro
- ❏ Fresh herbs (as needed)
- ❏ Green onions
- ❏ Hot peppers
- ❏ Lemons
- ❏ Limes
- ❏ Parsley
- ❏ Additional fruits and vegetables or juices you like

Menu-Planning Worksheet

No matter which cooking strategy you use, using menu-planning worksheets like the one in this appendix helps streamline the process. Even a loose plan—you don't have to fill in each and every category if that's not your style—will significantly cut down on extra trips to the grocery store for forgotten ingredients.

Fill in the plan with a combination of foods you plan to prepare along with selections from the stockpile in your freezer. When life interferes with the plan—and it will!—it's easy to swap days. You'll always have something on hand for dinner, so no more last-minute dashes for fast food because there's nothing in the house to eat.

Meal	Sunday	Monday	Tuesday	Wednesday	Thursday	Friday	Saturday
Breakfast							
Lunch							
Dinner							
Snacks							
Breakfast							
Lunch							
Dinner							
Snacks							

Meal	Sunday	Monday	Tuesday	Wednesday	Thursday	Friday	Saturday
Breakfast							
Lunch							
Dinner							
Snacks							
Breakfast							
Lunch							
Dinner							
Snacks							

Freezing Timetable

When it comes to predicting how long you can keep foods in the freezer, the answer is: it depends. Be diligent about cooling foods before freezing, wrapping them well, and keeping your freezer running optimally, and your freezer cooking creations should emerge from reheating as good as fresh.

Most of the recommendations in the following table come from the U.S. Department of Agriculture. In practice, I've kept frozen foods far longer than the recommended times with no quality sacrificed. Experiment to see what works for you. If you're able to keep your freezer's temperature consistent (see Chapter 2), you can get away with keeping foods for much longer.

Note: freezer storage times are for *quality* only. Frozen foods remain *safe* indefinitely.

Food	Recommended Storage Time
Baked goods	2 or 3 months
Butter	3 or 4 months
Casseroles	2 or 3 months
Eggs (whites, scrambled, substitute)	12 months
Fish:	
Cooked	2 or 3 months
Raw pieces	6 months
Frozen dinners and entrées	3 or 4 months
Meat:	
Cooked	2 or 3 months
Ham, bacon, sausage, cured meats	1 or 2 months
Hot dogs, lunchmeats, processed meat	1 or 2 months
Uncooked ground	3 or 4 months
Uncooked roasts	4 to 12 months
Uncooked steaks and chops	4 to 12 months
Poultry:	
Cooked	4 months
Uncooked giblets	3 or 4 months
Uncooked parts	9 months
Uncooked whole	12 months
Soups and stews	3 or 4 months
Vegetables:	
Delicate	3 months
Hearty	12 months
Wild game, uncooked	8 to 12 months
Yeast dough, unbaked	3 months

Index

C

G

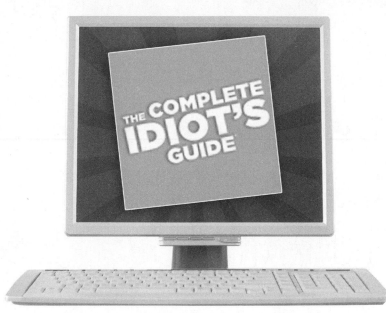